Toronto

*City*Guide ®

A FIREFLY BOOK

Published by Firefly Books Ltd. 2001

U.S. Cataloging-in-Publication Data
(Library of Congress Standards)

Must, John.
    Toronto city guide / John Must.—1st ed.
[208] p. : ill., maps ; cm.
Includes index.
Summary: A guide to tourist attractions, restaurants, night life and shopping, supplemented by sixty-eight detailed maps.
ISBN 1-55297-537-1 (pbk.)
1. Toronto (Ont.)—Guidebooks. 2. Toronto (Ont.)—Description and travel.
3. Toronto (Ont.)—Maps, Tourist. I. Title.
 917.1/ 354/ 1   21   2001   CIP

National Library of Canada Cataloguing in Publication Data

Must, John
        Toronto city guide

Includes index.
ISBN 1-55297-537-1

1. Toronto (Ont.)—Guidebooks. I. Title.

FC3097.18.M88 2001917.13'541044   C2001-901293-4
F1059.5.T683M88 2001

Design by John Must
Printed and bound in Canada by Friesens, Altona, Manitoba

Published in the United States in 2001 by
Firefly Books (U.S.) Inc.
P.O. Box 1338, Ellicott Station
Buffalo, New York, 14205

Published in Canada in 2001 by
Firefly Books Ltd.
3680 Victoria Park Avenue
Willowdale, Ontario
Canada, M2H 3K1

Contents

*City*Food

Visiting*TheCity*

*City*Streets

General index   195

*The*City

 1615 – 2001. Once a city of churches, it's now a place of neighbourhoods. Originally Anglo-Saxon, our new voices speak over 100 languages. The world has come here to live.

For centuries, this part of North America was Iroquois territory. Aboriginal peoples came through here to take advantage of trails leading north to Lake Simcoe and for canoe routes that provided a short cut between lakes Ontario and Huron.

In 1615 the French explorer Etienne Brûlé was the first European to see Lake Iroquois (now Lake Ontario) and it soon became well known to French fur traders. A small settlement took root in 1720 and a modest fort was erected in 1748. It wasn't long before British soldiers captured the place and Loyalists from the American Revolution ventured north to this and other sites further downstream along the St Lawrence River. The area became known in 1791 as Upper Canada, because it was upstream from the French settlements in Québec, which were known as Lower Canada.

Today, the Greater Toronto Area extends along that historic curve in Lake

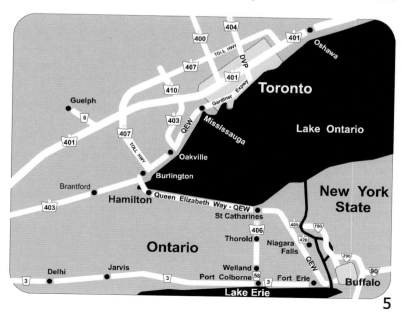

Ontario from Burlington to Clarington. Often referred to as the 'Golden Horseshoe', its population of 5,284,000 people makes it one of the continent's largest urban areas. It's home to a third of Ontario's residents and represents about 17% of Canada's population.

The region, which has one of the world's strongest economies, is the national centre for performing arts, communications, finance and banking, business, medical research, manufacturing, transportation and media enterprises.

The focal point is Toronto, Canada's largest city.

During the 1950s it was known as 'Toronto the Good', or 'Toronto the Sanctimonious'. This was not surprising considering the then *Lord's Day Act* had almost completely shut down any commercial activity on a Sunday. As far as anyone can remember there was only one half-decent restaurant open downtown on the Sabbath. And it wasn't allowed to serve alcohol. We rushed in droves over the border to Buffalo, NY for food, some shopping, a drink and excitement.

Toronto, back in those days, was a very conservative and thoroughly boring place. A member of Oxford University's debating team said: "Toronto is so boring the Indians don't want it back."

That was then and this is a new millennium.

In 1996, *Fortune* magazine noted that we were the best international city in which to live and work. *Fortune's* article was only one of many such observations. European-based international surveys throughout the last decade of the twentieth century had consistently placed us among the world's top five cities. And, for the last seven years of the twentieth century, the United Nations named Canada the best country in which to live. In 1999 the United States ranked third behind Norway.

News like this would have been heady stuff for residents of almost any other city. But it caused hardly a ripple in our media. That's because we don't have the brash impatience of New Yorkers, or the eccentric self-importance of Londoners. We are that unusual breed of people who can be seen on a deserted street corner at three in the morning waiting for the light to change.

On January 1, 1998, Toronto amalgamated with five surrounding municipalities - most being cities in their own right - to bring our collective population of 2,400,000 people into a common and better organized form of government. We became the fourth most populous city in North America after New York, Los Angeles and Chicago and were dubbed 'The Megacity' by local media. To our embarrassment, the name has stuck.

However, it's the smaller parts of the so-called megacity that make us unique. Unlike other places that insist on a cultural melting pot, we take the opposite view and vigorously promote the preservation and individualism of our diverse cultural communities.

Safe streets take on a European flavour and are crowded on a summer's night. We hear more resident languages spoken around our open-air markets and sidewalk cafés than we'd notice in either London or New York. The new millenium dawned with more than half our population being foreign-born, and less than half Anglo-Saxon. The United Nations has designated Toronto "the world's most ethnically diverse city" for the last five years.

Because of this cultural diversity and low crime rate, Toronto has become a vibrant and interesting place. It shows how people of every race, social group and creed from around the world can come together and share a truly international experience.

We have come a long way since 1788 when the Mississauga Indians traded the place to the English for a bit of money and 149 barrels of provisions. Today, they might even want it back.

*City*Quotes

"I found here good bread and wine…" *Fr. Picuet, at Fort Rouillé, 1751*

"Toronto makes a Sunday in a Scotch village seem like a hashish dream." *Aleister Crowley, British writer, 1913*

"It couldn't be any worse. You can't imagine it. I'm not going to describe it." *Ernest Hemingway, American journalist and author, 1923*

"We all hate Toronto. It's the only thing Canadians have in common." *Lister Sinclair, Canadian author and broadcaster, 1948*

"It's like New York run by the Swiss." *Sir Peter Ustinov, British actor and raconteur, 1976*

"Vandalism hits Toronto! They found a scratch on one of the subway seat covers." *Eric Korn, English businessman, The New Statesman, 1977*

"It's the cleanest city. And it works." *Buckminster Fuller, American urban guru, 1978*

"I've never been to a city I've fallen in love with more than Toronto." *Billy Graham, American evangelist, 1978*

"Toronto is still a jewel. It's a great place to live and work. But if you want something extra, you still have to go to Paris." *David Crombie, former Toronto mayor, 1979*

"Not only is it serendipitous, peripatetic, arboreal, eclectic and relatively hygienic, but it's also a wonderful city for children." *Margaret Atwood, Canadian author, 1982*

"I love Toronto. It's like New York with all the crap scraped off." *Ed Feldman, American television personality, 2000*

"It's the greatest city in the world!" *Mel Lastman, Toronto mayor, 2001*

City of **Toronto**

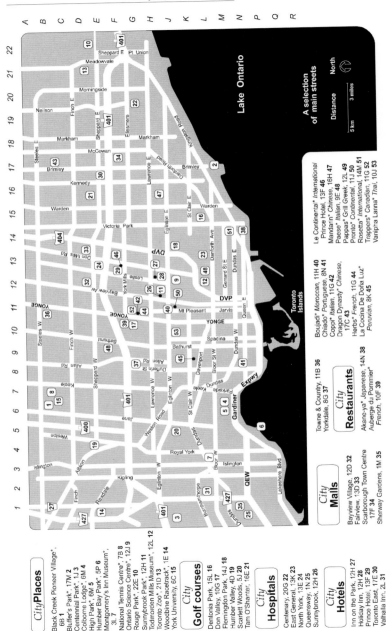

A selection of main streets

Distance   North

5 km   3 miles

Lake Ontario

Toronto Islands

DVP

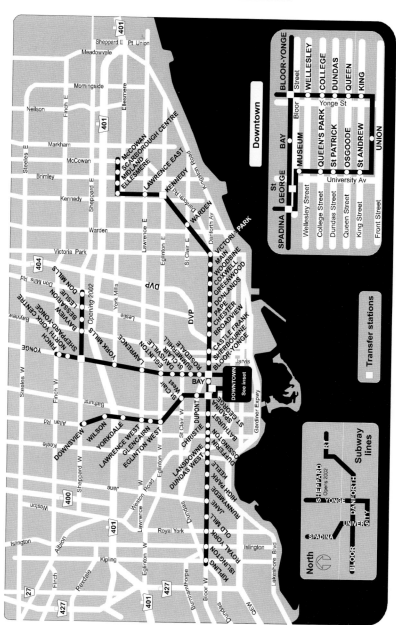

Downtown *Toronto*

A selection of some key streets.
See neighbourhood maps for complete detail.

Approximate distance

650 m   700 yd

North

WEST *of Yonge Street*   **EAST** *of Yonge Street*

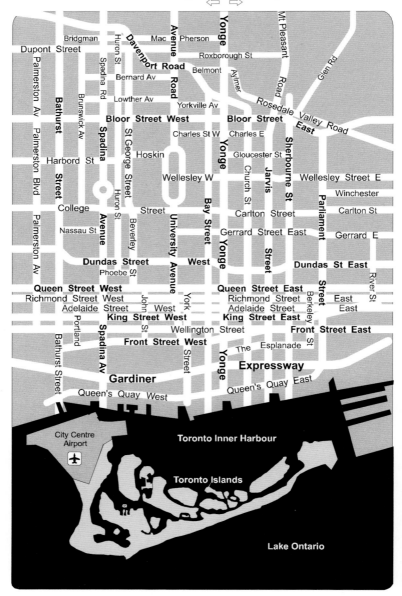

Bloor Street *Underground walkway*

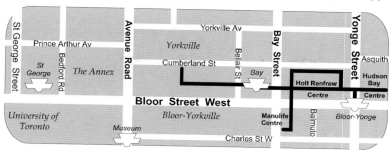

P A T H *Underground walkway**

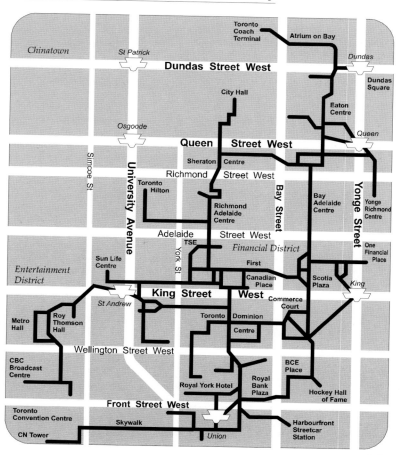

11

City-wide**Neighbourhoods**

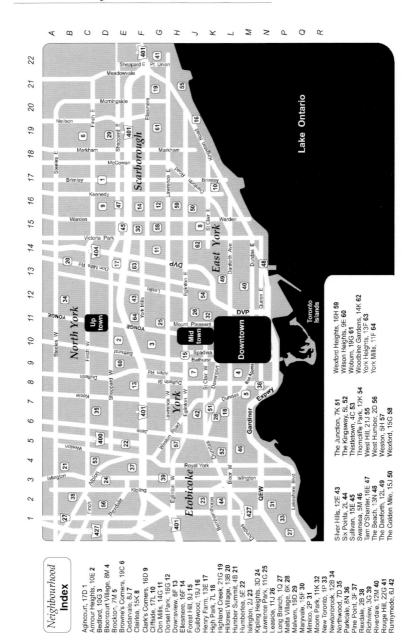

Lake Ontario

Scarborough

North York

Uptown

Midtown

Downtown

York

Etobicoke

East York

Toronto Islands

12

Yonge Street is the north-south spine that connects Toronto's inner-city neighbourhoods. It's also the dividing line between east and west.

Downtown, midtown and uptown have been organized into 35 detailed inner-city neighbourhood maps. They take you to street level to pin-point and index over 1,500 places.

These maps include:

● All highways, streets, lanes, parks and walkways – making them the most detailed available.

● Street numbers and one-way streets clearly marked every couple of blocks. All parking lots and gas stations are included.

● An *Area of Detail* at the top of each map shows you how that map fits into the city's neighbourhood layout.

22 Pointer tabs show numbers of joining maps.

✱ An asterisk to alert you to a detailed listing in the *City***Places**, *City***Life & entertainment**, or *City***Food** sections.

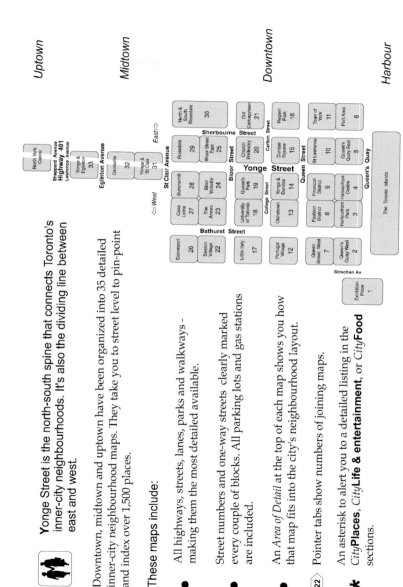

Uptown

Midtown

Downtown

Harbour

Distance

185 m   200 yd

North

Area of detail

BLOOR
COLLEGE   CARLTON
BLOOR
CARLTON

Islands

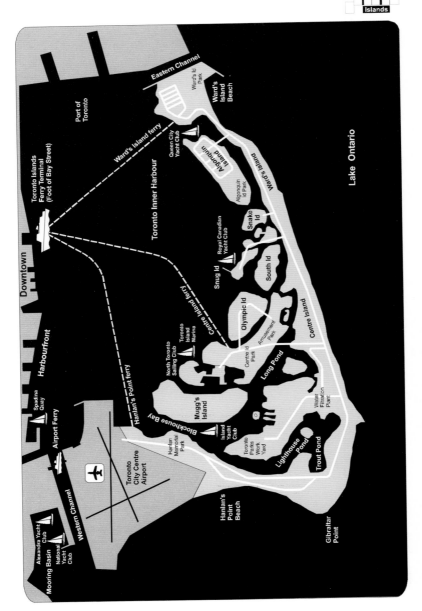

Eastern Channel

Ward's Id Park

Ward's Island Beach

Port of Toronto

Ward's Island ferry

Queen City Yacht Club

Algonquin Island

Algonquin Id Park

Ward's Island

Toronto Islands Ferry Terminal (Foot of Bay Street)

Toronto Inner Harbour

Snake Id

Royal Canadian Yacht Club

South Id

Snug Id

Lake Ontario

Centre Island ferry

Olympic Id

Centre Id Park

Amusement Park

Centre Island

Downtown

Harbourfront

Hanlan's Point ferry

North Toronto Sailing Club

Toronto Island Marina

Long Pond

Water Filtration Plant

Spadina Quay

Airport Ferry

Blockhouse Bay

Mugg's Island

Island Yacht Club

Lighthouse Pond

Trout Pond

Toronto Parks Work Yard

Alexandra Yacht Club

National Yacht Club

Mooring Basin

Western Channel

Hanlan Memorial Park

Toronto City Centre Airport

Hanlan's Point Beach

Gibraltar Point

14

*Neighbourhood***Profile**

For thousands of years, this is where people have come to relax. And that's the naked truth.

Before the arrival of the first Europeans here in the early part of the 17th century, the delta of what is now the Don River spilled out around two islands into what we know today as Lake Ontario. The delta, where Ashbridges Bay is now, was part of a large marsh that extended almost as far east as the Scarborough Bluffs. Off-shore there was a sand bank, formed from the Don's silt, that became an archipelago just west of the Don's delta. The isolation and tranquility of this finger of land with its small islands and sandy beaches became a kind of Caribbean vacation spot for the Aboriginals throughout the region. They came here to harvest medicinal plants, relax in sweat lodges and generally rejuvenate their bodies and spirits. The Iroquois called the place 'Taronto', which meant 'a meeting place near trees in the water.'

Early French explorers named the islands 'Presq'ile', or 'nearly an island'. Elizabeth Simcoe, wife of the first British lieutenant-governor, referred to them as "my favourite sands." In 1858 a violent storm tore at the sandbank and separated the archipelago at a point where the Eastern Channel now stands. By then, Toronto's early settlers had already begun to fill the marshes around the mouth of the Don and join many of the scattered islands with construction debris and soil from the expanding city. The idea was twofold: to give the city more room to grow, and to secure a more solid southern coastline for the harbour.

Today's archipelago is one of the largest public parks in the city, except for a couple of small and stalwart communities that have claimed parts of Ward's Island and Algonquin Island as their own. Over the years, the residents have been hassled unsuccessfully by civic fathers to renounce their communities so the city can extend the islands' popular public facilities. The residents have always won.

Centre Island, with its Centreville Amusement Park, is where a lot of us like to get away from the city with our kids and have a good time. It's also the place to be for the post-parade Caribana party and the International Dragon Boat Races. Mugg's Island is usually taken over by birds, and Snug Island is taken over by some of us who can afford to be members of the Royal Canadian Yacht Club. Olympic Island, with its snack bars and nice sandy beach, is for folk without cell phones and international portfolios.

But it's Hanlan's Point Beach that attracts a really note-worthy crowd. On July 17, 1894 the city passed a by-law permitting nude swimming and sunbathing there "at all times".

*Neighbourhood***Experience:** Go sailing around the Inner Harbour • take pictures of a great skyline view • get an overall sun tan.

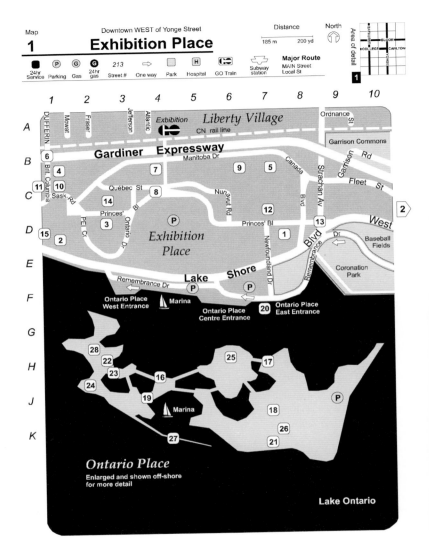

Map

1

Downtown WEST of Yonge Street

Exhibition Place

Distance — 185 m — 200 yd

North

Area of detail

■	Ⓟ	Ⓖ	**G**	213	⇨	▢	Ⓗ	⊫	⬇	Major Route
24hr Service	Parking	Gas	24hr gas	Street #	One way	Park	Hospital	GO Train	Subway station	MAIN Street Local St

ExhibitionPlace*

Automotive Building, 7D **1**
Bandshell, 1D **2**
Better Living Centre, 2D **3**
Centennial Square, 1B **4**
Coliseum, 7B **5**
Dufferin Gate, 1B **6**
Food Products Building, 4B **7**
Halls of Fame, 4C **8**
Horse Palace, 6B **9**
Horticultural Building, 1C **10**

Medieval Times, 1C **11**
National Trade Centre*, 7C **12**
Princes' Gate, 8D **13**
Queen Elizabeth Building, 2C **14**
Scadding Cabin Museum, 1D **15**

OntarioPlace*

Atlantis, 4H **16**
Bumper Boats, 7H **17**
Children's Village, 7J **18**
Cinesphere Imax®, 3J **19**

HMCS Haida*
   Historic naval ship, 7F **20**
Hydrofuge, 7K **21**
Island Club Stage, 2H **22**
Japanese Temple Bell, 3H **23**
Megamaze, 2H **24**
Molson Ampitheatre*, 6G **25**
Rush River Raft Ride, 7K **26**
Sunken Ships, 4K **27**
Wilderness Adventure Ride, 2G **28**

*Neighbourhood*Profile

There's been human activity around here since 8,000 BC. The first European settlers were French and they built Fort Taronto. Some will argue it was the birthplace of the city.

A year later, Fort Rouillé replaced Fort Taronto and in 1759 the French garrison burned it to the ground as they fled from British forces. During the next 30 years minor trading took place on this site before the British bought it from the Mississauga Indians and built a permanent settlement, the Town of York, a few kilometers to the east.

As the centuries changed, this area went from a place of conflict to one for leisure, entertainment and discovery.

The transition started in 1878 when 20 ha of land were leased to start a permanent fairground. Twenty-three wooden buildings and a spectacular Crystal Palace would house the Toronto Industrial Exhibition. Twenty-five years later the fairgrounds were the first to be lit by electricity and the following year saw the introduction of an electric railway. In 1912 the fair expanded to cover 141 ha and was re-named the Canadian National Exhibition. 'The Ex', or 'CNE', had entrenched itself into our psyche.

It became one of the world's finest permanent amusement and exhibition sites, featuring celebrity concerts, entertainment spectaculars, vast agricultural and industrial shows and the first television broadcast in the country. Every summer we flocked to the grounds like so many pilgrims. Being first through the Princes' Gate on opening day was to guarantee your name on the front page of that evening's newspaper.

The CNE magic began to wane in 1967 when Montréal staged the hugely successful Expo '67. It seemed the CNE, by comparison, was not all that inspiring anymore. The second blow came four years later when three man-made islands joined the CNE's shoreline to form Ontario Place. The old CNE grandstand shows were challenged by Ontario Place's 16,000 seat Molson Amphitheatre, one of the country's largest and most popular outdoor stages. The islands spawned parks, *avant-garde* architecture and dozens of fun places for kids. They provided a home for the first permanent Imax® theatre and a real Canadian naval destroyer. The venerable Ex never really recovered.

Some suggest Ontario Place was built to show Montréalers that Toronto was ready to up the ante when it came to creating a spectacular public playground that the world might also envy. Others muse, tongue in cheek, that Expo '67 was Montréal getting back at us for the defeat at Fort Rouillé.

> *Neighbourhood*Experience: Enjoy some fun at the CNE • attend a concert at the Molson Amphitheatre • sail around the Inner Harbour • walk through the parks inside Ontario Place • have an unusual dinner at Medieval Times.

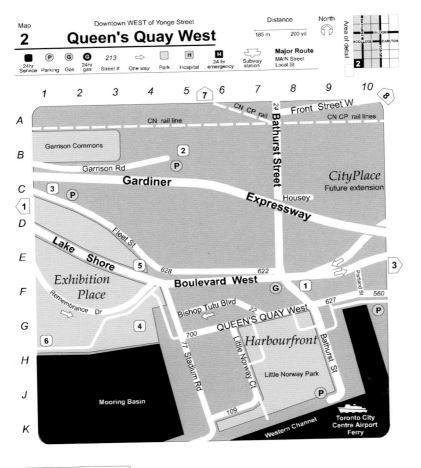

Map
2

Downtown WEST of Yonge Street

Queen's Quay West

Distance
185 m   200 yd

North

Area of detail

CityPlaces

CFMT-TV, 8F **1**
Fort York* (1793), 5B **2**
Fort York Armoury, 1C **3**

HMCS York (Department of National Defence), 3G **4**
Queen's Wharf Lighthouse (1861), 3E **5**
Victory Garden, 1G **6**

CityDevelopment

Over the next 15 years, the area east of Portland Street will undergo a massive redevelopment.

For decades the city has been debating the future of what's known as the 'railway lands' - that large tract bordered by Front Street West, Lakeshore Boulevard West, Bathurst Street and Spadina Avenue.

Finally, the area's future has been determined.

Construction has begun on CityPlace, a 557,000 sq m, 6,000-unit housing complex that's the biggest of its kind in Toronto.

An area of 17.8 ha will eventually see the construction of 20 highrise condominium towers, lowrise residential properties and commercial space. All buildings will be connected by parkland.

The total cost is believed to be in excess of $1,500,000,000

*Neighbourhood*Profile

In 1812, America declared war on Upper Canada. Twelve months later Fort York surrendered. The following year British forces retaliated in a most ungentlemanly fashion.

Fort York was built in 1793 to provide protection for the fledgling Town of York against the United States. But, on April 27, 1813 superior numbers of Americans stormed ashore just west of here and defeated a comparatively small band of British, Canadian, Mississaugan and Ojibway forces. Before retreating, the British blew-up Fort York's gunpowder magazine that led to the death of America's commander, Brigadier-General Zebulon Pike. It was a nasty six-hour battle with defenders outnumbered nearly four to one by the invaders. When it was all over, British forces had lost 157 men and the Americans 320

Americans occupied the Town of York for six days and went on a rampage of looting homes and pillaging supplies. They even burned down Upper Canada's parliament buildings and government house. It was a week the British wouldn't easily forget.

Toronto took over restoration of Fort York in 1924 and it later became a national historic site, housing Canada's largest collection of original War of 1812 buildings.

During World War II, this part of the city became directly involved in war once again. This time it opened its doors to Norwegian air force pilots who trained at the nearby island airport. Their barracks occupied what is now Little Norway Park. On the northeast corner there's an ancient stone brought from Norway to commemorate the wartime alliance. A bit further west, on the shore of Mooring Basin, is the quiet dignity of Victory Garden. The understated circle of memory was dedicated to peace on the 50th anniversary of the end of World War II.

There's an almost anonymous piece of naval history wedged between Lake Shore Boulevard West and Fleet Street near the entrance to Stadium Road. It's the operating portion of a lighthouse that began guiding ships into Toronto harbour from 1861.

This was the same year that this neighbourhood was on a war footing once again, fearing another American invasion. It never materialized. Perhaps the Americans remembered what happened the last time that they attacked here: within a year the British had retaliated for the American attack on Fort York by raiding Washington, DC. While they were there they burned down the Capitol and White House.

*Neighbourhood*Experience: Learn some history at Fort York • explore Little Norway Park's alcoves on Queen's Quay West • pause at the Victory Garden • enjoy the view around the Mooring Basin.

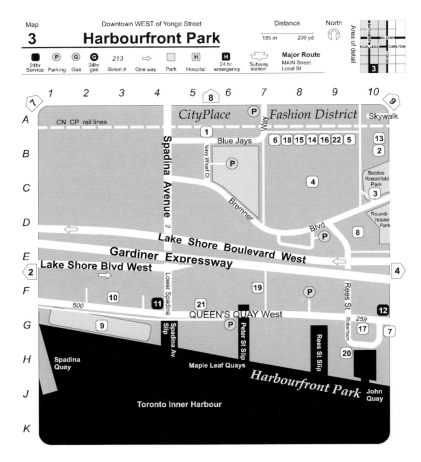

Map

3 Harbourfront Park

Downtown WEST of Yonge Street

Distance: 185 m / 200 yd

North

Area of detail

24hr Service | Parking | Gas | 24hr gas | 213 Street # | One way | Park | Hospital | 24 hr emergency | Subway station | Major Route MAIN Street Local St

---

CityPlaces

Chinese Workers monument, 5A **1**
CN Tower*, 10B **2**
Salmon Run*, 10C **3**
SkyDome*, 8C **4**
The Audience, Part 1*, 9B **5**
The Audience, Part 2*, 7B **6**
The Pier Museum*, 10G **7**
The Roundhouse, 10D **8**
Toronto Music Garden*, 2G **9**
Walter Carson Centre,
   National Ballet of Canada, 3F **10**

CityFood

24 hr Coffee shop, 4F **11**
24 hr Food mart, 10F **12**
360 Restaurant* (CN Tower)
   International, 10B **13**
Hard Rock Cafe American, 8B **14**

Sightlines American, 8B **15**
Windows on Sightline International, 8B **16**

CityHotels

Radisson Plaza Hotel, 10G **17**
Renaissance at SkyDome Hotel,
   8B **18**

CityServices

Beer Store, 7F **19**
Toronto Police Marine Unit, 9H **20**

CityShops

Antique Market Antiques, 5F **21**
Blue Jays Bullpen Blue Jays' stuff,
   9B **22**

*Neighbourhood***Profile**

Here's where you'll find lots of those postcard places. But there's more to address in this part of town.

Looking east along Queen's Quay from Lower Spadina Avenue there's a continuous line of high-rise condominium towers. Look straight up and the CN Tower dominates the sky. These are modern counterparts of ancient pine forests that once inspired Aboriginal people and became a source of lumber for European settlers.

Few neighbourhoods in the city have been so thoroughly stamped with Toronto's modern icons than Harbourfront Park. The CN (Canada's National) Tower has become the city's signature, while SkyDome is an integral part of North America's sporting vocabulary. But, if you look closer at less obvious things, the place can evoke other kinds of powerful emotions.

On Blue Jays Way at Navy Wharf there's the moving *Chinese Workers* monument. It is a stark memorial to the 4,000 people from Kwangtung, China who died between 1880-1885 while building the trans-continental Canadian Pacific railway through Alberta and British Columbia. Eldon Garnet conceived the monument and Francis Le Bouthillier sculpted the two working figures. The 13,000 Chinese labourers who survived didn't have enough money to return home and gradually disappeared into Canadian anonymity.

On the other side of SkyDome is another aspect of the realities of western Canada. It's Susan Schelle's sculpture, *Salmon Run.* The strangely realistic sight of two-dimensional salmon swimming and jumping up through waterfalls on their way to spawn has a serene strength that rivals the surrounding concrete. It draws us to it and provides a relaxing spot to sit for a while.

Another place for quiet contemplation is the Toronto Music Garden that evokes botanical themes for classical music. Look up to the old Canada Malting silos. One day it might become the Metronome, "an international symbol of a vital Canadian music community." In the midst of concrete icons, this neighbourhood is also becoming a place for art in its many forms.

Go east along Queen's Quay, just past Rees Street, and you'll find The Pier Museum. This is where you can go back to the days when Harbourfront was a pine forest where Aboriginal people met, and beyond that to the Ice Age.

As an inscription on the *Chinese Workers* monument reads:

"Rich is the hand that holds the stone of memory."

*Neighbourhood***Experience:** Have dinner at the 360 atop the CN Tower • shop for stuff at the Antique Market • take in a game at SkyDome • walk along Bremner Boulevard • stop and look at the street art • go back a few thousand years at The Pier Museum.

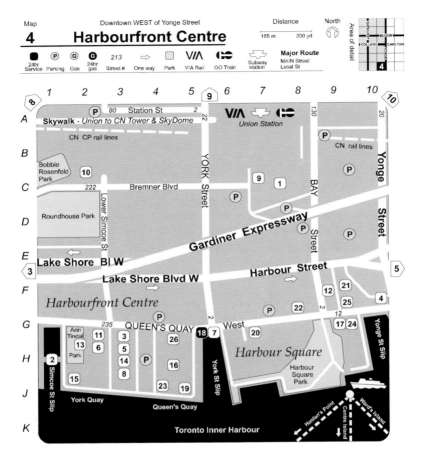

Map
4
Harbourfront Centre

Downtown WEST of Yonge Street

Distance
185 m   200 yd

North

Area of detail

■ 24hr Service   ℗ Parking   Ⓖ Gas   **G** 24hr gas   213 Street #   ⇨ One way   ☐ Park   VIA VIA Rail   ⬤ GO Train   Subway station   **Major Route** MAIN Street   Local St

22

*Neighbourhood***Profile**

Not too long ago, this is where you'd find crumbling warehouses and decaying docks. Today, it's a place where people come to play.

In 1974 the city began a significant 4 ha redevelopment of the waterfront between York and Simcoe slips. A quarter century later that modest beginning had escalated into a more ambitious project that spread west to Exhibition Place. This lake side stretch of playground south of the Gardiner Expressway is known simply as Harbourfront, while the original 4 ha at the bottom of York Street is called Harbourfront Centre.

This is a very busy area. About 4,000 events take place in this neighbourhood every year. They range from music and dance performances on several stages, to art exhibitions, ethnic festivals, literary readings and international marketplace activity. And there's CanadaPlace, a wired building open seven days a week, where you can use the latest technology to surf the Canadian government's databases. The LED monitors, at more than $5,000 each, are alone worth a visit.

On the other side of the expressway, south from Union Station, another massive development has been taking place. Following completion of the CN Tower and SkyDome, the barren lands to the east underwent a transformation that has changed them dramatically. The stub of Bremner Boulevard - that had previously not ventured much past SkyDome - was pushed eastward to join with York Street. Book-ending this section of the boulevard is the Air Canada Centre and the southern entrance to the Toronto Convention Centre.

Ground broke for the Air Canada Centre in February, 1997 on the site of the old Canada Post Delivery Building. It was designed to accommodate basketball (Toronto Raptors), ice hockey (Toronto Maple Leafs), concerts, trade shows and circuses. Seating capacity ranges from 19,000 for hockey to 22,000 for concerts. The old post office building's historic eastern façade was blended into the new stadium's architecture. On the west side of the arena is John McEwen's rusted 11-ton sculpture *Search Light, Star Light, Spot Light.*

When the Toronto Convention Centre on Front Street West was expanded towards the lake, its southern entrance spilled out on to Bremner Boulevard. There, on the edge of Bobbie Rosenfeld Park, sit two huge birds on the dauntingly black *Woodpecker Column.*

The total economic benefit over the next decade generated by the Air Canada Centre, Harbourfront Centre and Convention Centre should come to over $4,000,000,000. That's a lot of play money.

*Neighbourhood***Experience:** Spend time watching the boats • enjoy a live show • attend something at the Air Canada Centre • take a ferry to the islands • see what's inside the Power Plant and CanadaPlace.

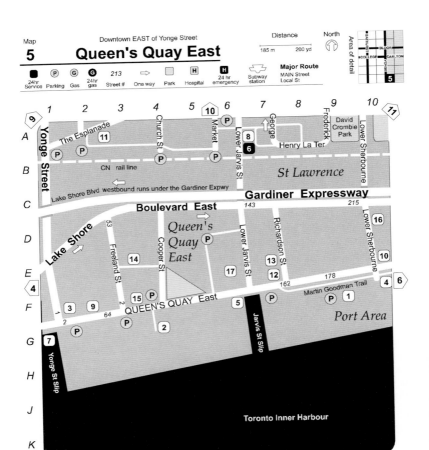

Map
5

Downtown EAST of Yonge Street

Queen's Quay East

Distance
185 m   200 yd

North

CityPlaces

Cinespace studios, 9F **1**
Redpath Sugar Museum*, 4G **2**
Toronto Star Newspaper, 1F **3**
Waterfront Tennis & Squash Club, 10F **4**
Whale mural, 6F **5**

CityFood

24 hr Food market, 7B **6**
Captain John's *Seafood*, 1G **7**
Casa di Giorgio *Italian*, 7A **8**
Grandma Lee's *American*, 2F **9**
Town & Country *Buffet*, 10E **10**

CityHotels

Hotel Novotel, 2A **11**

CityEntertainment

The Guvernment *Club*, 7E **12**
The Warehouse *Club*, 7E **13**

CityServices

LCBO Specialty Store *Wines*, 3E **14**
Liquor Store, 3F **15**

CityShops

Eurolite *Lighting fixtures*, 10C **16**
Queen's Quay Market, 6E **17**
 Caban Home décor
 Holy Smokes *Cigars*
 Liquor Store
 Loblaws *Supermarket*
 Moneysworth & Best *Shoe repair*
 Mövenpick Marché *Specialty food market*

*Neighbourhood***Profile**

The world's longest street starts here and goes northwest to the Ontario-Michigan border.

Yonge Street is also one of the oldest thoroughfares in the city.

It started as an Aboriginal trail that headed north from what was Lake Iroquois (Lake Ontario) to Lake Simcoe. Using this pathway as a rough guide, early settlers mapped out Yonge Street to serve as the north-south spine for the Town of York. The first few muddy kilometres were completed on February 16, 1796 and named after Sir George Yonge who was the British Secretary of War and an authority on Roman roads.

At the beginning of the 20th century, docks at the bottom of Yonge Street were a busy place. Steamers berthed here for their passenger and freight runs from Toronto to Buffalo, NY, Niagara Falls and Grimsby. The area now occupied by the *Toronto Star* building and Westin Harbour Castle hotel was crowded with horse-drawn wagons and merchants. The only marine memories left are the tour boats and a permanently moored ferry housing Captain John's Restaurant.

The area roughly south of The Esplanade is built entirely on landfill. In fact, The Esplanade gets its name because it was once literally an esplanade along the lake's shore and a popular spot for early residents during the summer. By 1900, Yonge Street had reached about as far south into the lake as it has today.

A significant redevelopment of the lake shore west of Yonge Street hasn't yet spilled over into Queen's Quay East. However, the large and trendy Queen's Quay Market at the bottom of Lower Jarvis Street, and a couple of popular clubs a block further east, have begun to bring this area to life. The former has attracted people from the condominium high rise neighbourhoods along Queen's Quay West, and the clubs act as a magnet for the young crowd from all over the city. The obvious sculpture on the northwest corner of Yonge Street and Queen's Quay West isn't supposed to represent an eggbeater. Its official name is *Between the Eyes*.

The Redpath Sugar Refinery holds the distinction of being one of the few, if not the only, commercial building in the city that was opened by Queen Elizabeth II. Tucked away at the back is a small, informal museum devoted to all you would ever want to know about sugar and its manufacture. Just go to reception in the main building and ask to be shown around.

They say that a long journey starts with the first step. So, if you really want to go all the way up Yonge Street, remember that it's 1,896 km long. And that's quite a hike.

*Neighbourhood***Experience:** Get out and go to a club • browse around the Queen's Quay Market shops • buy an expensive wine.

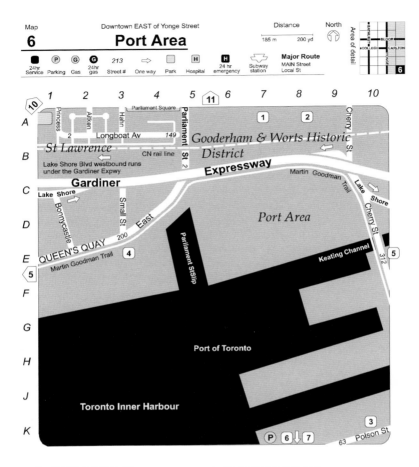

Map
6
Downtown EAST of Yonge Street
Port Area
Distance
185 m   200 yd
North
Area of detail

■ 24hr Service   ℗ Parking   ⓖ Gas   ❻ 24hr gas   *213* Street #   ⇨ One way   ▢ Park   Ⓗ Hospital   🅷 24 hr emergency   Subway station   **Major Route** MAIN Street Local St

CityPlaces

Gooderham & Worts Distillery (1832),
   7A **1**
Gooderham & Worts Historic District (1832),
   8A **2**
Lafarge Cement, 10K **3**
Royal Canadian Yacht Club private ferry,
   3E **4**

CityFood

Irish Rovers *Pub*, 10E **5**
The Docks *International*, 8K **6**

CityEntertainment

The Docks *Nightclub and activity centre*,
   8K **7**

CityDevelopment

This area and that to the east of Cherry Street could undergo a massive redevelopment. It is being considered as one of the three prime waterfront areas for Olympic venues.

Several scenarios have been put forward for Toronto. One suggests building the Olympic Village on this site and converting it into affordable housing once the games are over. It is also being eyed as a possible location for the Olympic Stadium.

Similarly disadvantaged neighbourhoods in both Sydney and Barcelona were converted into major sporting venues and village accommodation for athletes. The proposed sites are detailed on page 96.

Whatever plans come and go, a successful Olympic bid could totally change this neighbourhood.

*Neighbourhood***Profile**

The port area was once lying in marshland off the mouth of the Don River. Today, you're standing on lots of solid landfill.

The shoreline from the mouth of the Don River east to Scarborough Bluffs was one long marsh when European settlers arrived. John Graves Simcoe, who established the Town of York in 1793, had a vision for the place: convert land around the Don River delta into a public park. Accordingly, early layouts for the settlement included a significant allotment for parks east of Parliament Street.

Within 40 years commercial interests had redefined the future of the delta and that future didn't include Simcoe's visionary parkland. To satisfy an appetite for more industrial room and additional workers' housing - especially by the emerging brewing and distilling companies, including liquor giant Gooderham and Worts - the neighbourhood was redesigned to accommodate business rather than pleasure. By the end of the 1800s the place was a thriving industrial complex.

Gooderham and Worts was the largest 19th century distillery in the country. It started in 1832 as a gristmill to convert surplus grain into whiskey. Exploiting the technology of the day, the company grew steadily, paralleling Toronto's rise as a manufacturing centre. The stone distillery that remains today was built between 1859-61 and the rest of the complex was completed before the turn of the century. The distillery is no longer in business, but what remains is a national historic site and the city's best example of Victorian industrial design. Gradually, the complex is being converted into condominiums and commercial spaces.

On the other side of the Gardiner Expressway, south on Cherry Street, is the Port of Toronto. It does a modest business with ships carrying mainly sugar and cement for the nearby Lafarge Cement plant and Redpath Sugar refinery.

In an otherwise deserted part of the city, with its flat and anonymous landscape, there has emerged one of Toronto's largest and most successful entertainment complexes. The Docks is a bar, restaurant, activity centre, nightclub, midway, swimming pool, putting course and virtual reality kind of place. It attracts thousands of our twentysomethings to Polson Street - and to one of the best views of the downtown skyline.

Go further down Cherry Street towards the lake and you can look across to an evolving bird sanctuary on Tommy Thompson Park that's open to us on weekends. Perhaps it's the closest the city will get to accomplish the 200-year-old vision of John Graves Simcoe.

*Neighbourhood***Experience:** Be like everyone else and go to The Docks • jog and roller blade along the Martin Goodman trail.

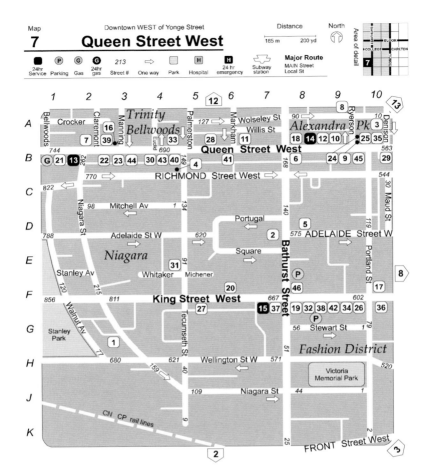

Map

7

Downtown WEST of Yonge Street

Queen Street West

Distance

185 m   200 yd

North

Area of detail

● 24hr Service   (P) Parking   (G) Gas   **G** 24hr gas   213 Street #   ⇨ One way   □ Park   H Hospital   **H** 24 hr emergency   Subway station   Major Route MAIN Street Local St

---

CityPlaces

Buddhist Temple, 3G **1**
St Mary's Church (1885)
  Roman Catholic, 7D **2**
St Stanislaus Kostka (1879)
  Roman Catholic, 10A **3**
Ukrainian Baptist Church, 5B **4**

CityEntertainment

Factory Theatre, 8D **5**
  John Mulvey House (1869)
Reverb *Club*, 8B **6**
Sanctuary *Club*, 2B **7**
Théâtre Passe Muraille*, 9A **8**
Velvet Underground *Club*, 9B **9**
Zen *Club*, 9A **10**

CityServices

Beer Store, 6A **11**
Wine store, 8A **12**

CityFood

24 hr Coffee shop, 1B **13**
24 hr Coffee shop, 8A **14**
24 hr Food mart, 7F **15**
Alegria *International*, 2A **16**
Amsterdam Brewing Company
  Pub, 10F **17**
Azul *International*, 8A **18**
Banknote *Grill*, 8F **19**
Bloor Street Diner *International*,
  6F **20**
Cities* *Continental*, 1B **21**
Citron *International*, 2B **22**
Dufflet *Pastries*, 3B **23**
Epicure *Cafe*, 9B **24**
Friendly Thai *Thai*, 10A **25**
Innocenti *Italian*, 9F **26**
Jalapeño *Mexican*, 5F **27**
La Hacienda *Spanish*, 5A **28**
Left Bank* *American*, 10B **29**
Munster Hall *Pub*, 4B **30**

Nonna's *Italian*, 5E **31**
Oscar's *Bistro*, 8F **32**
San *Korean*, 4B **33**
Susur *International*, 9F **34**
Taro *International*, 10A **35**
Toshi Sushi *Japanese*, 10F **36**
Wheat Sheaf (1849) *Pub*, 7F **37**

CityHotels

Executive Motor Hotel, 8F **38**

CityShops

Doc's Leather *Cycle gear*, 2B **39**
Future *Bakery*, 4B **40**
Jalan *Antiques*, 6B **41**
Navaro *Art gallery*, 8F **42**
Pavilion *Home décor*, 4B **43**
Quasi Modo *Home décor*, 3B **44**
Six One One *Fine arts*, 9B **45**
YTI *Home décor*, 8F **46**

*Neighbourhood*Profile

At the end of the 1800s the Polish community moved into this area along Queen Street West. Since then, their presence has dwindled and the neighbourhood has turned into a place where anti-establishment folk can relax and do their thing.

The Poles moved here from the notorious slums of The Ward, about a kilometre to the east, attracted by employment opportunities in the light manufacturing industries. The Roman Catholic faith was the cornerstone of their lives and places like St Stanislaus Kostka on Denison Avenue became the focal point to help families through some rough times. It is the oldest of the Polish churches in this area and keeps traditions alive with Polish language classes for kids and Polish dance lessons for adults. However, the community has largely moved on again. This time it has settled into what's known as Little Poland along Roncesvalles Avenue between Dundas Street West and King Street West.

The vacuum was filled with a wider cultural mix of people and for the last 40 years there's been a feeling of the Sixties here. Nowhere else in town will you see such a concentration of funky shops, nerdish people reading obscure literature in coffee shops, off-beat clothes hanging in windows and strange neon-coloured street art. It's all part of a modern-day hippiedom that this working class neighbourhood preserves for its residents. The young crowd comes here for an earthy urban experience, the clubs and a plethora of reasonably priced restaurants devoted to almost any cuisine your mood dictates. It's a place to take it easy and browse around on the weekend. 'Queen West' is a distinctive kind of place. And it's quite content believing that it's not really part of the predictable and stressed-out city.

This section of town also has stories to tell as far back as the days when a British garrison was in charge. Even the streets tell a story: Niagara was named after the original capital of Upper Canada; Tecumseth was the great chief of the Shawnee; Wellington after Lord Wellington. Garrison Creek, which flowed through Stanley Park, provided fresh water to the British forces at Fort York. It now flows anonymously through an underground Victorian brick sewer. The park is named to commemorate Stanley Barracks that once stood on the present Exhibition Place.

The men who died as a result of the American attack on Fort York in 1813 are remembered in Victoria Memorial Park. This is where you'll see some of the old headstones that were collected and placed here for a final acknowledgement of their acts of courage.

*Neighbourhood*Experience: Read the pavement inscriptions and map at Walnut and Wellington streets • visit the 24/7 hot dog stand at Queen and Spadina • take in a show at the 130 year-old Factory Theatre • have a drink at the 150 year-old Wheat Sheaf Pub.

Map

8

Downtown WEST of Yonge Street

Fashion District

Distance — 185 m   200 yd

North

Major Route
MAIN Street
Local St

Area of detail

- ■ 24hr Service
- Ⓟ Parking
- Ⓖ Gas
- **Ⓖ** 24hr gas
- 213 Street #
- ⇨ One way
- Park
- Ⓗ Hospital
- Ⓗ 24 hr emergency
- Subway station

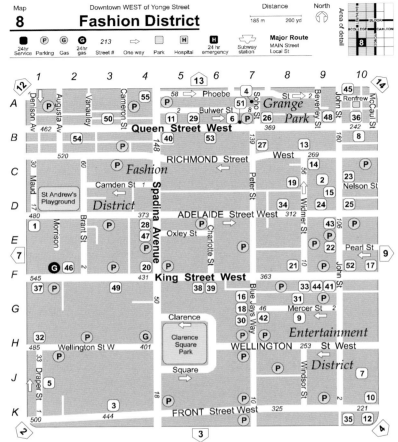

CityPlaces

eye Newspaper, 1D **1**
Festival Hall, 9C **2**
Globe and Mail, 3K **3**
Heritage houses (1889), 7A **4**
Heritage houses, 1J **5**

CityEntertainment

Bamboo Club, 6B **6**
CBC Broadcast Centre, 10J **7**
CITY-Muchmusic-Bravo!, 10B **8**
Digital Club, 8G **9**
Glenn Gould Studio, 10K **10**
Horseshoe Tavern, 5B **11**
John Bassett Theatre, 10K **12**
Joker Club, 8B **13**
Paramount IMAX®, 9C **14**
Playdium, 9C **15**
Playhouse Theatre, 7G **16**
Princess of Wales Thtr*, 10F **17**
Second City Comedy, 7G **18**

CityHotels

Canadiana Backpack, 8C **19**
Global Village Backpack, 4F **20**
Holiday Inn on King, 8F **21**

CityFood

Acme Grill American, 9E **22**
Al Frisco's International, 10C **23**
Alice Fazooli's Italian, 9D **24**
Avalon*, Continental, 10D **25**
Black Bull (1833) Tavern, 7B **26**
Fez Batik Eclectic, 7B **27**
Imagine Vegetarian, 4E **28**
Le Select French, 5A **29**
Leoni's Italian, 7G **30**
Mercer St Gr* Continental, 8G **31**
Mercini Café lounge, 1H **32**
Milano Italian, 8F **33**
Picante Spanish, 8D **34**
Planet Hollywood* American,
    10K **35**

Queen Street Market, 10B **36**
Sangria Spanish, 1F **37**
Solo International, 6G **38**
Thai Princess Thai, 6F **39**
Tortilla Flats* American, 5B **40**
Urban International, 9F **41**
Wayne Gretzky* Amer'cn, 7G **42**
Xango* Latin American, 9E **43**
Yamase Japanese, 8F **44**
Young Thailand Thai, 10A **45**
Zoë's Bakery, 2F **46**

CityShops

Art at 80 Galleries, 4E **47**
Caban Home accents, 9B **48**
De Leon White Gallery, 3F **49**
Fabric stores, 3B **50**
Flea Market (Seasonal), 7A **51**
Legends Sport memoribilia, 10F **52**
Pam Chorley Fashions, 6B **53**
Peach Berserk Fashions, 2B **54**
Peter Samaras Furs, 4A **55**

*Neighbourhood*Profile

Fur and discount clothing shops influence the upper part of this neighbourhood. But, if it's something in Versace or Hilfiger you're looking for, you'll have to check out the clubs.

York Hospital, built in 1829 to replace an existing military hospital, stood at the corner of King and John streets. It was so over-burdened by the cholera epidemic of 1847 that makeshift wooden sheds had to be constructed to the north to take care of patients. It was not a warm welcome for Toronto's fledgling Jewish community who came to this neighbourhood in the early 1830s. Nevertheless, 60,000 people banded together to build synagogues and open a variety of small businesses, including tailoring and furrier enterprises. It wasn't the greatest place to set-up shop, because it bordered a district known as 'The Ward'. Few would disagree that The Ward was the worst slum in Canada, if not North America. Nevertheless, large red brick industrial buildings began housing a flourishing needle trade that eventually included some of the city's most sought after furriers.

For all practical purposes, the Jewish community has moved away from Spadina Avenue to more affluent neighbourhoods. They've been replaced with a mainly Asian population. Even though the people and traditions have visibly changed, you'll still find Jewish-owned businesses carrying on the needle trade of their forebears. The short Queen Street West strip between Vanauley and Denison, for example, has the city's largest concentration of fabric and needlework shops. However, the big old buildings east of Spadina Avenue that once housed hundreds of tailors and seamstresses have largely made way for another fashion: the club scene.

The neighbourhood from Queen Street West down to Front Street is where our affluent young crowd - and those who wish they were - head for a night on the town. It's a blossoming mélange of clubs, bars, restaurants and little *avant-garde* shops that spill into the traditional Entertainment District.

This is also the most concentrated mass media neighbourhood in Canada. The national English-language radio and television networks of the Canadian Broadcasting Corporation are centred here. So is the street-savvy *CITY-TV* organization that runs a half-dozen cable networks, including the hip *MuchMusic* channel and the prestigious *Bravo!* arts channel. A few blocks away is the *Globe and Mail*, a newspaper that covets its position as 'Canada's newspaper of record.' Hip dot.com businesses are everywhere.

In the midst of it all is Draper Street, one of the city's least known enclaves. Its impeccable heritage cottages are so close to this playground of the Now Generation, yet so far away in time.

*Neighbourhood*Experience: Hit the clubs • be seen on a restaurant patio • walk down Draper Street • rant at *CITY-TV*'s 'Speaker's Corner' • get something strange at the Flea Market on Saturday.

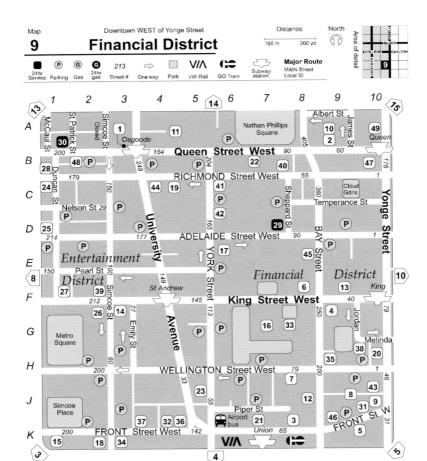

Map

9

Downtown WEST of Yonge Street

Financial District

Distance

185 m   200 yd

North

Area of detail

24hr Service · Parking · Gas · 24hr gas · 213 Street # · One way · Park · VIA Rail · GO Train · Subway station · Major Route · MAIN Street · Local St

Albert St
James St
Queen

Nathan Phillips Square

Osgoode

Queen Street **West**

RICHMOND Street West

Cloud Gdns

Nelson St 29

Temperance St

Entertainment

ADELAIDE Street West

District

Financial

District

Pearl St

St Andrew

King

King Street West

Metro Square

Emily St

University Avenue

Melinda

WELLINGTON Street West

Simcoe Place

Piper St

Airport bus

Union

FRONT Street West

FRONT ST W

---

*City*Places

Campbell House* (1822), 3A **1**
Cenotaph, 9B **2**
*City People**, 7K **3**
Commerce Court*, 9F **4**
Dominion Public Building, 9K **5**
First Canadian Place*, 8F **6**
Gallery of Inuit Art, 7H **7**
Heritage Square (BCE PI)*, 9J **8**
Hockey Hall of Fame*, 10J **9**
Old City Hall* (1899), 9A **10**
Osgoode Hall* (1832), 4A **11**
Royal Bank Plaza*, 8J **12**
Scotia Plaza, 9F **13**
St Andrew's Church
  Presbyterian (1876), 3F **14**
Toronto Convention Centre*,
  1K **15**
Toronto Dominion Cntr*, 7G **16**
Toronto Stock Exchange*, 6D **17**

*City*Hotels

Crowne Plaza Hotel, 2K **18**
Hilton Hotel, 4C **19**
Hotel Victoria, 10G **20**
Royal York Hotel*, 6K **21**
Sheraton Hotel, 7B **22**
Strathcona Hotel, 5J **23**

*City*Entertainment

Fluid *Club*, 1C **24**
Limelight *Club*, 1D, **25**
Roy Thomson Hall*, 2F **26**
Royal Alex Theatre*, 1F **27**
Whiskey Saigon *Club*, 1B, **28**

*City*Food

24 hr Coffee shop, 7D **29**
24 hr Food mart, 1A **30**
Acqua* *Italian*, 10J **31**

Armadillo *Texan*, 4K **32**
Canoe* *Canadian*, 8G **33**
East Side Marios *Italian*, 3K **34**
Far Niente *Continental*, 9H **35**
Fish House* *Seafood*, 4K **36**
Joe Badali's *Italian*, 3J **37**
Jump* *International*, 9H **38**
Kama *Indian*, 2F **39**
Le Bifthéque, *Steakhouse*, 8B **40**
Little Anthony's *Italian*, 6C **41**
Mövenpick* *Continental*, 6C **42**
Mövenpick Marché* *Continental*,
  10J **43**
Ruth's Chris* *Steakhouse*, 4C **44**
Szechuan *Chinese*, 8E **45**
Takesushi* *Japanese*, 8J **46**

*City*Shops

Bay *Department store*, 10B **47**
Condom Shack *Adult*, 2B **48**
Tower *Records*, 10A **49**

*Neighbourhood***Profile**

Four of Canada's 'Big Five' banks have built their monuments to wealth on the corners of King and Bay streets. If all their towers were placed end to end they would top 323 storeys. They call it 'Mint Corner'.

There are more banks, accountants, money traders and lawyers in this area than anywhere in the country. One of the buildings they occupy is made of matched Italian white marble. Another, a block south, is clad with $750,000 worth of real gold, calculated on the 2001 price for bullion. (Mint Corner is an acronym for the Bank of **M**ontreal, Canadian **I**mperial Bank of Commerce, Bank of **N**ova Scotia and the **T**oronto Dominion Bank.) The Toronto Stock Exchange is the fourth largest in North America in terms of market capitalization. During an average trading day about $2,000,000,000 changes hands. The five major banks here each make much more than a billion dollars in profit annually. Some of the legal firms in this area have more than 190 lawyers on staff. After a while, statistics in this part of town rise above the comprehension of mere mortals.

The mind boggled around here as far back as 70 years ago. The 34-storey Bank of Commerce building was the tallest in the British Empire when it opened in 1931. The Royal York hotel, which welcomed its first guests in 1929, was the largest hotel in the Empire and commanded the downtown skyline in both height and width.

Despite the intensity of size, this neighbourhood has been able to make room for quiet little parks and a spawning of street art. Catherine Widgley's cut-out *City People* can be seen scurrying up a staircase outside the south entrance to Royal Bank Plaza; Joe Fafard's *Reclining Cows* rests on lawns in the Toronto Dominion Centre; and Anish Kapoor's *Untitled Mountains* are forever catching the eyes of wandering camera buffs in Simcoe Place. Francesco Pirelli's The *Monument to Multiculturalism*, which was a gift to the city from the Italian community, stands outside Union Station. The park in First Canadian Place, fronting King Street West, has a full-length waterfall cascading down its northern wall. These are all favourite summer spots for office workers brown-bagging their lunches.

In 1869, at the northwest corner of Queen and Yonge streets, Timothy Eaton opened his first shop in Toronto. Just across the street, Robert Simpson set-up competition in the department store business. For generations both Simpson's and Eaton's were household names in Canadian merchandising. Today they're both gone. Simpson's was taken over by the Hudson's Bay Company and Eaton's became part of Sears in the fall of 1999.

Business can be rough in this part of town.

*Neighbourhood***Experience:** Gawk at skyscrapers • eat at trendy places • go to a club or show • explore the impressive PATH walkway.

Map
10
Downtown EAST of Yonge Street
St Lawrence

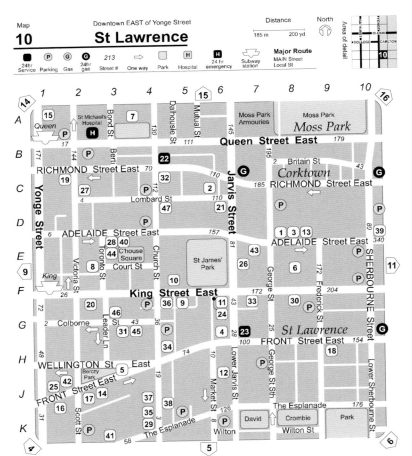

CityPlaces

Bank of Upper Canada (1827), 7D **1**
Central Fire Hall (1886), 6C **2**
De La Salle Institute (1871), 8D **3**
Farmers' Market, 6G **4**
Flatiron Building* (1892), 3H **5**
George Brown College, 8E **6**
Metropolitan Church* (1870), United 3A **7**
Post Office (1853), 2E **8**
Sculpture Garden*, 5F **9**
St James Cathedral* (1853) Anglican, 5F **10**
St Lawrence Hall (1850), 6F **11**
St Lawrence Market*, 6H **12**
York Post Office Museum* (First Post Office 1835), 8D **13**

CityEntertainment

Bluma Appel Theatre, 3J **14**
Elgin & Winter Garden Theatres*, 1A **15**
Hummingbird Centre*, 1J **16**
St Lawrence Centre*, 2J **17**
YPT Theatre*, 9H **18**

CityHotels

Cambridge Suites Hotel, 1C **19**
King Edward Hotel, 2F **20**
Quality Hotel, 6C **21**

CityFood

24 hr Coffee shop, 4B **22**
24 hr Restaurant, 6G **23**
Biagio* Italian, 6F **24**
Biff's French bistro, 1J **25**
Bombay Palace* Indian, 6E **26**
Conchy Joe's Seafood, 2C **27**
Fig Leaf Italian, 3D **28**
Fionn MacCool's Irish Pub, 4K **29**
Galileo* Italian, 8F **30**
Ginga Sushi Japanese, 3G **31**
Golden Thai* Thai, 4C **32**
Hiro Sushi* Japanese, 7F **33**
Hot House Italian, 4H **34**
Keg Steakhouse, 4K **35**
La Marquette* International, 4F **36**
Le Papillon* French, 4J **37**
Me-Gumi Japanese, 4J **38**
Montréal Bistro Jazz eatery, 10D **39**
Nami* Japanese, 3D **40**
Old Spaghetti Factory* Italian, 3K **41**
Penelope Greek, 1J **42**
Rodney's* Oyster House, 6E **43**
Rosewater* International, 3E **44**
Spinello Italian, 4G **45**
Tom Jones* Steakhouse, 3G **46**
Young Thailand* Thai, 4C **47**

Few neighbourhoods enlighten us about the city's deadly past more than St Lawrence. Gallows once stood under the spire of a church. And one of the buildings here is haunted.

Nothing reminds us more about the deadly history of this part of town than little Courthouse Square. Almost hidden among buildings and filled with lunchtime office workers, it is where the last public hangings took place. Three men, convicted for their part in the 1837 Rebellion, were put to death here in April, 1838. Their crime was to demand that the British crown hear the voices of concerned farmers. Queen Victoria commuted their sentences, but news of this didn't arrive in the colony in time to stay the executions.

The spire across the street from the gallows was that of St James' Church, which burned to the ground less than a year after the hangings. A replacement building suffered a similar fate in 1849. Today's Georgian-styled cathedral opened in 1853. In the porch wall is the tombstone of John Rideout, killed in 1817 during the last fatal duel held in the Town of York.

A few blocks further east is the 1827 Bank of Upper Canada building, the oldest surviving bank building in town. Founded by some of York's powerful élite, it became one of the most influential financial institutions on the continent. It collapsed in 1886. Next door is the De La Salle Institute, representing the first Jesuit foothold in what was then a staunchly Church of England colony. The next building to the east is the York Post Office, built a year before York changed its name to Toronto. It then became known as 'The First Post Office' in Toronto and is now the oldest continuously operating post office in Canada. The other famous old post office building is at 10 Toronto Street. It was modelled after a Grecian temple and had two front entrances – one for gentlemen and the other for ladies. After serving time in this capacity, it was turned into government offices and later sold to the Bank of Canada. The building today shows refurbishing done by its current occupants, the Argus Corporation.

British architect William Thomas, who imprinted a Gothic style on to the city's landscape, designed more than 100 buildings in only 17 years. One major project that remains is the still elegant 150 year-old St Lawrence Hall, where Ralph Waldo Emerson and D'Arcy McGee once spoke.

As for the ghost, it's believed to be that of Sister Vincenza. She was one of the Sisters of St Joseph who owned and operated St Michael's Hospital. She died in the late 1950s, but is still apparently doing her rounds switching lights on and off. Witnesses know it's Sister Vincenza because she's now the only 'person' in the hospital who wears a nun's habit.

*Neighbourhood***Experience:** Be inquisitive and walk through history • applaud good theatre • graze in popular restaurants • do the St Lawrence Market ritual on a Saturday morning.

Map

11

Downtown EAST of Yonge Street

Town of York

Distance

185 m | 200 yd

North

Area of detail

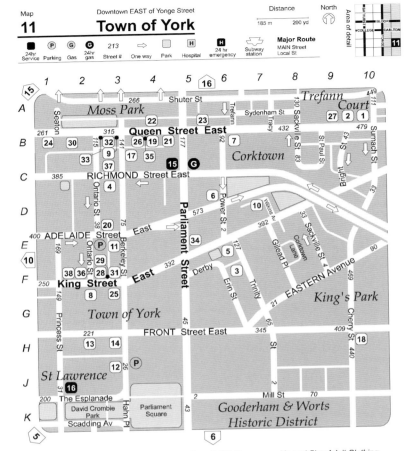

*Neighbourhood*Profile

In 1793 John Graves Simcoe established a garrison on the shore of Lake Ontario. A small settlement was built two kilometres to the east. He named it the 'Town of York'.

Simcoe was lieutenant-governor of Upper Canada, a not too inspiring colony in British North America. He was worried about an impending war with America and planned to establish a naval base here so the British could control Lake Ontario. Another part of his strategy was to move the capital of Upper Canada from Niagara to York to make it less vulnerable to American attack. York's town limits were set by what are now Parliament, Peter, Front and Queen streets. In the old days, Front Street East was called Palace Street, Richmond was Hospital Street, Adelaide was Newgate Street, and Queen was Lot Street. Lot Street was named that way for a purpose. In order to lure men of distinction to York, Simcoe offered them extensive lots of land fronting Lot Street and going as far north as present-day Bloor Street. Lot was then renamed Queen to add a little more tone.

The first parliament buildings, consisting of two single-storey structures, were erected in 1798 near the corner of Berkeley Street and The Esplanade. They were also used as a courthouse and for religious meetings. When the Americans finally attacked York in late April, 1813 they set fire to them. Seven years later the buildings were repaired, only to burn again in 1824 after a chimney fire. A third attempt was made in 1832 to establish a place for parliament at Front and Simcoe streets.

Not much of the old Town of York remains here. Three notable exceptions are Little Trinity Church, Dominion Square and the Enoch Turner School.

Little Trinity is the oldest church in town. It was built in 1842 to serve the hundreds of poor immigrants who had come here to work at places like the Gooderham and Worts distillery. People referred to it as "the poor man's church." Next door is Enoch Turner School, built in 1843. It's not only the oldest school building, but it was the first to offer free public education to underprivileged kids of working class parents. Inside, some of the original desks, stoves and blackboards remain as a reminder of much more stoic times. Dominion Square opened in 1873 in a neighbourhood known as Corktown. It got its name from the folk who came here from Cork, Ireland to work in the nearby distillery and brewing enterprises.

One of the last reminders of how they lived is tucked away along two tiny Corktown streets. Wilkins Avenue shows us a gentrification of the old workers' cottages, whereas Bright Street displays them in their original form. It's possibly the only street in the city that shows how Toronto's working class neighbourhoods might have looked in the days of York.

*Neighbourhood*Experience: Attend a live theatre • go to mass at the city's only basilica • see the best in modern furniture • explore history.

Map

12

Downtown WEST of Yonge Street

Portugal Village

Distance

185 m   200 yd

North

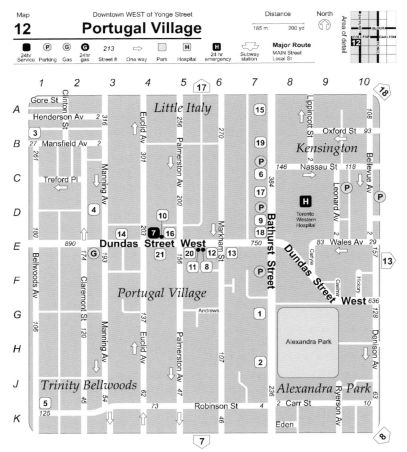

CityPlaces

Ching Kwok Temple *Buddhist*, 7G **1**
Church of the Assumption of the Virgin Mary *Ukrainian Catholic*, 7H **2**
St Francis of Assisi Church (1914) *Catholic*, 1B **3**
St Francis of Assisi School, 2D **4**
St Matthias Church (1873) *Anglican*, 1K **5**
St Vladimir Cathedral *Ukrainian Orthodox*, 7C **6**

CityFood

24 hr Cofffee shop, 4E **7**
Bar Vittoria *Italian*, 6E **8**
Kim Bo *Vietnamese*, 7D **9**

Lisbon by Night *Portuguese*, 4E **10**
Pane Vittoria *Bakery*, 6E **11**
Portuguese *Cafe*, 6E **12**
Tommy's Backyard *Greek*, 6E **13**
Torrefazione *Brazilian*, 3E **14**

CityServices

Beer Store, 7A **15**
De Sousa *Wine boutique*, 5E **16**

CityShops

Balloon King *Party supplies*, 7C **17**
Irene's *Florist*, 7D **18**
Kromer *Audio-Video*, 7B **19**
Liberal *Home accents*, 5E **20**
Portuguese Fish Market, 4E **21**

*Neighbourhood*Profile

Portuguese explorers got to know Canada as far back as the 15th century. And in 1705 Pedro Silva was the country's first letter carrier.

When the *SS Saturnia* docked in Halifax in 1953, it carried 85 Portuguese male passengers. Even though most of them were recruited as farm labourers, they soon made their way west to take advantage of Toronto's booming post-war construction industry. Since then the Portuguese community has grown from this modest number to about 160,000, making it the fourth largest cultural group in the city. Most have come from the Azores, but there's also a good representation from Madeira, Macao and the Cape Verde Islands.

They put down roots in the working-class neighbourhood around Dundas and Bathurst streets. This area goes back to the early 1800s when Samuel Smith owned much of the land. It was named Gore Vale after Lieutenant-Governor Francis Gore. There's a Gore Street in the neighbourhood and, interestingly, it runs into Clinton Street.

Except for a smattering of small front gardens displaying statues of Our Lady of Fatima, there's little about this part of the neighbourhood that is obviously Portuguese to the casual observer. The commercial corridor along this section of Dundas Street West is weighted heavily in favour of Asian businesses. The Ukrainian Orthodox Cathedral of St Vladimir stands just north of the Bathurst Street intersection. The impressive Ching Kwok Buddhist Temple faces Alexandria Park to the south. Little Italy presses down from College Street. East, across Bathurst Street, is the cultural mélange of Kensington.

The absence of noticeable Portuguese icons here may be due, in part, to the new generation of Canadian-born Portuguese who have moved into other parts of the city away from the comfortable traditions of their parents. You'll find the Portuguese restaurants these days further to the west, mostly along College and Dundas streets. And the city's two oldest Portuguese bakeries are still in business across on Augusta Avenue in Kensington, where they've been joined by a multi-national array of busy markets.

The real flavour of Portugal Village, however, comes not so much from food as it does from the Day of Portugal parade. The closest Saturday to June 10th brings thousands of traditionally dressed people out into the streets for Canada's largest Portuguese street festival.

It's something that would have made Pedro Silva proud.

*Neighbourhood*Experience: Spend time exploring a mix of the world's religious faiths • take advantage of that once-a-year opportunity to celebrate the Day of Portugal • say "*Dia de Nice*" to people sitting on their front porches.

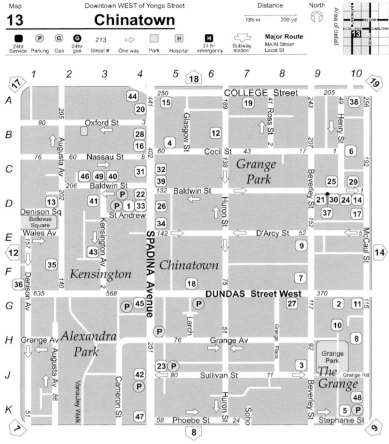

Map

13

Downtown WEST of Yonge Street

Chinatown

Distance
185 m   200 yd

North

Area of detail

24hr Service · (P) Parking · (G) Gas · (G) 24hr gas · 213 Street # · ⇨ One way · Park · (H) Hospital · (H) 24 hr emergency · Subway station · Major Route MAIN Street Local St

*City*Places

Anshei Minsk Synagogue (1930), 3D **1**
Art Gallery of Ontario (AGO)*, 9G **2**
Chinese Baptist Church (1886), 8J **3**
Cecil Community Centre (Church of Christ, 1890), 5B **4**
Church of St George the Martyr (1844), 10K **5**
Holy Trinity Russian Orthodox Church, 10C **6**
Italian Consulate (1872), 8F **7**
Ontario College of Art & Design, 10H **8**
Ontario Gallery of Chinese Arts, 8E **9**
The Grange (1817), 9G **10**
Two Forms, 10G **11**
Workers' cottages, 6B **12**

*City*Food

Amadeu's *Portuguese*, 1D **13**
Arugola *Italian*, 10D, **14**
Asean *Malaysian*, 5A **15**
Bangkok *Thai*, 4B **16**
Cassis *International*, 10E **17**
Champion House* *Chinese*, 5F **18**
Ein-stein *Pub*, 7A **19**
Fantastic *Chinese*, 4A **20**
Fujiyama *Japanese*, 9D **21**
Happy Seven* *Chinese*, 4D **22**
Hu Tieu Dai Nam *Vietnamese*, 5J **23**
Jodhpore *Indian*, 9D, **24**
La Bodega *French*, 9C **25**
Lee Garden* *Chinese*, 5D **26**
Lotus Garden *Vegetarian*, 8G **27**
Lucky Dragon* *Szechuan*, 4B **28**
Margarita's *Mexican*, 10C **29**
Mata Hari* *Malaysian*, 9D **30**
Miss Saigon *Vietnamese*, 4C **31**

Nha Hang *Vietnamese*, 5C **32**
Pho Hu'ng* *Vietnamese*, 4D **33**
Rol San *Seafood*, 5E **34**
The Boat *Portuguese*, 1F **35**
Vanipha* *Lao-Thai*, 1F **36**
Wah Sing* *Seafood*, 9D **37**
Woodlands *Vegetarian Thali* 10A **38**
Xam Yu* *Seafood*, 5C **39**

*City*Shops

Bakeries, 3C **40**
Cheese shops, 3D **41**
Chinatown Centre *Mall*, 4J **42**
Clothing shops, 3E **43**
Computer stores, 4A **44**
Dragon *Mall*, 4G **45**
Fish shops, 2C **46**
Fur stores, 4K **47**
Gallery Prime *Art pieces*, 10J **48**
Produce shops, 3C **49**

*Neighbourhood*Profile

Sam Ching's Chinese laundry was first listed in the telephone book in 1878. This is where you'll find his roots.

It's believed that our 248,000 Chinese residents have now formed the largest Chinese community in North America. Their roots go back to the 1870s when 17,000 of them came from China to work as labourers on the Canadian Pacific Railway. When the railway was completed many remained in Canada and some came east to start a new life in Toronto around the intersection of Bay and Dundas streets. Today, most of Chinatown has moved further west along Dundas Street towards Spadina Avenue and it's here that you'd be forgiven if you thought you were in Hong Kong.

The 1815 estate of Captain John Denison once occupied over 40 ha of dense forest on the west side of Spadina Avenue. His house, known as the Bellevue Homestead, was built on the present site of Bellevue Square. By 1870 the estate had been divided into a respectable middle class English neighbourhood with British street names such as Kensington, Oxford, St Andrew and Wales. Around 1900 the British moved north and Jewish people moved in to replace them. Many were new immigrants escaping persecution in Europe; others came here to avoid the persecution they had experienced in other parts of town. Jews were not welcomed into our business community during that time, so in 1905 they opened street stalls outside their homes and sold produce and merchandise to each other. This is how the century-old Kensington Market, around Kensington Avenue and Baldwin Street, came into being.

The Jewish community has now followed prosperity to North York and neighbourhoods along Bathurst Street, leaving behind only a couple of synagogues as a testament to the past. This part of town is now Chinese, Vietnamese, Portuguese, Malaysian and Laotian, making it easily the most colourful and exotic part of the city.

In the midst of all this is The Grange. It's about the last tangible reminder of the once huge old estates fronting Queen Street that were given to respectable citizens by Governor Simcoe in the early days of York. This one belonged to D'Arcy Boulton Jr. In 1911 it was bequeathed to the Art Museum of Toronto, which later became the Art Gallery of Ontario and the eighth largest gallery of its kind in North America.

Although this might be the original Chinatown, there are a few others in town: Chinatown East around Broadview and Gerrard and another in Scarborough's Agincourt neighbourhood. A fourth is the most affluent one of all. It's out of town in Markham. Like the British and Jews before them, the Chinese are prospering and moving north.

---

*Neighbourhood***Experience:** Discover Kensington Market on a Saturday • have lunch on Spadina Avenue and dinner on Baldwin Street.

Map **14** Downtown WEST of Yonge Street · **Yonge & Dundas**

Distance 185 m / 200 yd · North · Area of detail

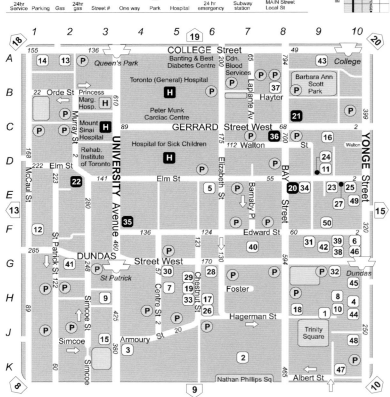

CityPlaces

Church of the Holy Trinity* (1847) *Anglican*, 9H **1**
City Hall*, 7J **2**
Court House, 4J **3**
Eaton Centre*, 10H **4**
Laughlen Lodge (1848), 6E **5**
Media Tower*, 10F **6**
Museum for Textiles*, 4H **7**
Old Rectory (1861), 9H **8**
Royal Cdn. Military Inst., 3H **9**
Scadding House (1860), 9H **10**
St George's Hall (1891), 9D **11**
St Patrick's *Catholic*, 1F **12**
Stewart Building (1894), 2A **13**
Toronto School Board, 1A **14**
United States Consulate, 3J **15**

CityHotels

Chelsea Inn, 9C **16**

Colony Hotel, 6H **17**
Marriott Eaton Centre, 8H **18**
Metropolitan Hotel, 5G **19**

CityFood

24 hr Coffee shop, 8E **20**
24 hr Food mart, 8C **21**
24 hr Food mart, 2D **22**
Adega* *Portuguese*, 9E **23**
Bangkok Garden* *Thai*, 9D **24**
Barberian's *Steakhouse*, 10E **25**
Chestnut Tree *American*, 6H **26**
Donatello *Italian*, 9E **27**
Garden *Chinese*, 6G **28**
Hemispheres *Continental*, 5H **29**
Hong Shin *Chinese*, 4G **30**
Indian Flavour* *Indian*, 9F **31**
J J Muggs *American grill*, 9G **32**
Lai Wah Heen* *Chinese*,
  2 Fl., Metropolitan Hotel, 5H **33**
Oro *Italian*, 9E **34**

CityServices

24 hr Business services, 3F **35**
24 hr Drug store, 8C **36**
Dental Clinic (Till 9.00 PM), 8B **37**
Liquor Store, 9F **38**
Post office, 9F **39**
Toronto Coach Terminal, 7F **40**
Toronto Police, 52 Div., 2G **41**

CityShops

Atrium on Bay *Mall*, 9F **42**
College Park *Mall*, 9A **43**
Eaton Centre *Mall*, 10H **44**
eatons *Department store*, 10G **45**
Gap *Clothing*, 10G **46**
Indigo *Books*, 9K **47**
Roots *Clothing*, 10J **48**
Sunrise *Recordings*, 10E **49**
World's Biggest Bookstore, 9F **50**

Neighbourhood **Profile**

During the latter half of the 19th century, this area housed the worst slums in North America. It's now the focal point of the city.

The neighbourhood was known as 'The Ward'. It was described as being "the Alsatia and St Giles of Toronto." Many building lots measured only three meters by six – about the same size as many of today's living rooms. There was a lack of running water, flush toilets and drains. Residents were charged 25 cents a week to live there.

A witness of the day wrote: "Worries about sanitation were exacerbated by suspicion of the increasingly non-British character of the area's population. The cultural and lifestyle differences that they attributed to Jews, Italians, and other southeast European immigrants were regarded as additional obstacles to 'improvement'." Another said: "It's a strange and fearful place. It is unwise to enter, even in daylight. No sane person would dream of running such a risk. Perhaps it is the dagger of an Italian desperado of which they dream, perhaps the bearded faces of the Sheenies are sufficient in themselves to inspire terror."

Gladys Marie Smith was born in The Ward in 1893 near the intersection of University Avenue and Elm Street. She's better known as Mary Pickford, the first genuine Hollywood film star and the first of an avalanche of talented Canadians who have since found fame and fortune south of the border. Her Broadway début was in 1907 and her first movie, *Her First Biscuits*, was released in 1909. All that's left of The Ward is Laughlen Lodge. It was built in 1848 as a charitable institution, known as the 'House of Industry', "to provide lodging, food and fuel to the needy. " It was modified by architect E J Lennox in 1898 and is now a retirement home for seniors.

The city gradually chipped away at The Ward's boundaries. The Victoria Hospital for Sick Children, the first pediatric hospital in Canada, was built on College Street in 1892. The Toronto General Hospital was erected next door in 1911. St George's Hall, designed as a place to help British immigrants, was opened in 1891. It's now the Arts and Letters Club that was often frequented by The Group of Seven. Along the Queen Street side, the (old) city hall was built, as was Osgoode Hall. Slowly, the ugly realities of The Ward, and all it stood for, were quietly and systematically erased.

These days, the neighbourhood houses city hall and the Eaton Centre. It has the largest concentration of medical facilities in Canada. University Avenue, with its eight lanes divided by a landscaped median filled with statuary, is Toronto's *grande allée*. The Media Tower projects 3-D electronic imagery over Yonge Street. No one is scared about coming here any more.

Neighbourhood **Experience:** Regain your sanity in Trinity Square • see the atrium in Sick Kid's hospital • try to imagine what this area was like a century ago.

Map
15
Downtown EAST of Yonge Street
Dundas Square
Distance
185 m   200 yd
North
Area of detail
15

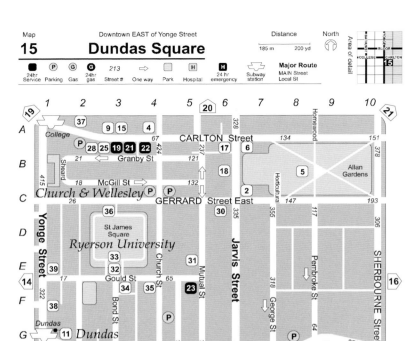

CityPlaces

Arena Gardens (1912), 5H **1**
Jarvis Street Baptist Church
  (1832), 7C **2**
Mackenzie House* (1859),
  3H **3**
Maple Leaf Gardens*, 4A **4**
Palm House (1910), 8B **5**
St Andrew's Lutheran Church
  (1878), 7B **6**
St Michael's Catholic Cathedral*
  (1848), 3K **7**
Torch on the Square (UC), 2H **8**

CityEntertainment

Carlton *Cinema*, 3A **9**
Massey Hall*, 2K **10**
Metropolis (UC) *Complex*, 1G **11**
Pantages Theatre*, 1H **12**

CityHotels

Bond Place Hotel, 3H **13**
Comfort Suites, 7G **14**
Day's Inn, 3A **15**
Grand Hotel, 7H **16**
Primrose Hotel, 6B **17**
Ramada Hotel, 6B **18**

CityFood

24 hr Coffee shop, 3B **19**
24 hr Coffee Shop, 6H **20**
24 hr Food mart, 3B **21**
24 hr Restaurant, 4B **22**
24 hr Supermarket, 5F **23**
Amalfi *Italian*, 4H **24**
Daio *Japanese*, 3A **25**
Hard Rock Cafe *American*, 1H **26**
Imperial *Pub*, 3G **27**
Peach *Vietnamese*, 2A **28**

Senator *International*, 2H **29**
Sorn Thai *Thai*, 6C **30**

RyersonUniversity

CJRT-FM, 5E **31**
Egerton Ryerson statue, 3E **32**
Normal and Model School (1851),
  3E **33**
O'Keefe House (1879), 3F **34**
Oakham House (1848), 4F **35**
Ryerson Theatre, 3C **36**

CityServices

CAA-AAA, 2A **37**

CityShops

HMV *Recordings*, 1F **38**
Sam the Record Man *Recordings*,
  1E **39**

This neighbourhood is more famous for three old arenas than it is for the promised glitz of Dundas Square. It was the place to be when anyone who was someone came to town.

The first of the great arenas was the Horticultural Pavilion. It was built in 1879 on the site of Allan Gardens and designed as a concert venue to raise money for the Toronto Horticultural Society. The building held 3,000 people, which was impressive for its day. Gradually the pavilion attracted a host of famous writers who came to Toronto to give readings. They included Mark Twain and Oscar Wilde. "I find that one great trouble all over is that your workmen are not given to noble designs", Wilde, then 27, said. "You cannot be indifferent to this, because art is not something which you can take or leave. It is a necessity to human life."

The Arena Gardens was the largest indoor facility in the country when it was built in 1912 on Mutual Street, just south of Dundas Street East. It was home to the Toronto Arenas, the city's first professional hockey team that would later become Toronto Maple Leafs. Glenn Miller dropped by the 'Mutual Street Arena' to give a concert in 1942, and so did Frank Sinatra in 1948. The first Boat Show opened here in 1954. But, perhaps the most famous event to take place on these grounds was on June 10, 1925. This was when Methodists, Congregationalists and Presbyterians came from across the country to this site to form the United Church of Canada.

The third arena is Maple Leaf Gardens. For nearly 70 years, 'The Gardens' hosted an almost endless parade of entertainment from the Metropolitan Opera Company and the Beatles to Frank Sinatra and Billy Graham. But its main focus was ice hockey. No other building in the city – including Sky-Dome and the Air Canada Centre – captures sports fans' memories more intensely than The Gardens. It was a place of triumph and tragedy for the Toronto Maple Leafs. They played 24,522 games here. The first was in 1931 against the Chicago Black Hawks. They lost 2–1. The last, also against the Blackhawks, was on Saturday, February 13, 1999. They lost 6–2. The only thing that changed was the way the Blackhawks spelled their name. Mercifully, between these two games, the Toronto Maple Leafs electrified the city by winning several Stanley Cups.

The latest baby to arrive on the block is a revamped Dundas Square, due to be born in the spring of 2002. Eventually, there'll be a $100-million complex on the north east side fronting a park with green granite walks, fountains, trees and benches. At the eastern end they're promising that the Torch on the Square will rise. The area is to be "Times Square with taste".

It would be interesting to hear what Oscar Wilde might have said.

*Neighbourhood***Experience:** Get that New York feeling without leaving town • then get away from it all and hide in St James Square.

Distance
185 m   200 yd

North

Area of detail

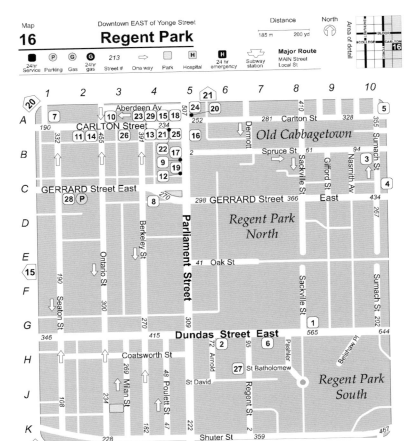

■ 24hr Service (P) Parking (G) Gas (G) 24hr gas 213 Street # ⇨ One way ☐ Park (H) Hospital **H** 24 hr emergency ⏚ Subway station **Major Route** MAIN Street Local St

---

*City*Places

Eastern Orthodox Church (1910), 8G **1**
Fire Hall #7, 6H **2**
Gerrard Street Methodist Church (1878), 10B **3**
Ontario Medical College for Women (1883), 10C **4**
Riverdale Zoo, 10A **5**
St Batholomew's Church (1873) *Anglican*, 7G **6**
St Peter's Church (1863) *Anglican*, 1A **7**
Toronto Public Library, 4C **8**

*City*Entertainment

Cabbagetown Community Arts Centre, 4B **9**

*City*Food

Asahi *Japanese*, 3A **10**
Barolo *Italian*, 2B **11**
Ben Wicks *British*, 4C **12**
Brass Taps *Pizza Pub*, 4A **13**
Cosmo *International*, 2B **14**
Daniel et Daniel *Fine food*, 4A **15**
Epicure Shop *Bakery*, 5A **16**
House on Parliament *Pub*, 4B **17**
Johnny G's *American*, 5A **18**
Jook Joint *Martini bar*, 4C **19**
Lettieri *Cafe*, 5A **20**
Margarita's *Mexican*, 4A **21**
Shanghai Gardens *Chinese*, 4A **22**
Tapas* *Spanish*, 3A **23**
The Peartree *Continental*, 5A **24**
Town Grill* *Continental*, 4A **25**

*City*Hotels

Amsterdam *Guesthouse*, 3B **26**

*City*Services

Police, 51 Division, 6H **27**
Beer Store, 1C **28**

*City*Shops

Micasa *Mexican décor*, 4B **29**

In the early 1940s this area supported the city's worst slums. Then came Canada's first large-scale housing project.

The existence of the neighbourhood enclosed by Queen, Parliament, Gerrard and the Don Valley has always been looked upon with a certain amount of derision. The ruling élite looked down on the original unskilled Irish workers who settled here from the mid-1800s. Those who came after them were poor immigrants from other lands. Between the two world wars the neighbourhood deteriorated into a major slum. And the derision worsened.

In the mid-1940s the city decided to knock down the entire neighbourhood of small, rat-infested houses and re-build. It was a bold and imaginative concept for its day. The area north of Dundas Street was designed for three-storey housing set amid enclosed open spaces, while south of Dundas accommodations would consist of high rise apartments. For people who had never had indoor plumbing or hot running water, the development bordered on Heaven. No one at the time seemed to realize that the whole project was designed without truly functioning streets. Those that did exist on maps were little more than dead-end lanes and walkways with no through traffic. Only Dundas Street East breathed any transportation into the area. And it managed to cut the project into two pieces: Regent Park North and Regent Park South. Each half then became an inward-functioning world unto itself.

The development was also a paternal, if not patronizing concept. Within two years of the first residents moving in at the beginning of 1949 there were confrontations with city fathers. People wanted to put up television aerials, but the mayor insisted this new form of entertainment was inappropriate for "the honest, though not entirely deserving, poor". One mother countered by saying that television in the home was necessary "to keep kids off neighbouring streets." The mayor threatened to have any aerials torn down.

By the mid-1980s, it became obvious to everyone that all good intentions to rectify "poverty, alcoholism, disease and broken families" were falling apart. The largely Caribbean, Tamil and Asian poor found themselves living in a neighbourhood rife with drug dealing and prostitution. The historic derision toward this part of town returned.

There are rumours circulating at city hall that the neighbourhood should be torn down again and built from scratch. And that's exactly the solution politicians had 150 years ago.

*Neighbourhood*Experience: Visit during daylight • stroll past nice Victorian houses north of Spruce Street • hang out with the Cabbagetown locals around Carlton & Parliament streets • expose yourself to earthy sights and sounds along Dundas Street East.

Map

17

Downtown WEST of Yonge Street

Little Italy

Distance

185 m   200 yd

North

Area of detail

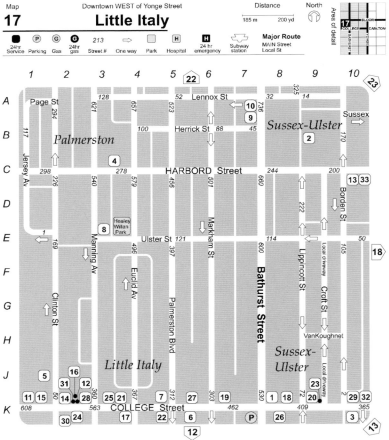

CityPlaces

Bank of Nova Scotia (1913), 8K **1**
Central Technical School, 9B **2**
Fire Station #8 (1878), 10K **3**
Harbord Collegiate Institute, 3C **4**
Holy Trinity Church *Greek Orthodox*, 1J **5**
Latvian House (1910), 5K **6**
Portuguese Seventh-Day Adventist Church
  (1888), 5K **7**
St Mary Magdalene Church (1888) *Anglican*, 3E **8**

CityEntertainment

Annex Theatre, 7B **9**
Bathurst Street Theatre, 7A **10**
Royal Cinema, 1K **11**

CityFood

Bar Italia *Italian*, 2K **12**
Boulevard Cafe* *Peruvian*, 10C **13**
Café Diplomatico *Italian*, 2K **14**

Coco Lezzone *Italian*, 1K **15**
Corso Italia *Italian*, 2K **16**
El Bodegon* *Peruvian*, 4K **17**
El Rancho *Latin*, 8K **18**
Gamelle *Bistro*, 6K **19**
Jing Peking *Chinese*, 9K **20**
Kalendar *Continental*, 3K **21**
Lava *Fusion*, 5K **22**
Maggie's *Bistro*, 9K **23**
Manzoni *Italian*, 2K **24**
Midtown West *Continental*, 3K **25**
Plaza Flamingo *Spanish*, 8K **26**
Pony *International*, 5K **27**
Riviera *Bakery*, 2K **28**
Roma *Italian*, 10K **29**
Trattoria Giancarlo *Italian*, 2K **30**
Utopia* *North American*, 2K **31**

CityShops

She Said Boom *Books/music*, 10K **32**
Things Japanese *Décor*, 10C **33**

The South Annex was touted in the 19th century as being "situated in the most healthy and pleasant part of the city". That pleasantness has been re-defined during the last 75 years *nello spirito di Italia.*

The South Annex is known for a lot of things. First, it was promoted during the 19th century as being close to the new University of Toronto and the parliament buildings, both of which came into being in the mid 1800s. Salesmen at the time promoted its 'location, location, location'. It was a place for people setting out in life. And, running north-south through the midst of it all, there was Palmerston Boulevard. Stone and iron gateposts grace its College Street and Bloor Street West entrances, and between these historic bookends you'll find the best of the neighbourhood's Victorian homes.

Between 1885 and 1925, the first wave of Italian immigrants settled just west along College Street and eventually took over most of the city's fruit markets. The second group came after World War II and made the area around Euclid Avenue and College Street their home. Bringing trade skills from the Old Country with them, they went on to make significant inroads into the construction business. Even today, it's almost impossible to find a construction crew anywhere around town that doesn't have a healthy Italian contingent.

We now have one of the largest Italian communities outside Italy. To honour this distinction the area around Euclid Avenue and College Street was named 'Little Italy'. And you'll understand why if you pass by Café Diplomatico's sidewalk eatery on a sunny weekend afternoon. But, if you really want to party, come here when Italy next reaches the final of the soccer World Cup.

Few neighbourhoods in the city have as many schools as the South Annex. The most imposing is Central Technical School with a Norman inspired tower rising above solid oak doors. Together with its playing fields, it occupies a city block. The second well-known school, though far less dramatic in appearance, is Harbord Collegiate Institute, built in 1931.

If you keep alert, you'll notice 148 Borden Street. It's a tiny worker's cottage that has survived as a reminder of times long gone. Another interesting discovery is St Mary Magdalene Church. Despite its name and location in a dominantly Italian Catholic neighbourhood, it's Anglican. The church is notable for two things: First, it had the world-famous musician Healey Willan as its organist and choirmaster from 1921-1968. Second, Queen Elizabeth the Queen Mother unveiled a plaque on the front wall in his honour in 1989. It's one of few plaques in the city bearing her name.

*Neighbourhood***Experience**: Get into the Italian spirit • sip a cappuccino anywhere along College Street • see some live theatre.

Map
18 **University of Toronto**
Downtown WEST of Yonge Street
Distance 185 m 200 yd
North
Area of detail

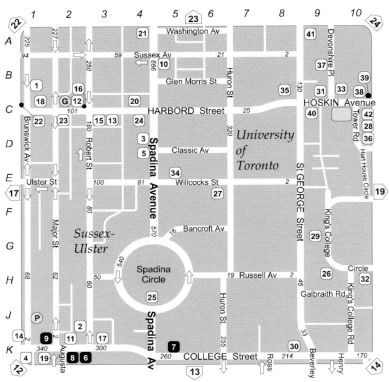

*City*Places

First Narayever Synagogue
(1890), 1B **1**
Hungarian Reformed Church
(1892), 2J **2**
Knox Church *Presbyterian*
(1907),4D **3**
St Stephen-in-the-Fields Church*
Anglican (1858), 1K **4**
Ukrainian Museum of Canada,
4D **5**

*City*Food

24 hr Coffee shop, 2K **6**
24 hr Coffee shop, 5K **7**
24 hr Food mart, 2K **8**
24 hr Food mart, 1K **9**
Élise *Café*, 5A **10**
Free Times *Cafe*, 2K **11**
Kensington Kitchen *Continental*,
2C **12**

Latitude* *International*, 3C **13**
Leao D'Ouro *Italian*, 1K **14**
Messis *International*, 3C **15**
Mo Mo's *Middle East*, 2B **16**
Rancho Relaxo *Mexican*,
3K **17**
Rowers *Pub*, 1C **18**
Simple Elegance *Taiwanese*,
1K **19**
Splendido *Italian*, 4C **20**

*City*Services

Post Office, 4A **21**

*City*Shops

Clay *Pottery*, 1C **22**
Harbord *Bakery*, 2C **23**
Toronto Women's Bookstore,
4C **24**

U of T

1 Spadina Crescent, 4H **25**
Convocation Hall, 9H **26**
Earth Sciences Centre, 6E **27**
Hart House, 10 C **28**
Knox College, 9G **29**
Koffler Student Services Centre
and Bookstore, 8K **30**
Massey College, 9C **31**
Medical Sciences Building, 10H **32**
Munk Centre for International
Studies, 10B **33**
New College, 5E **34**
Robarts Library, 8C **35**
Soldiers' Tower, 10D **36**
St Hilda's College, 9B **37**
Trinity College, 10C **38**
Trinity College Chapel*, 10B **39**
Whitney Hall, 9C **40**
Woodsworth College, 9A **41**
Wycliffe College, 10C **42**

*Neighbourhood***Profile**

An Ice Age relic stands erect in an area once dominated by the churches of England and Scotland.

The origins of Canada's largest university date back to 1827 when a Royal Charter was granted to King's College. It was the colony's first institution of higher learning, and the following year it was granted over 91,000 ha of Crown land. The campus cornerstone was laid in the middle of a forest on the site of the present-day provincial legislature. While the college was being built, lectures were held in the old parliament buildings near the corner of Front and Berkeley streets. In 1849 the government secularized the college from its Church of England origins and renamed it the University of Toronto. Construction of University College, the oldest building on campus, began in 1856.

Toronto's oldest newspaper, the *Globe and Mail,* once described the U of T this way: "The city has here a jewel, an eccentric but thoroughly charming mélange of architecture – Romanesque, Ruskinian, Oxbridgian, Arts and Crafts, high Victorian Gothic, late Gothic Revival, fussy Edwardian pomp (plus brutalism and the rest of the later stuff) – established 170 years ago in a sylvan, park-like setting designed to encourage spiritual and intellectual contemplation of the cosmos."

The campus is bounded by Spadina Avenue, Bloor Street West and College and Bay streets. A significantly re-styled St George Street, the official main street on campus, runs north-south proclaiming itself "at the heart of a great university." Everyone in town should visit the campus at least once, preferably on a summer or fall weekend.

The university tends to overshadow lots of other interesting places in the neighbourhood. There's St Stephen-in-the-Fields, a Gothic Revival church, that was designed in 1858 by Thomas Fuller "who later gained renown in fashioning Canada's parliament buildings." If you keep an eye open, you'll discover a very rare igneous boulder left here by a 12,000-year-old glacier. It's at the west side of Spadina Circle on the south corner of Russell Avenue. Knox Presbyterian Church on Spadina Avenue currently occupies the second oldest site in this part of town. Its predecessor was built here in 1821 and was the first Presbyterian church in Toronto.

The imposing old place at 1 Spadina Circle was built in 1844 as a Presbyterian seminary, then went on to become the Spadina Military Hospital and later the Connaught Medical Laboratories where insulin was first manufactured.

The *Globe and Mail* got it right about the spiritual and intellectual stuff.

NEIGHBOURHOOD EXPERIENCE: Go out and take one of the nicest walks in the city • join the students along St George Street •

51

Map

19

Downtown WEST of Yonge Street

Queen's Park

Distance

185 m   200 yd

North

Major Route
MAIN Street
Local St

Area of detail

■ 24hr Service   Ⓟ Parking   Ⓖ Gas   Ⓖ 24hr gas   213 Street #   ⇨ One way   ☐ Park   Ⓗ Hospital   Ⓗ 24 hr emergency   Subway station

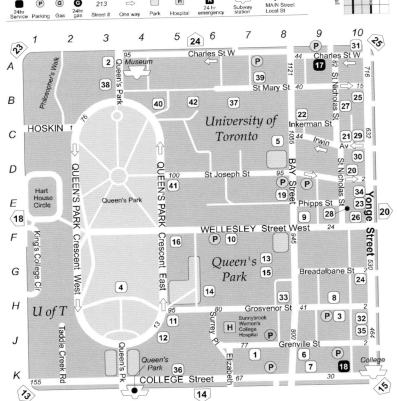

*Neighbourhood*Profile

For a long time, people have witnessed argument and opposition here. It's still popular public theatre. And Queen Victoria is not amused.

Queen's Park means different things to different people. It depends on who's talking. The northern extension of University Avenue is named Queen's Park. So is the southern extension of Avenue Road. The provincial legislature building has been called Queen's Park for so long that people - including some politicians - believe that's its real name. Bureaucrats refer to the civil service buildings to the east of the legislature as Queen's Park and they call the legislature building 'The Pink Palace'. Journalists, among themselves, call everything The Park. For the record, the real Queen's Park is the park just north of the legislature building. And a sombre, if not sullen, Queen Victoria sits on her bronze throne to the right of the legislature's front steps and oversees absolutely everything named in her honour.

Despite her regal presence, the front steps of the legislature provide a stage for rebellious citizens to rail against the government of the day. Whenever the legislature is in session, you're almost certain to see a demonstration of some sort outside. The most famous of these free-for-all events took place in 1872 when 10,000 members of the Toronto Typographical Union protested here to get themselves a nine-hour workday. Their efforts led the Canadian prime minister, Sir John A Macdonald, to pass a national law called *The Trade Union Act* that first established the legality of organized labour in the country.

But there was acrimony and screaming going on before the legislature was even built. It involved a competition for the building's design. A panel of judges couldn't agree on which concept to accept. In the end, and after many riotous debates, the award went to Richard Waite for the Romanesque Revival design you see today. The problem was that Waite was not only a member of the adjudication panel – but he was also an American from Buffalo, NY.

Not even the discovery of insulin here was without rancour. It happened on College Street in 1922 when a University of Toronto research team consisting of orthopedic surgeon Frederick Banting, J J R Macleod, J B Collip and Charles Best found this elusive treatment for diabetes. Banting was credited with the discovery and won the Nobel Prize for medicine in 1923. Only then did he find out that he would have to share the honour with Macleod - with whom he was completely incompatible. Banting showed his indignation by giving half of his prize money to Best.

Dissent seems to be in the genes in this neighbourhood.

*Neighbourhood*Experience: Attend Question Period when the legislature is sitting • walk through the university campus • catch up on crime at the Toronto Police Museum • join a demonstration.

53

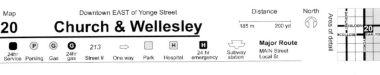

Map
20
Downtown EAST of Yonge Street
Church & Wellesley

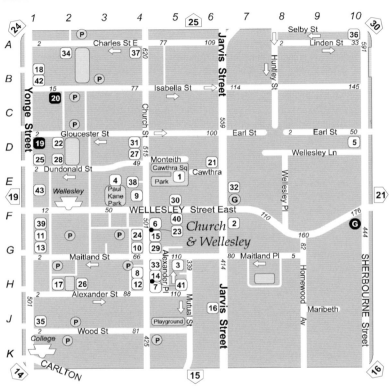

*City*Places

AIDS Memorial*, 5E **1**
Jarvis Collegiate, 7F **2**
National Ballet School, 5G **3**
Paul Kane House (1853), 3E **4**
Shrine of Our Lady of Lourdes
Church, *Catholic*, 10D **5**

*Gay*Places

Bar 501 *Bar*, 4F **6**
Black Eagle *Leather bar*, 4H **7**
Crews *Bar*, 4H **8**
Hassle Free *Clinic*, 4E **9**
Spa on Maitland *Sauna*, 4G **10**
St Marc *Sauna*, 1G **11**
Tango *Lesbian bar*, 4H **12**
Trax *Bar* 1G **13**
Woody's *Bar*, 4H **14**
XTRA! Newspaper, 4F **15**

*City*Entertainment

Betty Oliphant Theatre, 6J **16**
Buddies in Bad Times Theatre*,
2H **17**
New Yorker Theatre, 1B **18**

*City*Food

24 hr Coffee shop, 1D **19**
24 hr Food market, 2B **20**
Angelini's* *Italian*, 6D **21**
Bumpkin's *American*, 1D **22**
Byzantium *Continental*, 4F **23**
Cafe California *American*,
4F **24**
Caffe Volo *Italian*, 1D **25**
Carman's *Steakhouse*, 2H **26**
Diablo *Mexican*, 4D **27**
Miki Sushi *Japanese*, 2D **28**
P J Mellons *American*, 4G **29**

Satellite *American*, 5F **30**
Spiral *Continental*, 4D **31**
The Keg* *Steakhouse*, 7E **32**
Vagara Bistro *Continental*,
4G **33**

*City*Hotels

Comfort Inn Hotel, 2A **34**
Courtyard Marriott Hotel, 1J **35**
Hotel Selby, 10A **36**
Towne Inn Hotel, 4A **37**

*City*Services

Beer Store, 4E **38**
Liquor Store, 1F **39**
Wine Store, 5F **40**

*City*Shops

Priape *Adult clothing*, 4H **41**
Roberts Gallery *Art*, 1B **42**
Seduction *Adult*, 1E **43**

*Neighbourhood*Profile

This is where the first grand mansions proudly appeared. Today, pride has taken on a whole new meaning.

The most striking examples of what this neighbourhood must have looked like well over a century ago can be seen near the northeast corner of Jarvis and Wellesley streets. The buildings are McMaster House and Chester Massey House, constructed in 1868 and 1887. They were home to the founders of the Massey-Ferguson farm equipment empire, film star Raymond Massey and Vincent, the country's first Canadian-born governor-general. During the late Sixties McMaster House was the popular Julie's Restaurant and Bombay Bicycle Club bar. It's now The Keg Mansion steakhouse. The site is slated for 're-development'.

In the mid-1800s opulent estates dominated this part of town. William Jarvis, a provincial secretary of Upper Canada, owned a large tract of land here. The Home Wood Estate belonged to George Allen, a former mayor. And the Rideout family settled here after coming from Sherbourne in Dorsetshire, England. Street names are all that remain to remind us of them.

When the estates were sold and sub-divided, lesser homes were built. The best examples of these can be seen along Sherbourne and Jarvis streets, south of Wellesley. Many of these impressive residences, dwarfed by highrise neighbours, have deteriorated and remain boarded-up.

The area was once known as 'Molly Wood's Bush', named after magistrate Alexander Wood. He was infamous in the early 1880s for personally examining the genitals of young male rape suspects. Once discovered, his crime was deemed 'too odious' to investigate. It was in this neighbourhood that the core of our gay community openly emerged in the Sixties.

The long-gone St Charles Tavern over on Yonge Street was the most prominent gay bar in town when the community took root. It soon became an annual flash point for homophobic disturbances each Halloween. Today, our open and vibrant gay and lesbian community has integrated seamlessly into downtown.

The 1882 mansion of Charles Gooderham, head of the Gooderham & Worts distillery empire, became a hotel in 1913. Ernest Hemingway lived there. "I would sit at my table in the Café Selby and let the good and true whiskey warm my spirit and my soul", he once remarked. It's now a Howard Johnson's. On Gay Pride Day, climaxing a week of activities at the end of June, thousands of people from Toronto's gay community join with visitors from all over to celebrate community achievement. On occasions like this, it seems the St Charles Tavern on Halloween was a very long time ago.

*Neighbourhood*Experience: Sit on the Second Cup coffee shop steps and watch the guys go by • spend a quiet moment at the AIDS Memorial • enjoy dinner at the historic Keg Mansion.

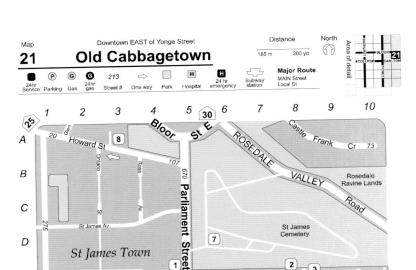

Map
21

Downtown EAST of Yonge Street

Old Cabbagetown

City**Places**

600 Parliament Street, 4E **1**
Heritage houses, 8E **2**
Heritage houses, 8E **3**
Heritage houses, 10E **4**
Necropolis, 10J **5**
Riverdale Park, 10K **6**
St James-the-Less Chapel (1860), 5D **7**
St Simon the Apostle Church (1887)
  Anglican, 3A **8**
Winchester Pub (1888), 5J **9**
Winchester Public School, 3J **10**

City**Entertainment**

Danny Grossman Dance Company
  & Canadian Children's Dance
  Theatre, 5K **11**
Toronto Dance Theatre &
  Winchester Street Theatre, 7J **12**

City**Food**

24 hr Coffee shop, 5J **13**
24 hr Coffee shop, 4G **14**
Chez Roger *Continental*, 5F **15**
Kiramathoo *Sri Lankan*, 5G **16**
Luciano's *Italian*, 5H **17**
Pelican *Fish & chips*, 5H **18**
Provence* *French*, 5G **19**
Rashnaa *Southern Indian*, 6F **20**
Timothy's *Indian*, 5H **21**

City**Services**

Beer Store, 4H **22**
Liquor Store, 4J **23**

City**Shops**

Green's *Antiques*, 5J **24**
Posterity *Prints*, 5K **25**

*Neighbourhood*Profile

We have nearly half a million residents of Irish descent. This is where many of their ancestors planted their roots - literally.

The original marshes at the mouth of the Don River were famous for three things: huge pine trees, disease-carrying mosquitoes and skunk cabbages. This is where the original Irish settlers built their homes and offered their unskilled labour to the Town of York's growing industries. It's likely that the skunk cabbages gave the neighbourhood one of its derogatory names: Cabbage Town. Others referred to it as Paddy Town.

Because of famine and potato crop failures in Ireland in the 1840s, more Irish began to arrive in what was now Toronto. They settled north of The Don marshes into an area bounded by The Don, Parliament and Queen streets and St James Cemetery. It, too, quickly became known as Cabbage Town - not because of skunk cabbages - but by the fact that the new arrivals planted cabbages in their front gardens.

There's little left of the original working class Cabbage Town south of Gerrard Street these days. What does remain, however, is the more affluent northern part of the old neighbourhood where the better-off residents built their homes. These old places got a new lease on life in the Seventies when upwardly mobile younger folk known as 'white painters' took over the area and spent a fortune on interior renovations. Over recent years, a growing number of Indo-Pakistani businessmen have opened restaurants and shops in the area, adding to its cultural mosaic.

The result is one of our proudest and most socially diverse communities. Local enthusiasts proclaimed it Old Cabbagetown and boasted that it had "the largest number of occupied Victorian homes in North America." True, or not, it's peppered with heritage buildings, with some of the most interesting houses on tiny Wellesley Avenue and out-of-the-way Alpha Avenue. These two enclaves give an insight into what the original community must have looked like 150 years ago.

To the northwest is St James Town, the most densely populated area in Canada. When the old workers' houses were demolished to make way for the complex in the late 1960s, one resident stood firm against developers and refused to sell. That house – which is now a laundromat – still stands at 600 Parliament Street.

This neighbourhood really shares its sense of community with the rest of us in September during the Old Cabbagetown Festival. But don't expect to see any cabbages growing in the front gardens.

*Neighbourhood***Experience:** Go to the festival and tour the open houses • stroll through St James Cemetery and count the number of historical figures laid to rest • roam around Riverdale Park • eat some Indo-Pakistani food.

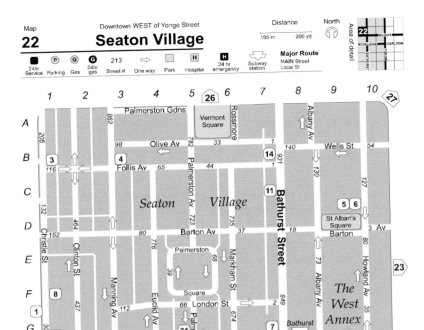

Map **22**

Downtown WEST of Yonge Street

Seaton Village

Distance 185 m 200 yd

North

Area of detail

Major Route
MAIN Street
Local St

24hr Service · Parking · Gas · 24hr gas · 213 Street # · One way · Park · Hospital · 24 hr emergency · Subway station

City**Places**

Christie Pits Park, 1F **1**
First Filipino Church *Baptist*, 8J **2**
Korean Beacon Church, 1B **3**
Orthodox Church, 3B **4**
Royal St George College Chapel, 9C **5**
St Alban the Martyr Church *Anglican*, 9C **6**
St Peter's Church *Catholic*, 7G **7**
Ukrainian Cultural Centre, 1F **8**

City**Entertainment**

Lee's Palace *Club*, 8H **9**

City**Food**

Aida *Lebanese*, 8H **10**

Black Roosters *Pub*, 7C **11**
Dooney's *Continental*, 9H **12**
Elixir *Persian*, 8H **13**
Grapefruit Moon *American*, 7B **14**
Hana *Korean*, 1H **15**
Il Bun Ji* *Korean-Japanese*, 2H **16**
Insomnia *Cyber bar*, 8H **17**
J J Muggs *American*, 8H **18**
Korea House* *Korean*, 2H **19**
Korean Central Market, 3H **20**
Korean Village *Korean*, 4H **21**
Montreal *Delicatessen*, 10H **22**
Moya *Japanese*, 4H **23**
Mul Rae Bang-A *Korean-Japanese*, 1G **24**
Paupers *Pub*, 8H **25**
Royal Thai *Thai*, 7H **26**
Se Jong* *Korean-Japanese*, 3H **27**
Seoul *Vietnamese*, 4H **28**

Victory Café *Eclectic*, 6K **29**
Zizi Trattoria *Italian*, 9H **30**

City**Services**

Public Library, 5G **31**

City**Shops**

Art Zone *Stained glass*, 5K **32**
Ashanti Room *African arts*, 7K **33**
Ballenford Books *Architecture*, 6J **34**
CD Replay *Used CDs*, 9H **35**
Cheese Dairy *Cheeses*, 9H **36**
Cinema Shoppe *Posters*, 6J **37**
David Mirvish *Art books*, 6J **38**
Experimental *Jewelry*, 6K **39**
Gallery Gabor *Art*, 6K **40**
Honest Ed's *Bargain store*, 7H **41**
Journey's End *Antiques*, 6H **42**
Plantation *Antiques*, 6H **43**

58

*Neighbourhood***Profile**

Pig farms and slaughter houses are part of the history of Seaton Village. Way before then, prehistoric elephants used to nibble on the tasty plants. The cuisine has now switched to Korean.

Many buildings constructed in Toronto in the early 1900s have a little bit of Christie Pits in them. This 3,000-year-old quarry provided the building trade with an almost inexhaustible supply of sand and gravel left behind by receding glaciers. It was vigorously mined to support a turn-of-the-century construction boom in the city. During early excavations a mammoth, or mastodon, was discovered buried in the pre-historic rubble. The pits have since been covered and landscaped to form the dish-shaped Christie Pits Park.

From the mid-Sixties to mid-Seventies, the first significant wave of Korean immigrants took place and new arrivals settled in and around Seaton Village. Although many of them have since taken up residence elsewhere in the city, the stretch of Bloor Street between Bathurst and Christie is still known as 'Korea Town'. This is where you'll find the best concentration of Korean restaurants in the city.

Although the Ukrainian community is better known further west along Bloor Street, the Ukrainian Cultural Centre on Christie Street remains the focus for those who had their Canadian roots in this area.

At the corner of Bloor Street West and Bathurst Street is one of our landmark stores. It's Honest Ed's, famed as much for its founder, Ed Mirvish, as it is for its flamboyant exterior and zany commercial signs. "Honest Ed's is the best place to find stuff you didn't know you needed!" is typical of what to expect.

A block-long section of Markham Street, south of Bloor, is known as 'Mirvish Village'. It came into being when the city planned to raze 24 little homes for a parking lot. Ed moved one step ahead of the city fathers and bought all the properties. He turned the place into a commercial colony for artists and things arty. Ed's son David owns one of the shops along here, David Mirvish Art Books. Together they own and operate the Princess of Wales and Royal Alexandra theatres, two of the city's premier stages. Ed also owned and refurbished London's venerable Old Vic theatre before handing it back to the British.

If he ever finds out that hairy elephants wandered around here, he might just commission a life-sized model of one for his store. He'd probably have it nibbling on a plate of kimshee or bibimbab. His rationale would be: "If it made sense, we'd be out of business!"

*Neighbourhood***Experience:** Humour yourself at Honest Ed's • have a Korean meal • spend an hour on Markham Street • play in Christie Pits Park.

Map
23

Downtown WEST of Yonge Street

The Annex

Distance
185 m   200 yd

North

Area of detail

■ 24hr Service ℗ Parking Ⓖ Gas **Ⓖ** 24hr gas 213 Street # ⇨ One way Park Ⓗ Hospital **Ⓗ** 24 hr emergency Subway station **Major Route** MAIN Street Local St

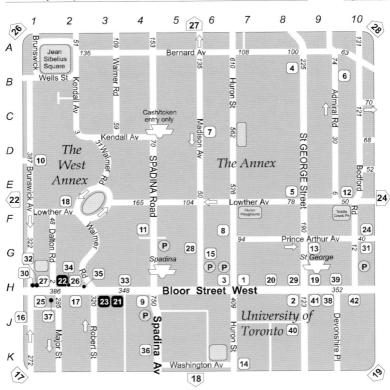

CityPlaces

Bahá'í Centre, 7H **1**
Bata Shoe Museum*, 8H **2**
Bloor Street Church (1887)
  United, 6H **3**
Chinese Consulate General,
  8B **4**
First Church of Christ Scientist,
  8E **5**
German Consulate, 10B **6**
Heritage houses, 6C **7**
Italian Cultural Institute, 6F **8**
Jewish Community Centre,
  4H **9**
Loretto College, 1D **10**
Native Canadian Centre, 4F **11**
Quakers Meeting House, 10E **12**
Royal Canadian Yacht Club,
  9G **13**
St Thomas Church (1893)
  Anglo-Catholic, 7K **14**

Tengye *Tibetan Buddhist*,
  6G **15**
Tranzac Club, 1J **16**
Trinity St Pauls *United*, 2H **17**
Walmer Road Church *Baptist*,
  2E **18**
York Club, 9H **19**

CityHotels

Quality Hotel, 8H **20**

CityFood

24 hr Convenience store, 3H **21**
24 hr Food market, 2H **22**
24 hr Supermarket, 3H **23**
Bedford Academy *Bistro*, 10F **24**
Brunswick House (1876) *Pub*,
  1H **25**
Goldfish *International*, 2H **26**
James Joyce *Pub*, 1H **27**

Madison Avenue *Pub*, 5G **28**
Mercurio *Italian*, 8H **29**
Nataraj *Indian*, 1H **30**
Opus *Italian*, 10G **31**
Rajputs *Indo-Pakistani*, 1H **32**
Real Thailand *Thai*, 3H **33**
Serra *Italian*, 2H **34**
Shakespeare's *Cafe*, 2H **35**

CityServices

Beer Store, 4K **36**
Kinko's 24 hr *Copy services*, 1H **37**

U of T

Admissions and Awards, 9H **38**
Ontario Institute for Studies in
  Education (OISE), 9H **39**
School of Continuing Studies,
  8J **40**
St George Graduate Residence,
  9H **41**
Varsity Stadium, 10H **42**

*Neighbourhood*Profile

In 1877, the middle classes moved north to where noise and pollution wouldn't interfere with their sense of well-being. Then the Aussies and Kiwis arrived.

It's known as 'The Annex' because it was annexed to the City of Toronto in 1887. To lure people here north of the city limits, builders and developers of the day promised an idyllic subdivision where homes were "subject to reasonable building restrictions, so as to prevent the erection in the district of business places, inferior houses or terraces."

They did a good job. There is still virtually no commercial activity between Bloor Street West and the Davenport Road corridor and the elegance of a Victorian subdivision remains intact. A forest of maple and oak trees cloaks large and dignified homes under a canopy of green in the summer and a rainbow of colours in the fall. Here you'll find Admiral Road, which is one of the city's most genteel streets. There's a peppering of historic buildings and two of our most exclusive clubs.

By 1890 an electrified public transit line had replaced horse-drawn carriages. Bloor Street was linked with Sherbourne and King streets and Spadina Avenue to form what was known as 'The Belt Line'. This was when most of the streets in The Annex were paved with cedar blocks, although St George Street claimed at the time to be the only one paved with asphalt.

Defining The Annex depends on historical lore or present-day legal precision. The area was designated as follows when annexation took place: "Boundaries being the western edge of Yorkville, Dupont Street, Bloor Street and a line between Brunswick Avenue and Walmer Road." Purists say the western edge of Yorkville is Bellair Street (right in the middle of present-day Yorkville), while modernists prefer Avenue Road.

Many of the old mansions have been taken over by the University of Toronto, or converted into rooming houses for students. But it doesn't take much imagination to realize that this is how the neighbourhood must have looked during Victorian times.

Even Ye Olde Brunswick House is still here. It opened in 1876 and welcomed the first post-war wave of travelling Australians and New Zealanders who hit Toronto in the 1950s. The Brunswick became their pub of choice and the beer flowed freely.

The Tranzac Club they founded in 1961 is still here. Predictably, it's just across the street.

*Neighbourhood*Experience: Walk along Admiral Road one afternoon • get someone to invite you to the York Club for lunch • join the university students at a pub • see Pope Leo XIII's slippers at the Bata Shoe Museum.

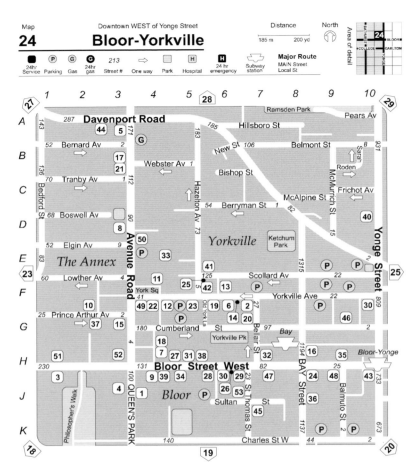

Map

24
Bloor-Yorkville

Downtown WEST of Yonge Street

Distance · 185 m · 200 yd

North

Area of detail

| ■ 24hr Service | ℗ Parking | Ⓖ Gas | **G** 24hr gas | 213 Street # | ⇨ One way | ▢ Park | Ⓗ Hospital | **H** 24 hr emergency | Subway station | **Major Route** MAIN Street Local St |

CityPlaces

Museum of Ceramic Art*, 4J **1**
Paisley Garden (1867), 6G **2**
Royal Conservatory of Music* (1881), 1J **3**
Royal Ontario Museum* (ROM) 3J **4**

CityFood

Arlequin* French, 3A **5**
Bellini's Italian, 6G **6**
Black & Blue French, 4H **7**
Boba* International, 3D **8**
Dynasty* Chinese, 4H **9**
Host* Indian, 2F **10**
Il Posto Nuovo* Italian, 4F **11**
La Pêcherie* Seafood, 4F **12**
Le Trou Normand French, 6F **13**
Little Tibet Tibetian, 6G **14**
Morton's Steakhouse, 3G **15**

Pangaea* International, 8H **16**
Pink Pearl Chinese, 3B **17**
Prego Della Piazza* Italian, 4G **18**
Remy's North American, 6G **19**
Sassafraz International, 6G **20**
Sotto Sotto Italian, 3B **21**
Truffles* (Four Seasons Hotel) International, 4F **22**

CityShops

Arctic Bear Native crafts, 5F **23**
Birk's Jewelry, 8H **24**
Budd Sugarman Antiques, 5F **25**
Bvlgari Jewelry, 6H **26**
Cartier Jewelry, 4H **27**
Chanel Womenswear, 5H **28**
Cole Haan Shoes, 6H **29**
Giorgio Clothing, 6H **30**
Gucci Accessories, 5H **31**
Harry Rosen Menswear, 7H **32**
Hazelton Lanes Mall, 4E **33**

Hermès Accessories 4H **34**
Holt Renfrew Clothing, 9H **35**
Indigo Books, 8J **36**
Issacs-Inuit Gallery Art, 2G **37**
Louis Vuitton Accessories, 5H **38**
Prada Handbags, 4H **39**
Ridpath's Home décor, 10D **40**
Sable-Castelli Gallery Art, 5E **41**
Sotheby's Auctioneers, 5F **42**
Stollery's Menswear, 10H **43**
Stubbe Chocolates, 2A **44**
Theatre Books, 7J **45**
Thomas Hinds Cigars, 9G **46**
Tiffany & Co Jewelry, 7H **47**
William Ashley China, 9H **48**

CityHotels

Four Seasons, 4F **49**
Howard Johnson's, 4D **50**
Inter-Continental, 1H **51**
Park Hyatt, 3H **52**
Windsor Arms, 6J **53**

*Neighbourhood*Profile

Yorkville has gone from an isolated 19th century village to a 20th century 'Hippie Haven' to the 21st century's most upscale commercial district.

It's hard to believe that this elegant part of town was once known as 'Haight Ashbury North'. The flower children of the Sixties, who made this neighbourhood a magnet for hippies from across North America, are long gone and so is the Mynah Bird that occupied the northeast corner of Hazelton and Yorkville avenues. It was the infamous club that tried to stage Toronto's first topless act. However, dense fog on stage and a bevy of police in the audience thwarted any thrills patrons might have been expecting.

This area, which was originally way north of the Town of York, was a forest until the 1830s when Joseph Bloor and Sheriff William Jarvis bought and subdivided a tract of land that was bounded roughly by today's Bloor Street, Avenue Road, Yonge Street and Marlborough Avenue. The Village of Yorkville was incorporated in 1853 and the first councilors were a brewer, butcher, carpenter, brick maker and blacksmith.

There are still a few reminders of those early days left. The 1867 house of John Daniels, the village constable, still stands at the corner of Yorkville Avenue and Bellair Street. It's now the Paisley Shop. A block further east is the 1876 fire hall that has been providing service to the neighbourhood for almost 130 years. At 105 Scollard Avenue you'll find one of the few remaining workers' cottages. It's now a tiny convenience store. On the corner of Hazelton and Yorkville avenues is the Olivet Congregational Church, built in 1876. It was converted into the Sable-Castelli Gallery. Next door is the 1909 Heliconian Club, once devoted to Women in the Arts. In 1883, Yorkville became the first village to be annexed by the City of Toronto.

After police moved the kids out of Yorkville during the summer of 1968, houses along Hazelton Avenue could be bought for $13,000. Today, some sell for more than a hundred times that price. That's because the Bloor-Yorkville neighbourhood has become Canada's epicentre for expensive restaurants and some of the world's most prestigious stores. During the summer try to get a sidewalk table at a fashionable area restaurant so you can watch the Porsche People trying to be unrecognizable behind dark glasses. Or, you can spend your life's savings on some baubles at the Bloor Street West marquees. If it's against your nature to be found inside Hermès, Gucci, Bvlgari, or Tiffany & Co, there's always the refurbished Hazelton Lanes, hidden almost too discreetly between Hazelton Avenue and Avenue Road. This is where the shops are not only a little less intimidating, but it gives us the pleasure of sitting in civilized atriums while sipping on designer coffees.

But don't expect the latte to be laced with the stuff they used in the Sixties.

*Neighbourhood*Experience: Shop till you drop • see and be seen at Prego Della Piazza • admire the heritage buildings in The Annex.

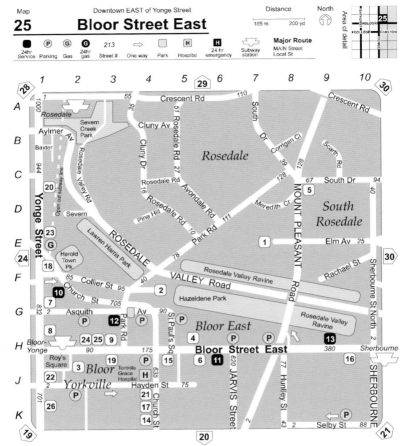

Map **25**

Downtown EAST of Yonge Street

Bloor Street East

Distance 185 m 200 yd

North

Area of detail

25

CityPlaces

Branksome Hall (1860), 7E **1**
Heritage houses, 4F **2**
Lotto Prize Office, 2J **3**
Manufacturers Life Building (1887), 5H **4**
Rosedale Presbyterian Church (1909), 8D **5**
St Paul's Church*, (1860), *Anglican*, 5H **6**
Toronto Reference Library*, 1G **7**

CityEntertainment

Plaza *Cinemas*, 1G **8**

CityHotels

Toronto Marriott Bloor-Yorkville, 2H **9**

CityFood

24 hr Coffee shop, 1F **10**
24 hr Coffee shop, 6H **11**

24 hr Food mart, 3G **12**
24 hr Food mart, 9H **13**
Ashai Sushi *Japanese*, 4K **14**
Cultures *Salads & light meals*, 4H **15**
Groundhog *Pub*, 9H **16**
Indian Hut *Indian*, 4K, **17**
Indochine* *French Vietnamese*, 1F **18**
Ithaca *Greek*, 3H **19**
Royal Angkor *Cambodian*, 1C **20**
Spirits *American*, 4J **21**

CityServices

Beer Store, 1J **22**

CityShops

Canadian Tire *Automotive & household*, 1E **23**
Hudson Bay Centre *Underground mall*, 2H **24**
Hudson's Bay Company (The Bay)
  Department store, 2H **25**
Kitchen Stuff *Kitchen needs*, 1K **26**

*Neighbourhood*Profile

Two influential men set a superior tone for this part of town 175 years ago. From then till now, this is where the city's Old Money resides.

In the early 1800s Toronto extended no further north than Queen Street. The hinterland was nothing but forest and a deep ravine carved by the retreating glacial claws of the Wisconsin Ice Age. It was the north side of this isolated ravine that attracted William Jarvis, and especially a spot near the present corner of Cluny Drive and Rosedale Road. His wife Mary fell in love with the wild roses that grew in abundance throughout the forest and she named their 1821 country estate 'Rosedale'. Chief Justice William Draper built his residence on the south side of the ravine where Collier Street is today, and the men joined their remote properties with a bridge.

Those residences are long gone, but Rosedale has retained its isolation and become one of the most prestigious places in Canada in which to live. Its mature, tree-lined streets and beautiful period homes bespeak the quiet respectability of Old Money, influence and power. The Rosedale Valley Ravine - filled with maple, oak, pine, beech, ash and basswood - provides a privacy wall to protect the moneyed scions of industry and commerce from those of us who are merely ordinary.

Bloor Street East, on the south side of the ravine, is the neighbourhood's stark divide. From here south is the much more mundane work-a-day world. Bloor East doesn't have the national *élan* attributed to Bloor West, with its Louis Vuitton and Chanel storefronts, on the other side of Yonge Street. But it does run through an area filled with almost forgotten bits of interesting history.

The hundreds of thousands of us who use the Bloor-Yonge subway interchange each week, for example, are probably unaware that we're walking through an old burial ground known as 'Sandhill'. Just up the street, where Canadian Tire now stands, our first significant brewery came into being in 1835. About a kilometre further north a Mr. Richards opened an ice house in the 1840s. He was the first Afro-Canadian businessman to set up shop in Toronto.

St Paul's Church on Bloor Street East is one of our most distinguished houses of worship. When the smaller church beside it, built in 1860, became inadequate to hold the congregation, the larger St Paul's was designed by architect E J Lennox to have the same seating capacity (2,500) as St Paul's Cathedral in London. It wasn't until renovations in 1991 that the seating was reduced to 1,700. Even so, it's the largest Anglican church in Canada and one of the most impressive churches in the country.

*Neighbourhood*Experience: Pamper yourself with a walk through Rosedale • stroll through Severn Creek Park into the ravine • see the Collier Street heritage houses • examine the library's Audubon collection.

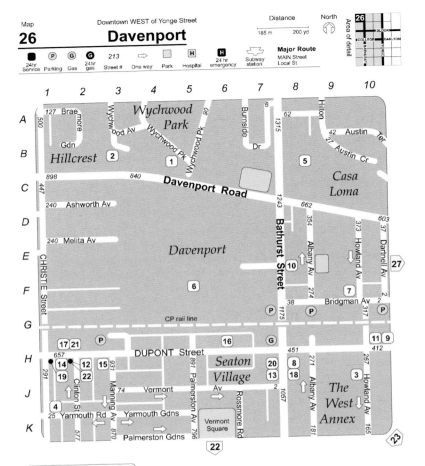

Map

26

Davenport

Downtown WEST of Yonge Street

Distance: 185 m, 200 yd

North

Major Route
MAIN Street
Local St

24hr Service | Parking (P) | Gas (G) | 24hr gas (G) | Street # 213 | One way | Park | Hospital (H) | 24 hr emergency (H) | Subway station

Area of detail

CityPlaces

6 Wychwood, 4B **1**
22 Wychwood, 3B **2**
Fire Station 23 (1910), 9J **3**
Korean Presbyterian Church (1914), 1J **4**
Rehabilitation Institute of Toronto, 8B **5**
TTC Hillcrest Yard, 5F **6**

CityEntertainment

Tarragon Theatre*, 9F **7**

CityFood

Annapurna* *East Indian vegetarian*, 8H **8**
Bistro Tournesol* *Continental*, 10H **9**
Dos Amigos *Mexican*, 8E **10**
Indian Rice Factory* *Indian*, 10H **11**
Lobster House *Chinese*, 1H **12**
Mayday Malone's *Pub*, 7J **13**
Mount Pinatubo *Filipino*, 1H **14**

Papamios *Italian*, 3H **15**

CityServices

Beer Store, 6H **16**
Wine Market (inside Loblaws), 1H **17**

CityShops

Annex Books *Used and rare*, 8J **18**
Candy Machine *Candy*, 1H **19**
La Parette *Print gallery*, 7H **20**
Loblaws Supermarket 1H, **21**
  Mövenpick Marché foods
  Ziggy's deli
Marlene's *Baby needs*, 1H **22**

66

Davenport Road is one of the oldest thoroughfares in the city. Perhaps more than ten thousand years old.

A very long time ago, the Iroquois used to travel along a trail that ran parallel to the shore of Lake Iroquois between the Humber and Don rivers. That was when the shores of Lake Iroquois (Lake Ontario) extended this far north. As the lake receded, leaving a plain on which the City of Toronto would eventually be built, the same path was used by missionaries and French fur traders. It appeared on maps for the first time with the settlement of Toronto's predecessor, the Town of York. That trail is now Davenport Road. It got its name from an isolated house built on the hill by John McGill in 1797.

The working class Davenport neighbourhood runs in a narrow swath between Davenport Road and the railway tracks west to past Dufferin Street. In this section the community is dominated by the Toronto Transit Commission's vehicle yards.

The land rises steeply from the north side of Davenport Road, giving homes on top of the hill a commanding view over the city and lake. Perched up here among a lot of trees is Wychwood Park. It's one of the most carefully hidden, intensely private and somewhat eccentric small neighbourhoods in the city.

Marmaduke Matthews, who was a landscape painter, wanted to start an artists' colony here in the 1870s. He named the tract of land after Oxfordshire's Wychwood Forest in England and set about creating one of the first planned communities in the area. Matthews' house is now number six Wychwood and that of his friend, Alexander Jardine, is number 22. They were built around 130 years ago.

Today, Ontario Heritage Conservation has designated the enclave an historic district. Each of the few dozen houses is listed in the Toronto Historical Board's inventory of heritage properties, even though some were built only 50 years ago.

Wychwood Park and the neighbouring Hillcrest and Casa Loma districts are in complete contrast to the much more modest streets of Seaton Village and The West Annex. There, mansions give way to less pretentious Victorian duplexes with street-front verandahs. No executive council meets to oversee private roads and parkland. No loosely gated entry deters the casual jogger. On this southern side of the railway tracks people much prefer life's more simple pleasures. Like watching their kids play in Vermont Square.

*Neighbourhood***Experience:** Say "Hi" to folks on their verandahs in Seaton Village • take a discreet stroll through Wychwood Park • mix with the locals along Dupont Street • take in a show at the Tarragon Theatre.

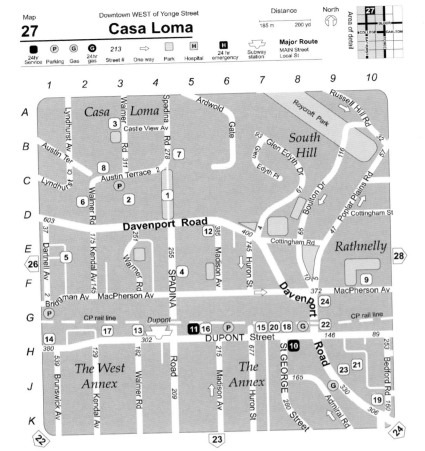

Map

27

Downtown WEST of Yonge Street

Casa Loma

Distance 185 m 200 yd

North

Area of detail

| 24hr Service | (P) Parking | (G) Gas | (G) 24hr gas | 213 Street # | ⇒ One way | Park | (H) Hospital | (H) 24 hr emergency | Subway station | Major Route MAIN Street Local St |

CityPlaces

Baldwin Steps, 4D **1**
Casa Loma* (1913), 3D **2**
Casa Loma Stables (1905), 3A **3**
City of Toronto Archives, 5F **4**
George Brown College,
    Casa Loma Campus, 1E **5**
Lenwil (1915), 2D **6**
Spadina House* (1886), 4B **7**
The (Pellatt) Lodge (1905), 2C **8**
Toronto Hydro Sub Station H (1910),
    10F **9**

CityFood

24 hr Coffee shop, 8H **10**
24 hr Food market, 5G **11**
Corner House* *French*, 5D **12**
Castle Dragon *Chinese*, 3H **13**

Dish *Cafe*, 1H **14**
Dolce Vita *Cafe*, 6H **15**
Madoka *Japanese*, 5G **16**
News Cafe *Resto-Bar*, 2G **17**
Red Raven *Thai*, 7G **18**
Tiffany *Tea room*, 10K **19**

CityServices

Liquor Store, 7G **20**

CityShops

Designers Walk *Home design*, 9H **21**
    Complex of five buildings
Martin Daniel Interiors *Home décor*,
    9G **22**
Mojtahedi *Persian carpets*, 9H **23**
Summerhill *Garden design*, 9G **24**

*Neighbourhood*Profile

Toronto is not well known for any grandiose quirkiness, or outrageous eccentricities. The exception is Casa Loma.

On the hill overlooking this section of Davenport Road is a collection of residences that typify the personalities of three turn-of-the-century people with money and power. One of those residences is a castle.

Casa Loma was the fantasy of Sir Henry Pellatt. He rose to prominence as one of the founders of Ontario's vast hydroelectric system anchored at Niagara Falls. He also fancied himself as a military man. After being knighted in 1905 he decided to build himself a home that not only befitted a knight but could serve as a place to entertain royalty royally. He toured the leading castles of Europe with local architect E J Lennox before deciding on a 17th century design that would be appropriate. The result was the largest home ever built in Canada. Although Sir Henry went bankrupt trying to complete his project, the monolith stands today as one of our top eccentricities and tourist sites.

If the castle was a testament to Pellatt's ostentatious display of wealth, then The Stables attached to it through a 244 m tunnel attest to his bizarre venture into financial extravagance. They are the most lavish and expensive stables ever built in North America. Gauntly ornate vertical stone turrets rise above stalls handcrafted from mahogany. The floors are covered with Spanish tile and laid in a herringbone pattern so horses wouldn't slip. Windows are hinged at the bottom so the animals would be saved any discomfort caused by drafts.

It isn't known whether these architectural flourishes attracted the Royal Navy here in 1944, but this is where they assembled the forerunner to Sonar. It helped assure the Allies of victory at sea during World War II.

The castle intoxicated E J Lennox so much that he built his own house, Lenwil, across the street. His bedroom was designed to overlook Casa Loma so it would be the first thing he saw when he got up in the morning.

Just to the east of Casa Loma is Spadina House, the 1886 home of financier James Austin who introduced branch banking to Canada. The present structure, with its opulent interior and historic gardens, has undergone four expansions in the last century. It stands at the north end of Spadina Road, which was originally an old Aboriginal trail. The road was designed to be a grand thoroughfare leading from Queen Street to the residence site.

Perhaps Sir Henry Pellatt thought that if he couldn't have the equivalent of London's Mall, then he should at least have the palace.

*Neighbourhood*Experience: Take a leisurely stroll along Glen Edyth Drive and Admiral Road • climb the Baldwin Steps and read the plaques at the top • follow the trend and take a visitor to Casa Loma.

Map
28
Downtown WEST of Yonge Street
Summerhill

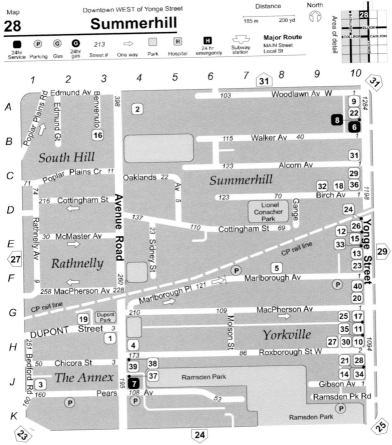

CityPlaces

Church of the Messiah (1891) *Anglican*, 3H **1**
De La Salle College, 4A **2**
Designers Walk Building 5, 1J **3**
Hare Krishna, 4H **4**
York Racquets Club, 8F **5**

CityFood

24 hr Coffee shop, 10B **6**
24 hr Food mart, 4J **7**
24 hr Food mart, 10A **8**
Blue Begonia *International*, 10A **9**
Espressimo *Caffeebar*, 10H **10**
Lakes *International*, 10H **11**
Musashi *Japanese*, 10E **12**
Pastis *French*, 10E **13**
Rebel House *American*, 10J **14**

Rosedale Diner *International*, 10E **15**
Scaramouche* *French*, 3B **16**
Thai Magic *Thai*, 10G **17**
The Nik *Eclectic*, 9C **18**
TrattoriaTata *Italian*, 2G **19**

CityShops

Absolutely *Antiques*, 10G **20**
Belle Epoque *Antiques*, 10J **21**
Braem & Minnetti *Antiques*, 10A **22**
Cadogan & Co *Prints*, 10F **23**
Conway & Gower *Tableware*, 10D **24**
Demarco Perpich *Home accents*, 10G **25**
Embros *Cookware*, 10E **26**
French Country *Antiques*, 10H **27**

Hollace Cluny *Home accents*, 10J **28**
Horse Feathers *Antiques*, 10C **29**
Hugo Quattrocchi *Antiques*, 10H **30**
L'Atelier *Antiques*, 10B **31**
Map Room *Antique maps*, 9C **32**
Matthew Berger *Antiques*, 10E **33**
Paul Hahn *Pianos*, 10J **34**
Putti *Home accents*, 10H **35**
R G Perkins *Antiques*, 10C **36**
Roots *Home accents*, 4J **37**
Touch Wood *Furniture*, 4H **38**
Vivian Shyu, *Women's fashion*, 4H **39**
Word of Mouth *Kitchenware*, 10F **40**

*Neighbourhood*Profile

Here's a part of 'Old Toronto'. And a Canadian sports hero is remembered.

It's been about 120 years since the area between Avenue Road and Yonge Street, north of the train tracks, started to blossom with Victorian and Edwardian residences. By 1900, this was a well established neighbourhood and the middle classes had settled themselves into a comfortable lifestyle.

About 12,000 years earlier, as the Ice Age was receding, waters of Lake Iroquois lapped the shores at the bottom of the Avenue Road hill. The hill remains as one of the very few steep grades in the city. Crowning its crest on the east side is an opulent old turreted mansion that's now part of De La Salle College.

Summerhill is not a grand place, but the mature homes along the magnificently treed Woodlawn and Walker avenues do create a sense of comfort and wellbeing. Scattered here and there are a few modern town homes that fit easily with the Victorian surroundings. Home décor stores along Yonge Street cater to trendy and fastidious tastes.

Across Avenue Road, you'll find Edmund Gate. It's one of our many little streets that provides a discreetly up-scale address for its residents. The house at the end has one of the finest views in the city.

A rather ordinary green space called Lionel Conacher Park on Birch Avenue sits right in the middle of this western half of Summerhill. It memorializes a Toronto athlete who was known as the "greatest all-round athlete in Canada" for the first 50 years of the 20th century. Conacher could break 10 seconds for the 100-yard dash. In 1921 he scored 15 of the points that gave Toronto a 23-0 victory over Edmonton's football team in the Grey Cup final. He played hockey for the Chicago Black Hawks and won the Canadian light-heavyweight boxing championship. World heavyweight champion Jack Dempsey fought an exhibition with him.

Conacher died of a heart attack on the baseball field after hitting a triple. It happened on May 26, 1954 while he was playing a charity game on Parliament Hill in Ottawa. He was 54.

As Ontario's Athletic Commissioner, Lionel Conacher worked hard to provide recreational facilities in parks, especially in his hometown of Toronto.

Except for a tiny and seldom used softball area, the park that was dedicated to him by the city in 1967 is devoid of sports amenities.

*Neighbourhood*Experience: Browse the antique shops along Yonge Street • drop in somewhere for a meal • take a walk through Ramsden Park • admire the big trees along Walker and Woodlawn avenues in the summer and fall.

Map
29
Downtown EAST of Yonge Street
Rosedale
Distance
185 m   200 yd
North
Area of detail

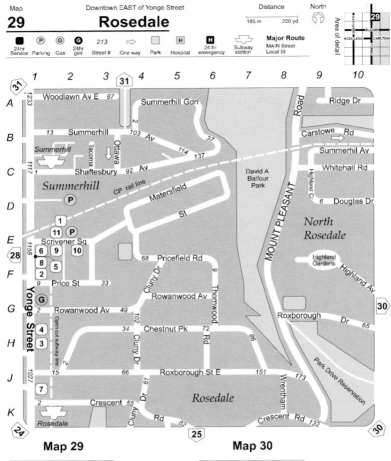

Map 29

CityPlaces

North Toronto Railway Station (1913), 2D **1**

CityFood

Patachou *French coffee house*, 1F **2**
Quail and Firkin *Pub*, 1H **3**

CityShops

Serendip *Antiques*, 1H **4**
All the Best *Fine foods*, 1E **5**
Harvest Wagon *Produce*, 1E **6**
House of Tea *Teas*, 1J **7**
Olliffe *Butcher*, 1F **8**
Pisces *Gourmet seafood*, 2E **9**

CityServices

Beer Store, 2E **10**
Liquor Store, 2E **11**

Map 30

CityPlaces

61 Bin-Scarth Road, 9E **1**
8 Castle Frank Road, 6L **2**
5 Drumsnab Road (1808), 9N **3**
44-66 Elm Avenue (1875), 1L **4**
89 Elm Avenue (1903), 5L **5**
1-7 Glen Road (1911), 2R **6**
6-8 Glen Road (1883), , 2K **7**
9 Glen Road (1888), 1K **8**
55 Glen Road (1891), 3M **9**
64 Glen Road (1894), 3M **10**
65 Glen Road (1891), 3L **11**
66 Glen Road (1894), 3L **12**
87-89 Glen Road (1901), 4K **13**
92-94 Glen Road (1900), 3J **14**
97 Glen Road (1901), 4K **15**
2 Hawthorn Gardens, 7K **16**
Rosedale United Church (1867), 8B **17**

*Neighbourhood*Profile

A touch of old Venice was supposed to add a bit more class to this 175-year-old community. But, like Venice itself, things started falling apart.

Here's where Rosedale really began. It's been said that Mary Jarvis, who gave this neighbourhood its name, was responsible for the meandering pattern of streets in the neighbourhood. They are supposed to follow the various trails she carved out on the forest floor when she went horseback riding. Two of those trails are now Cluny Drive and Crescent Road, where there is a collection of century-old residences listed by the city as heritage properties.

The one thing that dominates this part of town today has less to do with horses and more to do with the 42-metre clock tower that rises above the old North Toronto Railway Station. It's a stately and classical spire made of stone and modelled after the Campanile in Venice's St Mark's Square. The Canadian Pacific Railway opened the station in 1916. King George VI and Queen Elizabeth got off the royal train here in 1939 when they visited the city. During the next few years, it was the major embarkation point for Canadian troops on their way to fight in World War II.

After the war, the venerable old landmark ceased operating as a railway station. Downtown's Union Station, built in 1927 and comparable to the grand stations in New York and Chicago, took over as the city's only railway terminal building. As a consequence, the North Toronto Railway Station became vacant and generally ignored except for the presence of a 60-year-old liquor store on the main floor. Oldtimers will tell you that it's one of the best-known LCBO outlets in the city. As the years passed, the clock stopped working and the building started showing signs of premature age. It's no secret that the folk living in Rosedale found it embarrassing.

It wasn't the first time they'd been embarrassed. A long time ago, on the other side of Mt. Pleasant Road, they had to endure the lacrosse grounds. They have never quite forgotten the mayhem that ensued when the first Grey Cup game was played there. Sensitive and dignified feathers were truly ruffled.

In the spring of 1999 the large tract of vacant land just to the east of the old station came under residential development. To make the undertaking attractive to buyers and palatable to the old-time residents, it was proposed that the old station would be spruced-up with some kind of undefined rejuvenation.

And the clock in the Venetian tower is supposed to start ticking again.

> *Neighbourhood*Experience: Shop for prime produce, meats and seafood on Yonge Street around Scrivener Square • take a walk along Mary Jarvis's old riding trails.

30   North & South Rosedale

185 m   200 yd

Area of detail

30

The index for this map is shown with other Rosedale locations on map #29

1   2   3   4   5   6   7   8   9   10

A
119
55   Douglas Dr   109
137   Douglas Dr
200   Douglas Dr
6
154
Chorley Park

B
MacLennan
9
3
Edgar   Av   31
Roxborough
17
Dr
196

Rosedale Park

Scholfield Av   2

C
North Rosedale
138
5
Whitney   Av
41
Glen Rd   134

D
Highland   Av
106
Roxborough   Dr
65
94
Old George Pl

29
Roxborough   Dr   105

E
Highland Av
4
127
44   Bin-Scarth Rd
92
1

F
102

G
Park Drive Reservation
010
Beaumont   Rd
Don Valley Brickworks Park

H
C. Lamport Av
May Sq
14
Crescent Rd Jd
May St   2
Bell Line Trail

J
114
South Dr   138
Dunbar
South
Glen Rd
14
15
149
Nature Trail
BAYVIEW

K
13
Craigleigh Gardens
Rd
Avenue

L
4
51   Elm Av
74
12   11
5
99
Castle
54
Frank Rd   48
2
16
Hawthorm Gdns
Bayview & DVP ramp

25
Sherbourne
7
Maple
2
58
10
9
South Rosedale
Nanton Av
Hawthorn Av   2
43

M
Ancroft Pl
45   Glen Rd
Av   29
Powell Av
Castle Frank Rd

N
St North
2
20
63
Dale   Av   2
64
75
Drumsnab Rd
3

P
McKenzie Av 49

Q
SHERBOURNE
ROSEDALE VALLEY Road
Castle Frank
East
Sherbourne
Rosedale Ravine
Bloor Street East
Castle Frank Rd

R
6
Bloor
Rosedale Ravine
Bloor Street East
Castle
8
7
East
Frank Ct

20
Howard
Glen Rd
21

74

*Neighbourhood*Profile

Vancouver's 'West Van' is impressive. Montreal's Westmount is also a coveted address. But our Rosedale is still Canada's most respected residential neighbourhood.

Three neighbourhood maps - #25, #29 and #30 - detail one of the most eminent residential areas on the continent. Certainly nowhere else in Canada could you come across a more impressively mature, quiet and historically significant place to live – or have such a selection of some of the country's most influential people as your neighbours.

The best way to see Rosedale is on foot. Start at the Rosedale subway station (Map #25) and walk down the pathway through Severn Creek Park, along Rosedale Valley Road to Lawren Harris Park and on to the intersection of Park Road. You're now standing on the oldest road in the city. It was originally part of Davenport Road that followed a 10,000-year-old Aboriginal trail linking the Humber and Don rivers. Explorers, missionaries, fur traders and soldiers all came by here in the old days.

Go north along Park Road. Number 115 is the former home of Sir Ernest MacMillan, founder of the Royal Conservatory of Music and conductor of the Toronto Symphony Orchestra and Mendelssohn Choir. It contrasts with a controversial example of modern architecture at 111 Park Road. Near 30 Rosedale Road is where the original Rosedale House, owned by William Jarvis, stood. Continue up Park Road and go east along South Drive until you get to Glen Road (Map #30). Here you'll discover a cluster of Rosedale's historic homes.

In a neighbourhood drowning in splendid houses, you'll find 89 Elm Avenue, which was designed by the prolific social architect, E J Lennox. Five Drumsnab Road is the oldest continuously occupied house in the city. Built in 1808 on 81 ha of land, it has walls that are 76 cm thick. Eight Castle Frank Road, flanked along the front by five red maple trees, competes with the residence at 61 Bin-Scarth Road for being one of the most handsome houses in Rosedale. Each has one of the finest coach houses in the city. Another coach house can be found among the apartment residences at 2 Hawthorn Gardens. Don't overlook the old stone house on the northwest corner of Hawthorn and Dale avenues.

All that's left of the famous old Osler Estate – home of financier Sir Edmund Osler – are the gates. He willed his massive residence to the city. It was then torn down and absorbed into Craigleigh Gardens. Ironically, Osler founded the Rosedale Association in 1905 to protect homes in the area from the 'progressive' ideas coming out of city hall.

*Neighbourhood***Experience:** Walk south on Glen Road over the Rosedale Valley foot bridge. When you come out from under Bloor Street you'll experience the most dramatic social divide in the city. Within 200 m you go from abundant affluence into conspicuous poverty.

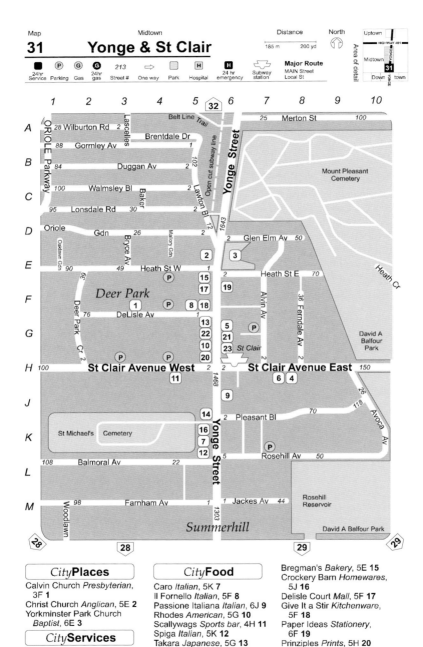

CityPlaces

Calvin Church *Presbyterian*, 3F **1**
Christ Church *Anglican*, 5E **2**
Yorkminster Park Church *Baptist*, 6E **3**

CityServices

Federal building, 7H **4**
Liquor Store, 6G **5**
Post office, 7H **6**

CityFood

Caro *Italian*, 5K **7**
Il Fornello *Italian*, 5F **8**
Passione Italiana *Italian*, 6J **9**
Rhodes *American*, 5G **10**
Scallywags *Sports bar*, 4H **11**
Spiga *Italian*, 5K **12**
Takara *Japanese*, 5G **13**

CityShops

Book City *Books*, 5J **14**

Bregman's *Bakery*, 5E **15**
Crockery Barn *Homewares*, 5J **16**
Delisle Court *Mall*, 5F **17**
Give It a Stir *Kitchenware*, 5F **18**
Paper Ideas *Stationery*, 6F **19**
Prinziples *Prints*, 5H **20**
Roots *Clothing*, 6G **21**
Sam *Records*, 5G **22**
St Clair Centre *Mall*, 6G **23**

*Neighbourhood***Profile**

Aboriginal people called this place 'Mushquoteh'. It was where deer came to feed in a forest meadow.

About 45 years after the founding of the Town of York in 1793, the Heath family ventured well north of the settlement and bought 16 ha of land. They named their new estate 'Deer Park'. In less than 20 years a small village emerged, complete with a racetrack. People who stayed at the Deer Park Hotel, on the present-day corner of Yonge and St Clair, had the pleasure of feeding a roaming herd of deer.

Not least among the community's landmarks was an 80 ha tract of land purchased in 1873 for use as a Protestant cemetery. Around the same time the Catholic church reserved another site close by for a burial ground. The combined capacity of these two cemeteries outnumbered the total population of Toronto. Deer Park was a place of tranquility.

The community lost its rural identity when the City of Toronto annexed it in 1908. Country life around the old meadow changed dramatically as people of mainly British stock came north to live. By the mid-Thirties it was known as one of Toronto's best neighbourhoods.

There's still a distinct Anglo-Saxon feeling about the place that some locals refer to as 'The Hill'. It's one of the few communities in town that lacks a broad and noticeable cultural diversity. Its three main churches – Christ Church, Yorkminster and Calvin - underscore the Protestant background of those who live here. All were built within a few years of each other during the Twenties, but it's Calvin Presbyterian that is perhaps the most interesting.

It came about when a minority of Presbyterians decided not to join the 1925 unification of Methodist, Congregational and Presbyterian faiths into the United Church of Canada. They wanted to continue their Presbyterian traditions and built a Greek and Gothic styled church designed along practical lines because the congregation "didn't have silver to waste." The bitter church schism still lingers, albeit in a civilized way, after more than 75 years. But those who stood by their Scottish religious heritage have given us one of our most interesting places of worship.

This is a generally low-key, upper-middle-class neighbourhood. The condominiums around Rosehill Avenue and Pleasant Boulevard rank among the best high-rise addresses in the city. The old single-family homes are gradually disappearing as the demand for elevated living moves forward.

And the deer have found somewhere else to roam.

*Neighbourhood***Experience:** Spend some time relaxing around the Rosehill Reservoir • take a walk along the Beltline Trail • stroll through the cemeteries.

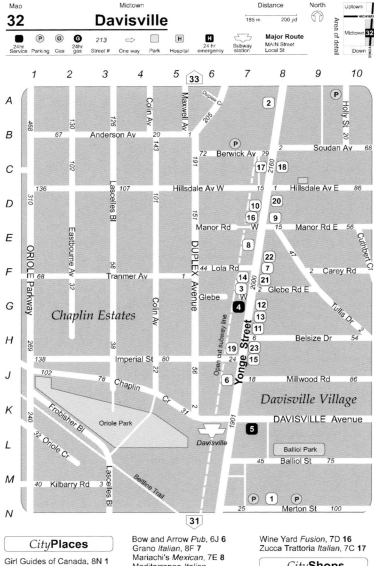

Map

32

Davisville

Legend:
- 24hr Service
- P Parking
- G Gas
- G 24hr gas
- 213 Street #
- ⇨ One way
- Park
- H Hospital
- H 24 hr emergency
- Subway station
- **Major Route** / MAIN Street / Local St

185 m   200 yd

Area of detail

HIGHWAY 401
Midtown 32
Downtown / YONGE

Chaplin Estates

Davisville Village

DAVISVILLE Avenue

Oriole Park

Balliol Park

---

*City*Places

Girl Guides of Canada, 8N **1**
TVOntario, 8A **2**

*City*Entertainment

Limelight *Supper club*, 7F **3**

*City*Food

24 hr Coffee shop, 7G **4**
24 hr Convenience store, 7K **5**

Bow and Arrow *Pub*, 6J **6**
Grano *Italian*, 8F **7**
Mariachi's *Mexican*, 7E **8**
Mediterraneo *Italian*,
  8D **9**
Quartier* *French*, 7D **10**
Sotto Terra *Italian*, 8H **11**
Stork on the Roof*
  Continental, 7G **12**
Sushi Supreme *Japanese*,
  8G **13**
Young Thailand *Thai*, 7F **14**
Vittorios Ristorante *Italian*, 7H **15**

Wine Yard *Fusion*, 7D **16**
Zucca Trattoria *Italian*, 7C **17**

*City*Shops

Art Shoppe *Furniture*, 8C **18**
Dell'Ernia *Lampmaker*, 7H **19**
Indoors Out *Gardening*,
  8D **20**
Lucca *Bedding*, 7F **21**
Rattan Shop *Furniture*, 8E **22**
Renaissance *Antiques*,
  7H **23**

As Yonge Street runs alongside the open subway tracks, it loses the *cachet* that has been bestowed on its better-known sections around Eglinton and St Clair. That changes when you go a block west.

This area is a combination of two important tracts of land. To the east of Yonge Street was the modest farming community of Davisville Village. The settlement was named after John Davis, who came to this part of the world in 1840 from Staffordshire, England. The village borders went from Eglinton Avenue south to Merton Street and from Yonge east to Bayview Avenue. Davis was the village's first postmaster and owned the pottery works that were the mainstay of the settlement's economy. It was, in its time, a peaceful little place with no pretensions.

Davis owned the lower half around Davisville Avenue and it was first subdivided in the 1860s. The top half, known as Davisville Glebe, was church property and it remained undivided until 1911. Some of the homes built in the southern half have since been replaced with commercial development, particularly along Merton Street.

It was an entirely different story on the west side of Yonge.

Around the same time that construction got underway in Davisville, the large, prestigious estate of William John Chaplin was being carved-up and promoted as a high-class residential district. It was bounded by Eglinton Avenue West, Yonge Street, Chaplin Crescent and over Oriole Parkway to Avenue Road. Anyone who thought of living here was forced to abide by a lengthy and bureaucratic array of complex building codes and zoning by-laws.

In the early Twenties the well-to-do were paying as much as $9,000 a lot. Despite this - or because of it - Tudor, Georgian and English cottage architecture began to fill the empty lots until the place was turned into one of the most distinguished residential areas in the city. It had, as they say, 'a nicer tone' than the settlement on the other side of Yonge.

Except for the high-rise complex on the south side of Oriole Park, this area remains one of our best and most sought-after addresses. To get the most out of this engaging neighbourhood, walk along Chaplin Crescent and north on Oriole Parkway to Hillsdale Avenue. Stroll through the streets south of Hillsdale, especially Colin and Tranmer avenues. This is definitely Mercedes territory.

And it has lots of *cachet*.

---

*Neighbourhood***Experience:** Get some high-end decorating ideas at the Art Shoppe • have dinner out along Yonge Street • check out one of the last lamp makers in the city • spend a summer's afternoon around Oriole Park.

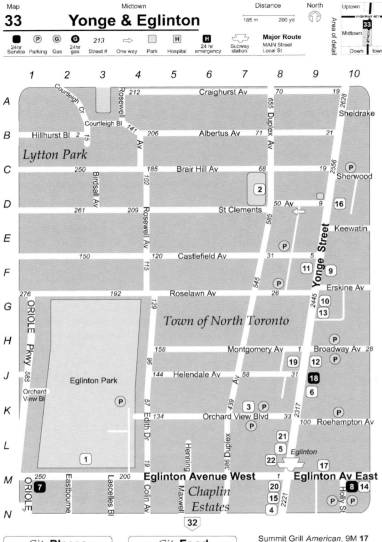

Map

33

Yonge & Eglinton

Distance

North

185 m   200 yd

Uptown

Midtown   33   Yonge

Area of detail

Down   town

HIGHWAY 401

Major Route
MAIN Street
Local St

■ 24hr Service (P) Parking (G) Gas (G) 24hr gas 213 Street # ⇨ One way ☐ Park H Hospital 🅷 24 hr emergency Subway station

CityPlaces

North Toronto Memorial
  Community Centre, 2L **1**
St Clement's *Anglican*, 7C **2**
Toronto Public Library
  North Branch, 7K **3**

CityEntertainment

Cineplex Odeon *Cinema*, 8N **4**
Silver City *Cinema*, 8L **5**
Yuk Yuk's *Comedy*, 9K **6**

CityFood

24 hr Coffee shop, 1M **7**
24 hr Restaurant, 10M **8**
Alize *Italian*, 9F **9**
Amore *Italian*, 9G **10**
Centro* *Canadian*, 9F **11**
Grazie *Italian*, 9J **12**
La Vecchia *Italian*, 9G **13**
Il Fornello *Italian*, 10M **14**
Mandarin* *Chinese buffet*, 8M **15**
North 44* *International*, 10D **16**

Summit Grill *American*, 9M **17**

CityServices

24 hr Drug store, 9J **18**
Post Office, 8J **19**

CityShops

Canada Square *Mall*,
  8M **20**
!ndigo *Books*, 8L **21**
Yonge-Eglinton Centre *Mall*,
  8L **22**

*Neighbourhood*Profile

One of Canada's most famous rebellions was hatched here. However, it was today's young urban professionals who eventually conquered the place.

Montgomery Avenue is named after the long-gone Montgomery Tavern that stood on land now occupied by the post office. It was the headquarters for William Lyon Mackenzie, who led the failed Upper Canada Rebellion of 1837. Despite the defeat, the disturbance precipitated the union of Upper and Lower Canada in 1841 that helped lead to the establishment of Canada as a nation.

Fifty years later, the energy of that anger had withdrawn into memory. The farm communities of Eglinton, Davisville and Bedford Park fused into a place they called 'New Toronto'. This was the northern terminal of the Metropolitan Street Railway that ran north on Yonge Street. And you could get here for five cents from downtown. Just before World War I, however, residents were getting fed-up with poor local services and voted to lose their independence and amalgamate with Toronto.

Except for the commercial corridors along Eglinton Avenue and up Yonge Street, this is largely a family-oriented neighbourhood. To the west of Yonge Street it's filled with mainly single-detached houses that were built between 1910-1940, even though development started here just before the turn of the century. Streets are lined with old trees that form leafy canopies over the sidewalks during the summer and fall.

It's in obvious contrast to the high-density buildings that have sprouted on the east side of Yonge. Some wry local folk point out that the urban professional families live with their designer dogs on the west side and the single wannabies live with their tabby cats on the east side.

The best time to experience the true flavour of Yonge and Eglinton is on a summer weekend. People are out jogging or taking chatty walks around the neighbourhood. Eglinton Park attracts hordes of summer kids into its playground and teams of energetic adults on to the playing fields.

Yonge Street is packed with pedestrian traffic and dogs on leashes. Folk relax in coffee shops, browse the book shelves at !ndigo, or wait for a brunch table at the Mandarin Restaurant. When the stars come out they can choose from two of Toronto's top five restaurants - North 44° and Centro – for dinner. There's a taste of success in the air.

The last thing on their minds is rebellion.

> *Neighbourhood*Experience: Splurge a bit on dinner at a good restaurant • hang out around the corner of Yonge and Eglinton and watch the locals • have Sunday brunch at the Mandarin • see the canines walking their human pets on a summer weekend.

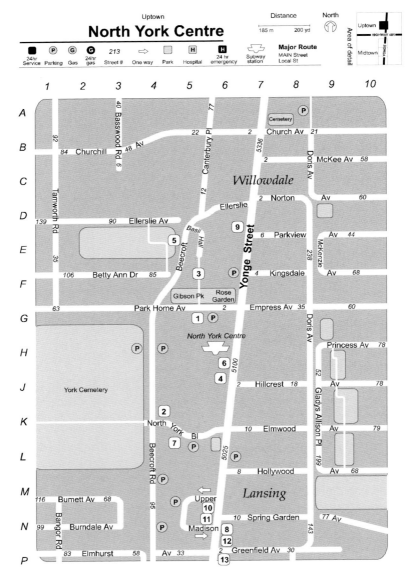

North York Centre

CityHotels

Novotel North York, 5G **1**

CityPlaces

Aquatic Centre, 4K **2**
Gibson House* (1851), 5F **3**
Mel Lastman Square*, 6J **4**

North York Archives, 5E **5**
North York Centre, 6H **6**

CityEntertainment

Toronto Centre for the Arts*,
4L **7**
George Weston Recital Hall
Main Stage

CityFood

Black Sheep *Pub*, 6P **8**
Cuisine of India* *Indian*, 6D **9**
Mazzone *Italian*, 6M **10**
Mr Greek *Greek*, 5N **11**
Smokey Joe's *American*, 6P **12**
The Keg *Steakhouse*, 6P **13**

*Neighbourhood***Profile**

North York came into being after two little rural communities – Lansing and Willowdale – finally grew into each other. Fast forward to Mel Lastman.

Jacob Cummer came to Lansing from Pennsylvania around 1797 to find a new life. The settlement was barely a year old when he built a modest log cabin near the present intersection of Church Avenue and Yonge Street. Thirty-five years later he erected what became known as 'Cummer's Chapel' - "a place where Divine services were to be held forever" in the Methodist Episcopalian tradition.

The chapel and its services no longer exist. In their place is a tiny cemetery with headstones going back more than 160 years. It's one of three sites in this area that links North York to its past.

The two others are Gibson House and the old Dempsey Store. A Scot named David Gibson built himself a Victorian farmhouse here in 1851 and then went on to become deputy land surveyor and an ardent political force. The house remains intact today as a popular museum.

The old Dempsey Store now sits in Willowdale after being rolled up Yonge Street from its original 1860 site in Lansing at the corner of Yonge and Sheppard. Taxpayers footed a $1-million bill to have it transformed into a museum and archives. In 2000 it was turned into a facility for autistic children.

A lot has changed since the days of Cummer and Gibson. This is the only area in Toronto that boasts a skyline to rival the downtown core. It was no accident. The rivalry between Toronto and North York - before they joined into one city in January, 1998 - raised civic political theatre into an art form. The lead character, who never missed a performance for almost a quarter-century, was Mel Lastman, North York's mayor.

It's impossible to separate Mel from North York. He was responsible for cutting a deal to build the then North York Centre for the Performing Arts so he could compete with Toronto's coveted downtown theatre district. He single handedly created what is now uptown. Mel Lastman Square rivals downtown's Nathan Phillips Square as the place for us to be seen on New Year's Eve. The carillon atop the North York Centre is known all over town as 'Mel's Bells'. There are lots and lots of portraits of Mel hanging along a single public corridor in the North York Civic Centre.

And, if all this wasn't enough, we elected him in December, 1997 as the first mayor of our new, amalgamated City of Toronto.

*Neighbourhood***Experience:** Hear some of the city's best acoustics at the George Weston Recital Hall • join one of the annual celebrations in Mel Lastman Square • explore what the city was like in the heyday of Gibson House •

*City*Places

If you went somewhere different every day, for the rest of your life, you still might not experience all the city has to offer. Here are some places that are well worth exploring.

Art galleries & street art

Toronto has many of the country's finest galleries, including the 8th largest art museum on the continent. And, over the last decade, a mass of art has appeared on the streets.

AIDS MEMORIAL
WHERE: Cawthra Square Park. MAP: 20 WHEN: 24 hr. ADMISSION: Free.
SUBWAY: Wellesley.

The memorial, designed by Patrick Fahn, is a plain curved row of concrete pillars set in the middle of the gay neighbourhood. It's a reflective reminder of past companions, friends and relatives. Hundreds of names and dates are engraved on stainless steel plates fixed to the pillars. They are arranged chronologically from 1984.

ART GALLERY OF ONTARIO (AGO)
WHERE: 317 Dundas Street West. MAP: 13
WHEN: Tuesday through Friday, 12 noon – 9.00 PM. Weekends, 10.00 AM – 5.30 PM. AD-
MISSION: $. TELEPHONE: 416-979-6648 (General information);
416-979-6649 (Today's showings); 416-979-6610 (Gallery Shop). WEB SITE: **ago.on.ca**
SUBWAY: St Patrick.

A French critic once lauded the AGO's architecture. Others felt a yawn was more exciting. Inside, it ranks as the 8th largest art museum on the continent. Ambitious visiting collections from around the world find their way here every year. There's a rental and sales gallery, plus the AGO Gallery Shop with 930 sq m of floor space for books, jewelry and reproductions.

CANADIAN AIRMEN'S MEMORIAL
WHERE: University Avenue at Dundas Street West. MAP: 14 WHEN: 24 hr.
ADMISSION: Free. SUBWAY: St Patrick.

This once controversial statue created by Oscar Nemon is known locally as 'Gumby Goes to Heaven' and was erected as a private initiative. Other war-related works in the area include *The Great War* memorial by Charles Adamson on University Avenue at Elm Street and the Cenotaph fronting the old city hall on Queen Street West at Bay Street.

CITY PEOPLE
WHERE: Front Street West at Bay Street in front of the Royal Bank Plaza. MAP: 9
WHEN: 24 hr. ADMISSION: Free. SUBWAY: Union.

Catherine Widgley's multi-piece cutout sculpture is one of our most whimsical pieces of public art. Depicting hurried and harried folk dashing off up the stairs to who knows where, the work seems to blend inconspicuously with real people on the sidewalk.

FLATIRON MURAL
WHERE: On the west wall of the Flatiron Building overlooking Berczy Park. MAP: 10
WHEN: 24 hr. ADMISSION: Free.
SUBWAY: Union. Go one and a half blocks east along Front Street East.

Derek Besant's 1980 *Flatiron Mural* is one of the city's most photographed works of street art. The plaque underneath says little about the mural, but lots about the politicians who made it possible.

FLYING GEESE
WHERE: Inside the Eaton Centre. MAP: 14 WHEN: Daily. ADMISSION: Free.
SUBWAY: Dundas or Queen.

A flock of Canada geese seems perpetually in flight down the inside length of the Eaton Centre. Michael Snow was the artist - and he makes sure the work isn't sullied by tying Yuletide red ribbons around the geese's necks.

HARBOURFRONT CENTRE
WHERE: 235 Queen's Quay West in the York Quay building. MAP: 4
WHEN: Daily, 10 AM – 11.00 PM. ADMISSION: Free. TELEPHONE: 416-973-3000
WEB SITE: **harbourfront.on.ca** SUBWAY: Union and take the Harbourfront 509 streetcar.

A one-of-a-kind arts centre offering visual arts and crafts programs. At the Craft Studio you can watch working professionals designing in glass, metal, textiles and ceramics. Items can be purchased from the Bounty Shop.

HENRY MOORE SCULPTURES
MAP: 13 and 14

We have two large public bronzes by Henry Moore. *Two Forms* is on the southwest corner of Dundas Street West and McCaul Street outside the Art Gallery of Ontario. *The Archer* (1966) is displayed in Nathan Phillips Square fronting city hall on Queen Street West at Bay Street.

JUSTINA M. BARNICKE GALLERY
WHERE: 7 Hart House Circle, inside Hart House, University of Toronto. MAP: 19
WHEN: Monday through Friday, 11.00 AM – 7.00 PM. Weekends, 1.00 PM – 4.00 PM. Closed Sundays in July and August. ADMISSION: Free. TELEPHONE: 416-978-8398
WEB SITE: **utoronto.ca/gallery** SUBWAY: Queen's Park.

The gallery houses the finest examples of *beaux-arts* Gothic Revival in Canada. It offers a display of works by promising Canadian artists as well as historical exhibitions curated from the Hart House permanent collection.

MEDIA TOWER
WHERE: Northwest corner of Yonge Street and Dundas Street West. MAP: 14
WHEN: 24 hr. ADMISSION: Free. SUBWAY: Dundas.

By the time Dundas Square opens officially in the spring of 2002, the Media Tower will have been projecting imagery over Yonge Street for some time. It's believed to be the first of its kind in the world. The whole area is being designed to elevate advertising into an art form.

MUSEUM OF CONTEMPORARY CANADIAN ART

WHERE: 5040 Yonge Street inside the Toronto Centre for the Arts.
MAP: *North York Centre*. WHEN: Tuesday through Sunday, 12 noon – 5.00 PM.
ADMISSION: Free. TELEPHONE: 416-395-0067 SUBWAY: North York Centre.

The two-floor, 465 sq m gallery devoted to challenging contemporary Canadian works was opened in 1994. It also features changing exhibits. The gallery is open for ticket-holders at the Toronto Centre for the Arts before shows and during intermissions. It was previously called the Art Gallery of North York.

POWER PLANT

WHERE: 231 Queen's Quay West. MAP: 4
WHEN: Tuesday through Sunday, 12 noon – 6.00 PM. Wednesdays, 12 noon – 8.00 PM.
ADMISSION: $, but free Wednesdays from 5.00 PM – 8.00 PM.
TELEPHONE: 416-973-4949 WEB SITE: **culturenet.ca/powerplant/**
SUBWAY: Union and take the Harbourfront 509 streetcar.

Here's our main public gallery for innovative contemporary art. The various forms include photography, sculpture, painting and new media. The Power Plant is a non-collecting gallery specializing in solo and group exhibitions from across the country.

PRINCESS OF WALES THEATRE MURAL

WHERE: Pearl Street. MAP: 8 WHEN: 24 hr. ADMISSION: Free. SUBWAY: St Andrew.

When Ed Mirvish built the Princess of Wales Theatre in 1993 for the Canadian première of *Miss Saigon,* he commissioned American Frank Stella to provide 930 sq m of murals. One of the largest of these is displayed on the exterior Pearl Street wall of the theatre. Inside, Stella's work graces the hall, foyers and ceilings.

ROSE WINDOWS

WHERE: St Paul's Anglican Church, 227 Bloor Street East. MAP: 25
WHEN: Lunch-hour weekdays and services Sunday. ADMISSION: Free.
TELEPHONE: 416-961-8116 WEB SITE: **anglican.ca** SUBWAY: Bloor-Yonge.

The windows are placed in each transept and are among the largest of their kind. Other stained glass windows that are outstanding are on the east wall. They're dedicated to those in the congregation who gave their lives in World War I.

SALMON RUN

WHERE: Southeast corner of SkyDome. MAP: 3 WHEN: 24 hr. ADMISSION: Free.
SUBWAY: Union and take the Skywalk to SkyDome.

This is one of the most engaging pieces of public sculpture we have in the city. Cascading waterfalls splash as two-dimensional salmon swim and jump upstream. Susan Schelle created the work in 1991 for this location.

SCULPTURE GARDEN

WHERE: 115 King Street East opposite St James' Park. MAP: 10 WHEN: Dawn to dusk. ADMISSION: Free. TELEPHONE: 416-485-9658 SUBWAY: King.

This is a small park on the east side of the La Maquette restaurant. Exhibits change regularly and portray a wide range of themes from 'flying saucers' to animals and contemporary pieces. It was once the site of historic Oak Hall that was demolished in 1938 to make way for a tiny parking lot. The garden was opened in 1981.

ST ANNE'S ANGLICAN CHURCH

WHERE: 270 Gladstone Avenue. MAP: *City of Toronto* near the Dundas and Dufferin intersection, area 8M, and in detail below. WHEN: Sunday services.
TELEPHONE: 416-536-1202 WEB SITE: **stannes.on.ca** ADMISSION: Free.
SUBWAY: Dufferin and take a 29 bus south.

This is the only Byzantine-style Anglican church in Canada. It's one of those places that you've probably heard about, but haven't bothered to visit. Famous for its interior art, it has 11 canvas panels painted by three members of The Group of Seven: J E H MacDonald, Frank Carmichael and Frederick Varley. The spire rises 23 metres above the nave, giving the interior an unexpected feeling of space in all directions.

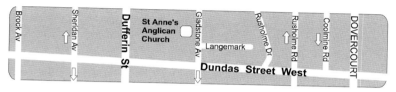

THE AUDIENCE

WHERE: North exterior wall of SkyDome. MAP: 3 WHEN: 24 hr. ADMISSION: Free.
SUBWAY: Union and take the Skywalk.

There are two parts to this conspicuous 1989 Michael Snow sculpture: *Audience 1* on the east side shows gargoyles cheering; *Audience 2* on the west side depicts jeering fans – including *Fat Man* and *Muscle Man*. The works, which are made of fibreglass and painted to look like bronze, dominate the north side of the stadium. Not everyone was enamoured with them when they appeared, but time has mellowed any initial controversy. Snow's other well-known public sculpture is *Flying Geese* inside the Eaton Centre.

UNTITLED MOUNTAINS

WHERE: Simcoe Place. MAP: 9 WHEN: 24 hr. ADMISSION: Free.
SUBWAY: Union, or St Andrew.

A lot of street art is emerging in this part of town. Anish Kapoor's metallic sculpture of ribbed, triangular mountain peaks stands just back from Front Street and dominates other pieces of sculpture and fountains around Simcoe Place and Metro Square. It isn't hard to find. All you have to do is head for the crowd of camera-happy tourists. After a while you realize that Kapoor's work has an uncanny resemblance to the signature mountain at Paramount Canada's Wonderland.

WOODPECKER COLUMN

WHERE: Bremner Boulevard outside the Toronto Convention Centre's south entrance.
MAP: 4 WHEN: 24 hr. ADMISSION: Free. SUBWAY: Union.

There are a few pieces of street art around town that reach out and grab you. One of the most obvious is a thick black vertical pole grasped by two giant woodpeckers. It rises above Bobbie Rosenfeld Park and dominates the immediate area. The 1997 work, which does not have a plaque acknowledging the artist, joins *Salmon Run*, just to the west, as one of many sculptures around downtown devoted to animals.

Buildings

We have two signature buildings in the city: the CN Tower and city hall. A third building - the longest of its type in the world – is underground.

CITY HALL
WHERE: Queen Street West at Bay Street. MAP: 14
WHEN: Weekdays and during public tours. ADMISSION: Free.
TELEPHONE: 416-338-0338 (Tours). WEB SITE: city.toronto.on.ca SUBWAY: Queen.

Before the CN Tower came along, city hall was Toronto's signature building. Finnish architect Viljo Revell won an international competition to design the complex that attracted more than 500 entries from 40 countries. Governor-General Georges Vanier opened the building on September 13, 1965, ten months after Revell's death. It's one of the best pieces of modern architecture downtown, with two concave wings enclosing an oyster-shaped council chamber. A stylized version of the building forms the city's official logo.

CN TOWER
WHERE: Front Street West at John Street. MAP: 3 WHEN: Daily. ADMISSION: $.
TELEPHONE: 416-868-6937 WEB SITE: cntower.ca SUBWAY: Union. Take the Skywalk.

At 553 m, this is the world's tallest free-standing structure. However, it could lose its top spot to hopeful projects already on drawing boards in Asia and Australia. Six glass-walled elevators get you to the top in 58 seconds. The tower wasn't built primarily for tourists. Its main function is to consolidate and improve the city's vast electronic communications systems. CN meant Canadian National when the tower was built. It now means Canada's National.

COMMERCE COURT
WHERE: Southeast corner of King and Bay streets. MAP: 9 WHEN: Weekdays.
ADMISSION: Free. TELEPHONE: 416-861-3475 SUBWAY: King.

Esthetically, the main CIBC tower's 57 storeys are secondary to the old building next door. This aging landmark at 25 King Street West was the original headquarters of the Bank of Commerce before it merged with the Canadian Imperial Bank to form the CIBC. It once held the distinction of being the tallest building in the British Empire and its observation deck 32 storeys above ground was the CN Tower of its day. The inside has been preserved and offers one of the most beautiful examples of corporate interior design in the city.

EATON CENTRE
WHERE: Yonge Street, between Dundas and Queen streets. MAP: 14 WHEN: Daily.
ADMISSION: Free. TELEPHONE: 416-598-8700 WEB SITE: torontoeatoncentre.com SUBWAY: Dundas, or Queen.

More people go through the centre each weekday than through any other place except the PATH underground walkway. It's also believed to be our top tourist attraction. The vast four-level atrium, inspired by Milan's galleria, has over 300 stores. In 1999, the Yonge Street side and west entrance were re-designed to make the complex more accessible. Outside the northwest entrance is historic Trinity Square that few of us even know exists. Without doubt, it's one of the most pleasant and historic squares in the city. The Eaton Centre was named after Timothy Eaton's first department store that opened on the southern Queen Street end in 1869. Although Eaton's went into receivership and was taken over by Sears Canada in the fall of 1999, the centre and its anchor department store have retained the historic Eaton's name. However, the store's name now has a small 'e' and no apostrophe.

FIRST CANADIAN PLACE
WHERE: Northwest corner of Bay and King streets. MAP: 9 WHEN: Daily.
ADMISSION: Free. TELEPHONE: 416-862-8138 SUBWAY: King.

The complex is owned by Olympia & York and has the highest office tower in Canada. The 74-storey skyscraper, built in 1972, is home to the Bank of Montreal and was constructed of matching white Italian marble. It arrived in the Financial District at a time when the major banks seemed to be out-building each other with ever more impressive edifices. Together with other major complexes at the King and Bay streets intersection, it forms a major component of the PATH underground walkway system.

HERITAGE SQUARE - BCE PLACE
WHERE: Bounded by Yonge, Bay, Wellington and Front streets. MAP: 9 WHEN: Daily.
ADMISSION: Free. TELEPHONE: 416-777-6480 WEB SITE: **bceplacetoronto.com**
SUBWAY: King, or Union.

The Heritage Square galleria in BCE Place is one of the most photographed indoor sights in the city. Several television commercials and movies have used this location because of its vaulted glass ceiling that towers above a dramatic pedestrian mall. Trendy restaurants, including the popular Mövenpick Marché and Acqua, open on to the public areas.

NATIONAL TRADE CENTRE
WHERE: Princes' Boulevard, Exhibition Place. MAP: 1
WHEN: During conventions and exhibitions. ADMISSION: Included in events.
TELEPHONE: 416-263-3000 WEB SITE: **ntc.on.ca**
SUBWAY: Union and take the Harbourfront 509 streetcar.

When the Trade Centre opened in the late 1990s it was the biggest in the country and the third largest in North America. Its modern curved design, with four signature cylindrical turrets, encloses almost 93,000 sq m of exhibition area.

OLD CITY HALL
WHERE: Northeast corner of Bay and Queen streets. MAP: 9 WHEN: Weekdays.
ADMISSION: Free. A security check is in effect. SUBWAY: Queen.

Before the 'new' city hall was built across the street, this was Toronto's seat of government. E J Lennox, the architect who was famous for designing Casa Loma, spared no expense. The final bill was $2,500,000 - up considerably from the budgeted $600,000. He created the 1899 Romanesque-style building from carved stone brought in from Credit River valley and New Brunswick. It was hailed as "one of the most magnificent municipal buildings in North America" and one of Canada's most important examples of monumentally scaled city halls. The beige-brown building, with its imposing clock tower facing down Bay Street, is used now mainly for law courts.

ONTARIO SCIENCE CENTRE
WHERE: Don Mills Road at Eglinton Avenue East.
MAP: *City of Toronto*, area 12J, and in detail below. WHEN: Daily, 10.00 AM – 5.00 PM.
ADMISSION: $. TELEPHONE: 416-696-3127 (Information).
OMNIMAX®: 416 696-1000 (Tickets and show times). WEB SITE: **osc.on.ca**
SUBWAY: Eglinton and take the 34 bus to Don Mills Road.

The centre was our ambitious project for Canada's centennial year in 1967. The building, which opened two years late and cost six times the estimated $5,000,000 budget, has a wide entrance fronted by a mass of fountains and the Omnimax® Theatre. Inside, the structure cascades down into a ravine. This is a fascinating hands-on place for fun and discovery and ranks among the finest science centres in the world. Architect Raymond Moriyama also designed the Bata Shoe Museum and Toronto Reference Library.

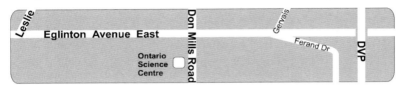

OSGOODE HALL
WHERE: Northeast corner of Queen Street West and University Avenue. MAP: 9
WHEN: During court hours. ADMISSION: Free. Security may be in effect.
TELEPHONE: 416-947-3300 (Law Society of Upper Canada). SUBWAY: Osgoode.

The building is named after William Osgoode, who was Upper Canada's first chief justice. It is the centre of judicial life in Ontario and houses the Superior Court of Ontario, judicial offices and the Law Society of Upper Canada. The Regency-styled east wing was completed in 1832 with other sections added in 1846 and 1860.

PATH UNDERGROUND WALKWAY
WHERE: From Front Street north to Dundas Street, and Yonge Street west to John Street.
MAP: PATH Underground Walkway, page 11 WHEN: Daily. ADMISSION: Free.
SUBWAY: Union, King, Queen, Dundas and St Andrew.

Our first underground public passage opened in 1900 and joined Eaton's main store at Yonge and Queen streets to its annex. Today's PATH began modestly in the Sixties with some underground shops around the Richmond-Adelaide and Sheraton centres. In 1973 these two complexes were joined underground and the idea, based on isolating pedestrians from traffic, took flight. It's now believed to be the longest continuous urban underground walkway in the world and the world's largest underground shopping mall. There are well over 1,000 shops along the climate-controlled 10 km of passageways that connect major hotels, transportation terminals, arenas, residential towers and commercial complexes throughout the inner-city. Therefore, it's possible to live downtown and never have to go outside.

PROVINCIAL LEGISLATURE
WHERE: Queen's Park. MAP: 19
WHEN: Weekdays, 8.30 AM – 4.30 PM. Security may be in effect.
TELEPHONE: 416-325-7500 WEB SITE: **gov.on.ca** ADMISSION: Free.
SUBWAY: Queen's Park.

This is the seat of government in Ontario. The building houses the legislative chamber, offices of the speaker, premier, leaders of the opposition parties and press gallery. When the house is sitting you can attend Question Period commencing at 2.00 PM. Passes are available in the lobby. For details on the history of the legislature building, see page 53.

ROYAL BANK PLAZA

WHERE: Northwest corner of Front and Bay streets. MAP: 9 WHEN: Weekdays. ADMISSION: Free. TELEPHONE: 416-974-3940 WEB SITE: **royalbank.com** SUBWAY: Union.

There's real gold in those twin towers. In fact, 70,900 g of 18-karat gold was used to coat the inner panes of 14,000 double-glazed windows. The reason for this seeming extravagance was to improve insulation. The towers cost $100,000,000 to build in the mid-1970s and the fountain outside was then the largest of its kind in North America.

ROYAL CONSERVATORY OF MUSIC

WHERE: 270 Bloor Street West. MAP: 24 WHEN: Weekdays, phone ahead. ADMISSION: Free. TELEPHONE: 416-408-2825 WEB SITE: **rcmusic.ca** SUBWAY: St George.

The building, known for its high Victorian architecture, opened in 1881 as a Baptist college named McMaster Hall. It later became McMaster University, which eventually moved to Hamilton in 1930. The present site was then taken over as the home of the Royal Conservatory of Music.

ROYAL YORK HOTEL

WHERE: 100 Front Street West. MAP: 9 WHEN: 24 hr. ADMISSION: Free for public areas. TELEPHONE: 416-368-2511 WEB SITE: **fairmont.com** SUBWAY: Union.

The 1,365-room Royal York - the most venerable of our hotels - sits on land that has seen a lot of changes. The first building here was a log cabin built in 1812. Thirty-two years later, Sword's Hotel was erected and 18 years after that the Queen's Hotel took over the site. During the 1880s circuses pitched their tents on this site. It wasn't until June, 1929 that the Royal York opened its doors. And when it did, it dominated the city's skyline in both height and width and became the largest hotel in the British Empire.

SCARBOROUGH CIVIC CENTRE

WHERE: Highway 401 at McCowan Road. MAP: *City of Toronto*. WHEN: Business hours. ADMISSION: Free. TELEPHONE: 416-396-7216 WEB SITE: **city.toronto.on.ca** SUBWAY: Kennedy. Transfer to the LRT and get off at Scarborough Centre.

Raymond Moriyama was the architect for many of our prominent public buildings, not least among which is the Scarborough Civic Centre. Its modern interior and exterior lines make it the most impressive building in the eastern part of the city. Fronted by the 0.9 ha Albert Campbell Square, it has become a focal point for community activities.

ST LAWRENCE MARKET

WHERE: Front Street East at Jarvis Street. MAP: 10 WHEN: Tuesday through Thursday, 8.00 AM – 6.00 PM; Friday, 8.00 AM – 7.00 PM; Saturday, 5.00 AM – 5.00 PM. ADMISSION: Free. TELEPHONE: 416-392-7120 WEB SITE: **stlawrencemarket.com** SUBWAY: UNION

As early as 1796 this site was being eyed as a market district for the Town of York. It wasn't until 1803 that Governor Peter Hunter proclaimed the area bounded by present-day Front, Church, Jarvis and King streets as the 'Market Block'. Few of us realize that the market site also housed the first city hall and police station from 1845 until 1899. Visitors are encouraged to see the city's art and archival collections in the Market Gallery on the second floor. It's housed in the original council chambers. Today, the St Lawrence Market's north and south buildings attract thousands of people in search of fresh produce, meat, cheese, baked goods and seafood. The north building is set aside mainly for district farmers who come into town to sell their products. Saturday morning is the busiest and best time to go shopping.

TORONTO CONVENTION CENTRE
WHERE: 255 Front Street West. MAP: 9 WHEN: Daily.
ADMISSION: Free when events are not scheduled. TELEPHONE: 416-585-8000
WEB SITE: **mtccc.com** SUBWAY: Union or St Andrew.

Canada's largest convention facility was built in two stages, finally cascading south from the main entrance on Front Street West to Bremner Boulevard. There are 185,800 sq m of space available and the complex can be rearranged into 70 fully-equipped meeting rooms ranging in size from 46 sq m to 4,600 sq m. The 1,330-seat John Bassett Theatre, with a full orchestra pit, forms part of the centre. There's underground parking for 1,700 vehicles and a further 17,000 spaces available within easy walking distance.

TORONTO DOMINION CENTRE (TD CENTRE)
WHERE: Southwest corner of Bay Street and King Street West. MAP: 9
WHEN: Site and buildings open daily. ADMISSION: Free. Tel: 416-869-1144
WEB SITE: **cadillacfairview.com** SUBWAY: King.

Internationally acclaimed Dutch architect Mies Van Der Rohe designed the complex over 30 years ago. The original 56-storey tower was built as the headquarters for the Toronto Dominion Bank, after which another four matched buildings were constructed for major corporations. This is the largest collection of Mies Van Der Rohe buildings in the world. The façade of the old Toronto Stock Exchange on Bay Street was incorporated into the complex. The area is laced with open spaces that are popular during lunch hours in the summer.

TORONTO REFERENCE LIBRARY
WHERE: 789 Yonge Street at Asquith Avenue. MAP: 25
WHEN: Monday through Thursday, 10.00 AM – 8.00 PM;
Friday & Saturday, 10.00 AM – 5.00 PM; Sunday, 1.30 PM – 5.00 PM. ADMISSION: Free.
TELEPHONE: 416-393-7131 SUBWAY: Bloor-Yonge. WEB SITE: **tpl.toronto.on.ca**
VIRTUAL LIBRARY: http://vrl.ptl.toronto.on.ca

This is the main library of the Toronto library system, which is the largest in Canada. The building houses both the Sir Arthur Conan Doyle and Audubon collections. The Doyle collection consists of 5,000 books and memorabilia housed in a replica of Sherlock Holmes' study at 221B Baker Street in London. The Audubon collection has a four-volume folio of 435 hand coloured, life-sized birds that was originally published between 1827 and 1838. Library staff answers about 8,000,000 questions annually.

TORONTO STOCK EXCHANGE (TSE)
WHERE: 130 King Street West at York Street. MAP: 9
WHEN: Summer tours Monday through Saturday, 10.00 AM – 5.00 PM. ADMISSION: $.
TELEPHONE: 416-947-4676 WEB SITE: **tse.com** SUBWAY: St Andrew.

Here's where billions of investment dollars race at computerized speed through North America's fourth largest and most modern stock exchange. It all happens quietly. You won't find any Hollywood drama on the trading floor because the TSE was the first exchange on the continent to get rid of all that Tinseltown hype. However, "friendly, nicely-dressed guides" will be delighted to tell you stories about the old-fashioned way of doing business here and, when you've been told everything you want to know, you can go away and play with the interactive games and exhibits.

UNION STATION
WHERE: 67 Front Street West. MAP: 9 WHEN: Daily. ADMISSION: Free. SUBWAY: Union.

The block on Front Street West from Bay to York streets is home to the largest and busiest passenger rail terminal building in Canada. Union Station was completed in 1927 and features a dramatic Great Hall measuring 76 m long, 27 m wide and 27 m high. The *beaux-arts* style uses 22 Doric exterior columns, each weighing 22 tons and rising 12 m from the sidewalk. John M Lyle, who created the Royal Alexandra Theatre, was the architect most responsible for Union Station's design. Well over 100,000 passengers pass through the terminal every business day.

Entertainment & sports

  Over 9% of Toronto's workforce is directly, or indirectly, involved in professional sports and the arts. Complementing their endeavours are some of North America's finest performance venues.

AIR CANADA CENTRE
WHERE: 40 Bay Street. MAP: 4 WHEN: During events. ADMISSION: $.
WEB SITE: **toronto.com** TELEPHONE: 416-815-5500 SUBWAY: Union.

The centre opened in February, 1999 on the site of an historic postal building and became home to the Toronto Maple Leafs and Toronto Raptors. Despite being known as 'The Hangar', it's considered North America's premier arena for basketball and ice hockey. With seating for up to 19,800 game fans or over 20,000 concert-goers, the building is famous for the 640 television screens scattered throughout the complex. You won't miss a play even if you're in a washroom. The Leafs and Raptors each won their opening game in the new venue.

BUDDIES IN BAD TIMES THEATRE
WHERE: 12 Alexander Street. MAP: 20 WHEN: During events.
ADMISSION: Pay what you can up to $25 TELEPHONE: 416-975-8555 (Box office);
416-975-9130 (Administration). WEB SITE: **buddies.web.net** SUBWAY: Carlton.

In a city supporting one of Canada's largest gay and lesbian neighbourhoods, it seems only natural that a theatre should specialize in productions of interest to the community. Buddies in Bad Times was founded in 1979 in a dishevelled space on George Street before moving to the 'gay ghetto' in 1991. The main space, seating 300, is the venue for award-winning drama, comedy, dance, solo acts and the Fringe Festival. It's best known for staging adventurous new works by Canadian writers, composers and performers.

CANADA'S WALK OF FAME
WHERE: King Street West along theatre row and Simcoe Street outside Roy Thomson Hall.
MAP: 9 WHEN: 24 hr. ADMISSION: Free. SUBWAY: St Andrew.

On June 28, 1998 fourteen prominent Canadian artists were honoured with their very own sidewalk stars. Inaugural inductees included John Candy and Rich Little, each of whom had their name imbedded in concrete along with other such luminaries as Pierre Berton, Anne Murray and Karen Kain. You'll also find Rush and Mary Pickford honoured. And, yes, they were born in Canada too. Any similarity to another walk on Hollywood's Sunset Boulevard is purely co-incidental.

ELGIN AND WINTER GARDEN THEATRES
WHERE: 189 Yonge Street. MAP: 10
WHEN: Tours, Thursdays 5.00 PM and Saturdays 11.00 AM. ADMISSION: $.
TELEPHONE: 416-872-5555 (Show tickets), 416-314-2901 (Tours).
WEB SITE: **heritagefdn.on.ca** SUBWAY: Queen.

During the great vaudeville days people like Burns and Allen, Edgar Bergen and 'Charlie McCarthy', Milton Berle and Sophie Tucker played here. These houses are the last operating double-decker theatres on the continent. They were completed a couple of months apart during the winter of 1913-14. When vaudeville lost its charm, they were turned into movie houses. After many years in the dark, they were completely refurbished at a cost of $29,000,000 and returned to their original décor and style.

EXHIBITION PLACE
WHERE: Lakeshore Boulevard at Strachan Avenue. MAP: 1 WHEN: Daily.
ADMISSION: $ for events only. TELEPHONE: 416-393-6000 WEB SITE: **theex.com**
SUBWAY: Union and take the Harbourfront 509 streetcar.

The personality of Exhibition Place has changed over the years. Once almost exclusively the domain of the Canadian National Exhibition and events at Exhibition Stadium, the site now houses the vast National Trade Centre. This is a complex rich in memories and tradition, and it has a special place in the hearts of most Torontonians. For the history of Exhibition Place, see page 17.

HOCKEY HALL OF FAME
WHERE: Northwest corner of Yonge and Front streets. MAP: 9 WHEN: Daily. Times vary.
ADMISSION: $. TELEPHONE: 416-360-7765 WEB SITE: **hhof.com**
SUBWAY: Union, or King and go through the PATH walkway to BCE Place.

This is Canada's shrine to ice hockey, housed in the reputedly haunted 1885 Bank of Montreal building. Play goalie against virtual reality shooters, or browse through the most comprehensive collection of hockey stuff anywhere. And, best of all, you can have your picture taken standing next to the Stanley Cup, which is on permanent exhibition here. The Spirit of Hockey store is the place for mementos and gear.

HUMMINGBIRD CENTRE FOR THE PERFORMING ARTS
WHERE: 1 Front Street East. MAP: 10 WHEN: For performances. ADMISSION: $.
TELEPHONE: 416-872-2262 (Tickets). WEB SITE: **hummingbirdcentre.com**
SUBWAY: Union.

On this site, 150 years ago, a pier jutted out into Lake Ontario. Charles Darwin disembarked here May 4, 1842 for his only visit to Toronto. That was Act 1. This is Act 2. When the O'Keefe Centre was looking around for some money, a software company came up with $5,000,000 and got its name on the marquee. This is where the world première of Lerner and Loewe's *Camelot* opened. Next morning the *Toronto Star's* theatre critic panned it unmercifully. Nathan Cohen stood by his original evaluation of the show until the day he died. Since then the theatre has seen more than its fair share of glitzy Broadway and West End productions, plus some of the world's leading solo acts. For years the 3,200-seat centre has been home stage for the Canadian Opera Company and the National Ballet of Canada. However, their aspiration is to have a ballet-opera house all their own. And city council often murmurs that the Hummingbird might be torn down.

MAPLE LEAF GARDENS
WHERE: 60 Carlton Street. MAP: 15 WHEN: During events.
ADMISSION: $ for most events. TELEPHONE: 416-977-1641 SUBWAY: College.

With the demise of the old Montréal Forum in the early 1990s, Maple Leaf Gardens was the last great hockey arena left in Canada. Every famous ice hockey player had been on the ice here during the past 60 years. Those great glory days of hockey disappeared when the Toronto Maple Leafs moved in 1999 to new digs at the Air Canada Centre. Apart from hockey, the Gardens had also played host to a myriad of celebrities and entertainers – from the Metropolitan Opera to the Beatles and from Billy Graham to a memorable speech delivered by Winston Churchill in 1932. Disgusted with the inadequacy of the public address system, he dispensed with the microphone and addressed the crowd of 10,000 with such forceful projection that everyone heard him perfectly. The 'Grand Old Lady of College Street' is being redeveloped to provide a 500-seat arena, restaurants, shops and possibly a condominium tower.

MASSEY HALL
WHERE: 178 Victoria Street. MAP: 15 WHEN: During performances.
ADMISSION: $. TELEPHONE: 416-872-4255 (Tickets). WEB SITE: **masseyhall.com**
SUBWAY: Dundas, or Queen.

When the hall opened in 1894 with a performance of Handel's *Messiah*, it was obvious that this was a space with stunning acoustics. The 2,750-seat red brick facility was a gift from the Massey family and for many years was the venerable home of Toronto Symphony Orchestra. Now well into its second century, it can look back on having welcomed a daunting international list of classical and pop artists to its stage, as well as people like G K Chesterton, Arthur Conan Doyle, John Masefield, J B Priestly and Grey Owl.

MOLSON AMPHITHEATRE
WHERE: Ontario Place. MAP: 1 WHEN: May through September for performances.
ADMISSION: $. TELEPHONE: 416-260-5600 WEB SITE: **universalconcerts.ca**
SUBWAY: Union and take the Harbourfront 509 streetcar.

A lot of folk will remember this stage when it was called the Ontario Place Forum. As the Molson Amphitheatre, it's a magnet for summer pop concertgoers who want to relax outdoors. There are now 5,500 reserved seats under its modern roofline, another 3,500 seats out in the open and a further 7,000 general admission places on surrounding lawns. A state-of-the-art sound system and two super video screens give everyone an intimate connection with what's happening on stage.

NATIONAL TENNIS CENTRE

WHERE: 4700 Keele Street at Steeles Avenue West. MAP: *City of Toronto*. ADMISSION: $.
TELEPHONE: 416-665-9777 WEB SITE: **tenniscanada.com**
SUBWAY: Keele and take the 41C bus.

The aging National Tennis Centre at York University, which is home base for the Canadian Open, is getting a little worse for wear. A $30-million overhaul is being planned for the site to bring it more in line with ATP standards by 2002. The Canadian Open, which has become a prime ATP event sandwiched between Wimbledon and the US Open, is well over 100 years old. The first person to win the singles event was American Delano Osborne in 1892.

OLYMPIC GAMES - PROPOSED SITES FOR 2008

WEB SITE: **to-2008.com**

In its bid for the 2008 summer Olympic Games, Toronto proposed that most of the major facilities would cluster around three re-developed pods along the waterfront.

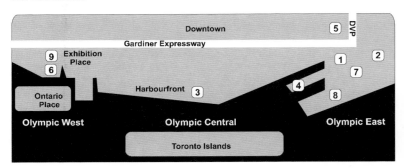

1	Aquatic Centre	4	Cultural Plaza	7	Olympic Stadium
2	Broadcast Centre	5	Media Village	8	Olympic Village
3	Central Plaza	6	Olympic Plaza	9	Velodrome

ONTARIO PLACE

WHERE: South of Exhibition Place. MAP: 1
WHEN: May through September. Cinesphere® open year round. ADMISSION: $.
TELEPHONE: 416-314-9900 WEB SITE: **ontarioplace.com**
SUBWAY: Union and take the Harbourfront 509 streetcar.

This series of man-made parks off-shore from Exhibition Place is filled with activity and entertainment areas during the summer. It's one of our most popular lake shore areas and the prime location for watching fireworks and other spectacles. Star-studded concerts are staged at the 16,000 seat Molson Amphitheatre. For more information, see page 17.

PANTAGES THEATRE

WHERE: 263 Yonge Street. MAP: 15 WHEN: During performances. ADMISSION: $.
TELEPHONE: 416-872-2222 (Tickets). SUBWAY: Dundas.

They spent an extraordinary amount of money in 1989 to refurbish this once decaying and historic 2,200-seat theatre for the opening of *Phantom of the*

Opera. Few theatres in the world can boast such restored turn-of-the-century elegance as this gem on Yonge Street. Sweeping staircases, rich woods and ornate décor have given us as much to applaud as anything that might happen on stage.

PRINCESS OF WALES THEATRE

WHERE: 300 King Street West. MAP: 8 WHEN: During performances. ADMISSION: $. TELEPHONE: 416-872-1212 (Tickets).
WEB SITE: **mirvish.com** (Information and ordering tickets). SUBWAY: St Andrew.

Ed Mirvish's companion theatre to the historic Royal Alexandra opened in May, 1993 with *Miss Saigon*. The building was designed by theatre architect Peter Smith to accommodate 2,000 seats and house the city's largest stage. Frank Stella created hundreds of square metres of modern murals for foyers, ceilings and the back exterior wall.

ROY THOMSON HALL

WHERE: Southwest corner of King and Simcoe streets. MAP: 9
WHEN: Monday through Saturday. ADMISSION: Free, except for performances.
TELEPHONE: 416-872-4255 (Tickets and information). WEB SITE: **roythomsonhall.com**
SUBWAY: St Andrew.

Arthur Erickson's design for a concert hall raised eyebrows when it opened in 1982. The circular glass-clad concrete structure caused added concern when acoustics didn't match those of the venerable Massey Hall that had been a distinguished home for concert-goers during previous generations. Even its name raised people's hackles. Canada's late press baron - Roy Thomson (Lord Thomson of Fleet) after whom the hall was named - was reputed never to have willingly attended a symphony concert. Roy Thomson Hall opened in 1982 at a cost of $38,000,000 and is home for the Toronto Symphony Orchestra and visiting concert artists.

ROYAL ALEXANDRA THEATRE

WHERE: 260 King Street West. MAP: 9 WHEN: During performances. ADMISSION: $. TELEPHONE: 416-872-1212 (Tickets).
WEB SITE: **mirvish.com** (Information and online ticket orders). SUBWAY: St Andrew.

Helen Hayes, John Gielgud, Edith Evans and the Barrymores have all played the 'Royal Alex' during the theatre's staging of more than 3,000 productions. When it opened in 1907 it was hailed as a technological triumph of its day. It was the first fireproof theatre built on the continent and is now the oldest legitimate theatre in Toronto. In 1962 the Alex was scheduled for demolition. Just before the wrecking ball was brought in, entrepreneur Ed Mirvish bought the property and launched a theatrical career that reached a pinnacle when he purchased London's Old Vic. The top balcony of the Royal Alex betrays the theatre's age: stairs are steep and seating is cramped.

SKYDOME

WHERE: 1 Blue Jays Way. MAP: 3 WHEN: During events and tours. ADMISSION: $.
TELEPHONE: 416-341-3663 (Information); 416-870-8000 (Tickets); 416-341-2770 (Tours).
WEB SITE: **skydome.com** SUBWAY: Union and take the Skywalk.

This landmark facility was the first multi-purpose stadium to have a retractable roof. The Jumbotron video screen is one of the largest in the world. 'The Dome' has 1,280 toilets, three-quarters of which are for women. The 11,000-ton roof - which spans 3.2 ha - takes 20 minutes to open or close. The Eaton

Centre, St Paul's Cathedral in London, or Rome's Coliseum could fit easily inside the 32-storey structure. SkyDome is home stadium for the Toronto Blue Jays and Toronto Argonauts. Seating capacity is just over 50,000 for games and 67,000 for concerts. The Jays went down 5-3 to the Milwaukee Brewers on opening day, June 5, 1989

ST LAWRENCE CENTRE FOR THE ARTS

WHERE: 27 Front Street East at Scott Street. MAP: 10 WHEN: During performances. ADMISSION: $. TELEPHONE: 416-366-7723 (Tickets). WEB SITE: **stlc.com** SUBWAY: Union.

With more than a quarter century under its belt, the St Lawrence Centre has provided us with a unique mix of theatre, music and social consciousness. The 876-seat Bluma Appel Theatre is home for the Canadian Stage Company and was chosen as the venue for the world première of *Kiss of the Spiderwoman*, which went on to spend a Tony Award winning season on Broadway. The smaller 497-seat Jane Mallett theatre is best for intimate music recitals, small theatre and public debates on issues of the day.

TORONTO CENTRE FOR THE ARTS

WHERE: 5040 Yonge Street. MAP: *North York Centre*. WHEN: During performances. ADMISSION: $. TELEPHONE: 416-870-8000 (Tickets); 416-733-9388 (Administration). WEB SITE: **tocentre.com** SUBWAY: North York Centre.

When North York was a separate city, it made a conscious effort to compete with Toronto's downtown theatre district. Mayor Mel Lastman and entrepreneur Garth Drabinsky teamed-up as the driving forces behind building the North York Centre for the Performing Arts, consisting of the Apotex Theatre, George Weston Recital Hall and the Studio Theatre. Its name changed to the Ford Centre and then to the Toronto Centre for the Arts. During the late 1990s the Apotex Theatre, with 1,800 seats and one of the city's largest stages, held the world premières of *Showboat, Ragtime* and *Fosse* - all of which originated in Toronto before their award-winning runs on Broadway. The Apotex is now called the Main Stage. The George Weston Recital Hall shares the best acoustics in the city with Massey Hall.

WOODBINE RACETRACK

WHERE: Rexdale Boulevard at Highway 27 MAP: *City of Toronto*, area 1E, and in detail below. WHEN: Race days. ADMISSION: $. TELEPHONE: 416-675-7223 WEB SITE: **ojc.com** SUBWAY: Islington, take 37A bus.

Since Greenwood Racetrack was closed and its land converted into mixed use building projects, Woodbine has become our only – and one of North America's best – tracks for thoroughbred and harness racing. In addition to the one-mile and 1½-mile tracks, there are four additional training surfaces, giving it more diversity than any other course on the continent. Daily purses average over $250,000

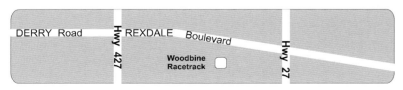

YPT - YOUNG PEOPLES THEATRE

WHERE: 165 Yonge Street East. MAP: 10 WHEN: For performances. Admission: $.
TELEPHONE: 416-862-2222 (Tickets). WEB SITE: **toronto.com**
SUBWAY: Union or King.

Few of us realize that in 1887-88 this building was a stable for the Toronto Street Railway's horses that pulled carriages up Yonge Street. Welcome now to a theatre devoted entirely to giving kids an introduction to the wonders of the stage. There are two theatres: the 468-seat Susan Rubes Mainstage and the 115-seat Nathan Cohen Studio Theatre. Youngsters won't remember that it was *Toronto Star* theatre critic Nathan Cohen who panned the daylights out of Lerner and Loewe's *Camelot* when it had its world premiere with Richard Burton and Julie Andrews at the then O'Keefe Centre just down the street.

History & museums

You could walk around a 140-year-old village, or decide to buy a quill pen and some sealing wax. Maybe you feel more like spending a day with 4,600,000,000 years of history. The choice is yours.

BATA SHOE MUSEUM

WHERE: 327 Bloor Street West at St George Street. MAP: 23
WHEN: Tuesday through Sunday. Hours vary. ADMISSION: $. TELEPHONE: 416-979-7799
WEB SITE: **batashoemuseum.ca** SUBWAY: St George.

This is where you'll find everything you ever wanted to know about shoes and shoe making: ten thousand exhibits and 8,000 pairs of shoes, including those worn by people as diverse as Pope Leo XIII, Queen Victoria, Imelda Marcos and Elton John. This museum, designed by prolific architect Raymond Moriyama, is the leading one of its type. A good place to take jaded New York friends who think they have everything.

BLACK CREEK PIONEER VILLAGE

WHERE: Jane Street at Steeles Avenue West. MAP: *City of Toronto.*
WHEN: Daily, May 1 through December 31, 10.00 AM – 4.30 PM. ADMISSION: $.
TELEPHONE: 416-736-1733 WEB SITE: **trca.on.ca** SUBWAY: Jane. Transfer to bus 35B

Costumed guides take you around original buildings that housed family and commercial life as it was 140 years ago in Upper Canada. Village crafts, which make unusual gifts, are available in some of the 35 homes and workshops. Good times to experience this 1860s Victorian living history village are during the annual Pioneer Festival held in mid-September, or around the Yuletide season.

CAMPBELL HOUSE MUSEUM

WHERE: 160 Queen Street West at University Avenue. MAP: 9
WHEN: Monday through Friday, 9.30 AM – 4.30 PM; Saturday and Sunday, May through September, 12 noon – 4.30 PM. ADMISSION: $. TELEPHONE: 416-597-0227
WEB SITE: **advsoc.on.ca** SUBWAY: Osgoode.

This 1822 building is the earliest surviving example of formal Georgian architecture from the Town of York. In 1972 the house was moved from its original site at Adelaide and Frederick streets to its present location.

CASA LOMA
WHERE: 1 Austin Terrace. MAP: 27 WHEN: Daily, 9.30 AM – 4.00 PM. ADMISSION: $. TELE-PHONE: 416-923-1171 WEB SITE: **casaloma.org** SUBWAY: Dupont.

Here's a genuine castle built in Norman, Gothic and Romanesque styles that towers over 2.4 ha of gardens and woodland. The Casa Loma Stables, just north on Walmer Road, and accessible through a tunnel from the castle, are worth a visit. One of our top ten tourist destinations. For some more background on Casa Loma, see page 69

CHILDREN'S OWN MUSEUM
WHERE: 90 Queen's Park at Charles Street West. MAP: 19
WHEN: Tuesday through Saturday, 10.00 AM – 5.00 PM; Sunday, 12 noon – 5.00 PM.
ADMISSION: $. Kids under one year free. TELEPHONE: 416-542-1492
WEB SITE: **toronto.com** SUBWAY: Museum.

The museum has taken over what used to be the MacLaughlin Planetarium. The new facility is a magical place designed to provide active learning through play for children aged two to eight years. Explore different museum areas such as the Construction Site, Sensory Tunnel, Garden, Animal Clinic and Theatre.

COLBORNE LODGE MUSEUM
WHERE: Colborne Lodge Drive, High Park. MAP: *City of Toronto*, area 6M, and in detail below. WHEN: Tuesday through Sunday, noon – 5.00 PM in the summer and weekends during the winter. ADMISSION: $. TELEPHONE: 416-392-6916
WEB SITE: **toronto.com** SUBWAY: Keele.

Finding an historic site in the city that's not smothered by close neighbours is quite an achievement. The lodge is situated in one of our largest parks and goes back to 1873 when the residence and most of the present green space belonged to John George Howard. It's not hard to imagine that this is what it must have looked like 130 years ago.

FIRST POST OFFICE MUSEUM (YORK POST OFFICE)
WHERE: 260 Adelaide Street East. MAP: 10 WHEN: Weekdays, 9.00 AM – 4.00 PM;
Weekends, 10.00 AM – 4.00 PM. Closed statutory holidays. ADMISSION: Free.
TELEPHONE: 416-865-1833 WEB SITE: **tha.on.ca/firstpo** SUBWAY: King

If a genuine quill pen and sealing wax are on your shopping list, then this is where you can get them. It's also the only post office in the country where you can buy American and British postage stamps. The First Post Office - which opened in 1813 and was called the 'York Post Office' - is the oldest functioning post office in Canada and one of the city's best-kept secrets.

FLATIRON BUILDING
WHERE: Intersection of Front Street East and Wellington Street East. MAP: 10
WHEN: Business hours. ADMISSION: Free. SUBWAY: Union.

There's little argument that this is one of the most photographed old buildings we have, especially when it's framed in front of the Financial District's modern skyscrapers. The old Flatiron was built in 1892 as the corporate headquarters for liquor giant Gooderham and Worts. It holds the distinction of being the first building in town to install an electric passenger elevator.

FORT YORK
WHERE: Garrison Road, off Fleet Street. MAP: 2
WHEN: Daily, 10.00 AM – 5.00 PM. Closed over Christmas season. ADMISSION: $.
TELEPHONE: 416-392-6907 WEB SITE: **toronto.com**
SUBWAY: St Andrew and take a 504, or 508 service to Strachan Avenue.

The fort comes alive with explosive charm on the first Monday in August (Simcoe Day) when soldiers put on a display of musketry. During the rest of the year this national historic site, built in 1793, re-creates conditions during the earliest days of the Town of York and its defence against the Americans during the War of 1812-13.

GIBSON HOUSE MUSEUM
WHERE: 5172 Yonge Street. MAP: *North York Centre*. WHEN: Tuesday through Friday, 9.30 AM – 4.30 PM; weekends and holidays, 12 noon – 5.00 PM. ADMISSION: $.
TELEPHONE: 416-395-7432 WEB SITE: **city.toronto.on.ca**
SUBWAY: North York Centre.

Costumed guides explain the home's interior furnishings and relate what country life north of Toronto must have been like during the mid-1800s. Exhibits, gift shop, activity programs and stuff for kids. The farmhouse was built for David and Eliza Gibson and their family in 1851.

HMCS HAIDA MUSEUM
WHERE: Ontario Place. MAP: 1
WHEN: Victoria Day through Labour Day, 10.00 AM – 7.00 PM.
ADMISSION: Free with Ontario Place Day Pass, otherwise there's a modest entrance fee.
TELEPHONE: 416-314-9755. WEB SITE: **toronto.com**
SUBWAY: Bathurst and take the 511 streetcar south.

This ship is the only surviving Tribal class destroyer in the world. It was built for the Canadian Navy in 1942 and saw action during WW2 and the Korean War. The vessel has been refurbished and audio and visual guides add to your enjoyment of the tour. Each day at noon, one of the ship's guns is fired.

MACKENZIE HOUSE MUSEUM
WHERE: 82 Bond Street. MAP: 15 WHEN: Tuesday through Sunday, Noon – 5.00 PM during summer; Tuesday through Friday, Noon – 5.00 PM in the fall; and weekends during winter.
ADMISSION: $. TELEPHONE: 416-392-6915 WEB SITE: **city.toronto.on.ca**
SUBWAY: Dundas.

Just around the corner from bustling Dundas Square there's a two-storey house that's got quite a history. It was the residence of William Lyon Mackenzie, the man who led the unsuccessful 1837 Upper Canada Rebellion. He was also Toronto's first mayor and a publisher and printer of note. The old print shop is still in working condition. It's an unusual place to visit during the holiday season for an interesting experience of Christmases past.

MONTGOMERY'S INN MUSEUM
WHERE: 4709 Dundas Street West. MAP: *City of Toronto*, area 3L, and in detail on the next page. WHEN: Monday through Friday, 9.00 AM – 4.30 PM; Weekends and holidays, 1.00 PM – 5.00 PM. ADMISSION: $.
TELEPHONE: 416-394-8113 WEB SITE: **montgomerysinn.com**
SUBWAY: Islington and take 37 bus to Dundas Street West.

Built around 1830, the inn is one of the last examples of late Georgian or Loyalist architecture we have in the city. You'll be treated to an authentically restored building of the period 1847-1850 staffed by folk dressed in attire of that much less hurried day. Worth visiting for the fine collection of British, Canadian and American antiques.

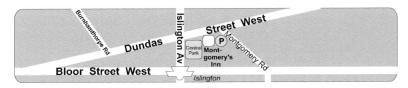

MUSEUM FOR TEXTILES
WHERE: 55 Centre Avenue. MAP: 14 WHEN: Tuesday through Friday, 11.00 AM – 5.00 PM; Wednesdays, 11.00 AM – 8.00 PM; Weekends, 12 noon – 5.00 PM. Admission: $
TELEPHONE: 416-599-5321 WEB SITE: **museumfortextiles.on.ca** SUBWAY: St Patrick.

This museum, which is tucked away on a quiet street in Chinatown, is internationally recognized for its collection of over 8,000 artifacts. It's the only museum in Canada devoted to the collection, exhibiting and documentation of textiles from around the world.

MUSEUM OF CERAMIC ART
WHERE: 111 Queen's Park. MAP: 24 WHEN: Tuesday through Sunday. Hours vary.
ADMISSION: Donation appreciated. TELEPHONE: 416-586-8080
WEB SITE: **gardinermuseum.on.ca** SUBWAY: Museum.

Formally called The George R Gardiner Museum of Ceramic Art, it houses one of the most outstanding collections of ceramics anywhere. Get involved in clay classes, browse through its 2,600 exhibits, or find something unique in the Gardiner Shop.

REDPATH SUGAR MUSEUM
WHERE: 95 Queen's Quay East. MAP: 5
WHEN: Phone ahead for days and times. ADMISSION: Free. TELEPHONE: 416-366-3561
WEB SITE: **redpath.com** SUBWAY: Union and take the 6 bus to Cooper Street.

The museum is an informal place that traces the history of sugar production through exhibits and a video presentation. You'll find it at the back of the Redpath Sugar Refinery, which was opened on June 29, 1959 by Queen Elizabeth II. Wyland's whale mural is on the outside wall of the raw sugar shed facing Queen's Quay East.

ROYAL ONTARIO MUSEUM (ROM)
WHERE: 100 Queen's Park. MAP: 24 WHEN: Monday through Saturday, 10.00 AM – 6.00 PM; Tuesdays till 8.00 PM; Sundays 11.00 AM – 6.00 PM. ADMISSION: $.
TELEPHONE: 416-586-8000 WEB SITE: **rom.on.ca** SUBWAY: Museum.

The ROM is one of the continent's leading museums, specializing in an extensive collection of decorative arts, archaeology and science. There are 6,000,000 objects and artifacts in over 40 permanent galleries. The Chinese collection is one of the world's best. Special changing exhibits year-round. It's a place where you can get your hands on 4.6-billion years of history and still find enough time to gaze at the 193-carat Star Sapphire.

SPADINA HOUSE MUSEUM
WHERE: 285 Spadina Road. MAP: 27
WHEN: Tuesday through Sunday, Noon – 5.00 PM. ADMISSION: $.
TELEPHONE: 416-392-6910 WEB SITE: **toronto.com**
SUBWAY: Spadina.

This historic 1866 furnished residence of the Austin family is one of our prized possessions. It has 2.4 ha of Victorian and Edwardian gardens with 300 varieties of flowers and vegetables. It's one of the top spots in town for taking wedding photos. With Casa Loma next door, this is an interesting place to take visitors.

THE PIER WATERFRONT MUSEUM
WHERE: 245 Queen's Quay West. MAP: 3 WHEN: Daily, May through October.
ADMISSION: $. TELEPHONE: 416-338-7437 WEB SITE: **toronto.com**
SUBWAY: Union and take the Harbourfront 509 streetcar to Rees Street.

Originally called the Marine Museum and housed at Exhibition Place, this better facility traces the story of Toronto harbour and the Great Lakes from the Ice Age to the present. Get involved with the interactive exhibits, models and historic artifacts.

TODMORDEN MILLS MUSEUM
WHERE: 67 Pottery Road. MAP: *City of Toronto*, area 12L, and in detail below.
WHEN: Tuesday through Friday, 11.00 AM – 4.30 PM; weekends, noon – 5.00 PM.
Closed Mondays. ADMISSION: $. TELEPHONE: 416-396-2819
WEB SITE: **city.toronto.on.ca** SUBWAY: Broadview and take the 87 bus to Pottery Road.

The mill worked away on the Don River during Victorian times and has been restored as an example of local industry in the 19th century. There are two historic houses to explore and an audio-visual presentation takes you behind the scenes of what went on here in days gone by.

TORONTO POLICE MUSEUM
WHERE: 40 College Street in the Toronto Police Headquarters building. MAP: 19
WHEN: Daily, 9.00 AM – 9.00 PM. Gift Shop, Monday through Friday, 9.00 AM – 3.30 PM.
TELEPHONE: 416-808-7020 WEB SITE: **torontopolice.on.ca/cos/cpsmuseum**
ADMISSION: Free. SUBWAY: College.

Friendly members of the Toronto police help you to find almost everything you need to know about the force and how it operates. See famous pieces of evidence associated with celebrated cases and select your own video subject for viewing in the Museum Theatre.

YORK POST OFFICE (FIRST POST OFFICE MUSEUM)
WHERE: 260 Adelaide Street East. MAP: 10 WHEN: Weekdays, 9.00 AM – 4.00 PM;
Weekends, 10.00 AM – 4.00 PM. Closed statutory holidays. ADMISSION: Free.
TELEPHONE: 416-865-1833 WEB SITE: **tha.on.ca/firstpo** SUBWAY: King

If a genuine quill pen and sealing wax are on your shopping list, then this is where you can get them. It's also the only post office in the country where you can buy American and British postage stamps. York Post Office, which opened in 1813, is also known as the 'First Post Office'. It's the oldest-functioning post office in Canada and one of our best-kept secrets.

Parks, gardens, zoos & squares

Toronto is renowned for its ravine woodlands and tree-lined streets. There are 2,000 parks in the city and 8,000 ha of green space - including the continent's largest urban wilderness. Check them out – and DO walk on the grass!

ALBERT CAMPBELL SQUARE
WHERE: Scarborough Civic Centre. MAP: *City of Toronto*, area 17F, and in detail below.
WHEN: Daily. ADMISSION: Free.
TELEPHONE: 416-396-7111 (Information), 416-396-7216 (Tours of Civic Centre).
WEB SITE: **city.toronto.on.ca/parks**
SUBWAY: Kennedy and take the LRT to Scarborough Centre.

This relaxing 9,300 sq m square, complete with art and a cascading water-fall, won the Vincent Massey Award for urban design. It forms an impressive entry to the Scarborough Civic Centre, which was designed by acclaimed architect Raymond Moriyama. The centre is one of our best examples of modern architecture, both inside and out. Three large pines in the square are turned into illuminated Christmas trees during the Yuletide season.

ALLAN GARDENS
WHERE: Carlton Street at Sherbourne Street. MAP: 15 WHEN: 24 hr. ADMISSION: Free.
TELEPHONE: 416-392-1111 WEB SITE: **city.toronto.on.ca/parks** SUBWAY: College.

The highlight of Allan Gardens is the Palm House greenhouse. It houses the best collection of tropical plants in the city. Historically, you could say that this might be the place where Toronto's formal parks system was born. The Prince of Wales, later King Edward VII, opened a 2 ha space here in 1860 at the behest of the Toronto Horticultural Society that was founded 26 years before. It later became known as Allan Gardens in 1901. It's best to avoid the park at night.

BLUFFER'S PARK
WHERE: South end of Brimley Road. MAP: *City of Toronto,* area 17M, and in detail on the next page. WHEN: Year-round. ADMISSION: Free. TELEPHONE: 416-396-7111
WEB SITE: **bluffersparkmarina.com** SUBWAY: There's no public transit into the park.

When Elizabeth Simcoe, wife of the first lieutenant-governor of Upper Canada, saw this area she said it reminded her of Scarborough Bluffs in Yorkshire. The name 'Scarborough' has remained and so have the bluffs. Before

Simcoe arrived, they were known as the Toronto Highlands – high cliffs that rose sheer from Lake Ontario to give Toronto its most dramatic topographical feature. Bluffer's Park is the largest and most accessible of many parks along the bluffs and includes a large marina, walking trails, impressive views and picnic sites. Joining it to the east and west are Cathedral Bluffs Park and Scarborough Bluffs Park. Together, they provide a perfect summer spot for thousands of us to get out and relax.

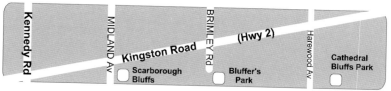

CENTENNIAL PARK
WHERE: Bounded by Eglinton Avenue West, Renforth Drive and Rathburn Road.
MAP: *City of Toronto*. WHEN: Daily.
ADMISSION: Free, though some facilities could charge a fee. WEB SITE: **toronto.com**
TELEPHONE: 416-394-8750 (Picnic sites). SUBWAY: Royal York and take the 2 bus.

This is one of our largest recreational parks. Facilities in the 212 ha area include picnic sites, an Olympic-sized pool, ski hills, golf, skating arena, baseball diamonds, tennis courts and a 2,200 seat stadium. At the end of Elmcrest Road, off Rathburn Road, you'll find the Centennial Park Conservatory. The gardens, which house a wide variety of plants, consist of three glass houses covering 1,100 sq m.

DISCOVERY WALKS
WHERE: Contact the city's Parks Department. TELEPHONE: 416-392-8186
WEB SITE: **city.toronto.on.ca/discovery/index**

When you want to escape the downtown concrete, you can enjoy a network of self-guided walks that link ravines, lost rivers, parks and heritage sites. Just get all the information from the city's Parks Department. It's amazing what you can accomplish. In fact, you can walk from one side of the city to the other without ever leaving a park or ravine. We've given 'taking a walk in the park' a whole new meaning.

EDWARDS GARDENS
WHERE: Lawrence Avenue East at Leslie Street. MAP: *City of Toronto*, area 12H.
WHEN: Daily, dawn to dusk. ADMISSION: Free. TELEPHONE: 416-392-8186
WEB SITE: **toronto.com** SUBWAY: Eglinton and take the 51 bus east to Leslie Street.

A lot of us regard this former estate as the best of the three formal public gardens in the city. It's renowned for its perennials, roses, wildflowers and rhododendrons. Alexander Milne, who began milling operations here shortly after he bought the property in 1812, originally owned the site. The Civic Garden Centre - one of the country's top gardening education facilities - uses the gardens as its base. As a bonus, you can see three apple trees here that are over 150 years old.

HIGH PARK
WHERE: Bloor Street West at Parkside Drive.
MAP: *City of Toronto*, area 6M, and in detail on the following page.
WEB SITE: **toronto.com** WHEN: 24 hr. ADMISSION: Free. SUBWAY: Keele.

From the corner of Bloor Street West and Parkside Drive (the extension of Keele Street), the park extends south to the Queensway and west half-way to South Kingsway. John George Howard, who built a lodge here in 1873, once owned most of this land. Since then the space has become one of the largest formal parks in the city. Its main feature is Grenadier Pond, which forms most of the park's western boundary. Those of us who live nearby make it a focal point for outdoor activities year-round. Historic Colborne Lodge is at the south entrance on Colborne Lodge Drive.

HUMBER ARBORETUM
WHERE: 205 Humber College Boulevard.
MAP: *City of Toronto*, area 1C, and in detail below.
WHEN: Daily, 9.00 AM – 3.30 PM. ADMISSION: Free. TELEPHONE: 416-675-5009
WEB SITE: **humberc.on.ca**
SUBWAY: Finch and take 36C bus west to Humber College Boulevard.

Situated on the west branch of the Humber River, this 96 ha of green space includes an extensive collection of over 5,000 trees, shrubs and herbaceous plants in a natural environment. The arboretum, which opened in the fall of 1982, offers over three kilometres of bike and walking trails, a nature club for kids, an area where you can get ideas for landscaping, and ways to explore wetlands, meadows and forests.

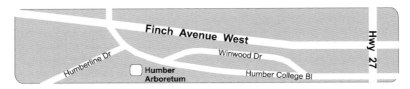

HUMBER BAY PARK
WHERE: Lake Shore Boulevard West at Park Lawn Road.
MAP: *City of Toronto*, area 5P. WHEN: Daily. ADMISSION: Free.
TELEPHONE: 416-392-8186 WEB SITE: **city.toronto.on.ca/parks**
SUBWAY: Old Mill and take 66D bus.

It's possible to walk from this spot on Lake Ontario up to Steeles Avenue on the northern side of the city without ever leaving ravine parkland. Humber Bay Park is the largest on the waterfront in the west end and is one of 39 parks along the Toronto lake front. Apart from being a popular mooring place for yachts and small boats, it's got some of the best views of the city skyline.

MEL LASTMAN SQUARE
WHERE: Yonge Street, fronting North York Civic Centre. MAP: *North York Centre*.
WHEN: 24 hr. ADMISSION: Free. TELEPHONE: 416-395-6050 WEB SITE: **toronto.com**
SUBWAY: North York Centre.

When North York was a city, it created a square in front of city hall to rival Toronto's Nathan Phillips Square. When the cities amalgamated in 1998, competition came to an end. Even though North York is now uptown Toronto, Mel Lastman Square remains this area's lively focal point for celebrations and general good times. Mel Lastman was the last mayor of North York and the first mayor of Toronto after amalgamation.

MOUNT PLEASANT CEMETERY
WHERE: 375 Mount Pleasant Road. MAP: 31 (Yonge Street entrance).
WHEN: 8.00 AM – dusk. ADMISSION: Free. TELEPHONE: 416-485-9129
WEB SITE: **findagrave.com/cemeteries** SUBWAY: Eglinton and take the 103 bus.

An example of practically every variety of tree that grows around Toronto can be found here. Hundreds of varieties include everything from Oriental elm and Babylon willow to oak trees that were mature when the cemetery opened in 1826. The area is a popular spot for walkers.

NATHAN PHILLIPS SQUARE
WHERE: Queen Street West at Bay Street. MAP: 9 WHEN: 24 hr. ADMISSION: Free.
TELEPHONE: 416-392-1111 SUBWAY: Queen, or Osgoode.

When we go out to celebrate something like New Year's Eve, we usually descend on Nathan Phillips Square. The new Dundas Square – scheduled to open late in 2001 - might take over as the trendy place to be during such events, but the open space in front of city hall will take some beating as the city's official square. It's one of the most photographed places in town and the skating rink is the place to be for winter activities.

ROSETTA McCLAIN GARDENS
WHERE: Kingston Road at Fishleigh Drive.
MAP: *City of Toronto*, area 16L, and in detail below. WHEN: Daily. ADMISSION: Free.
WEB SITE: **city.toronto.on.ca/parks** SUBWAY: Warden and take 69 bus south.

Just west of the Scarborough Bluffs parks complex is perhaps the most secluded and attractive public garden in the city. It's one of the few, if any, places along the eastern lake shore that is free of Canada Geese, bikes, dogs and people having picnics. The gardens, on a 16.2 ha site donated by Robert McClain in 1959, are a place for strolling among summer flower beds and leafy trees, or just sitting near a waterfall and looking out over the lake. It's one of many parks that has a site map in Braille.

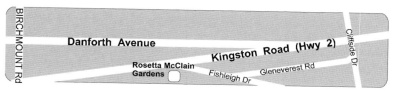

ROUGE PARK
WHERE: Sheppard Avenue East at Twyn Rivers Drive.
MAP: *City of Toronto*, area 22E, and in detail on the next page. WHEN: 24 hr.
ADMISSION: Free. TELEPHONE: 416-287-6843 WEB SITE: **city.toronto.on.ca/parks**
SUBWAY: Kennedy. Take an 86 bus to Sheppard.

This is the largest urban park in North America. It's situated along the Rouge River and preserved as a wilderness area. The ravine lands cover 5,400 ha, making them four times larger than the Toronto Islands and seven times bigger than New York's Central Park. It's one of our best-kept secrets (which makes local residents happy) and certainly the best place in town to see the fall colours. Natural walking trails only. Limited parking, camping, swimming and fishing.

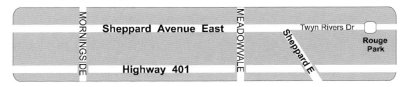

ST JAMES' CEMETERY AND CREMATORIUM
WHERE: 635 Parliament Street. MAP: 21 WHEN: Daily, 8.00 AM – 8.00 PM.
ADMISSION: Free. TELEPHONE: 416-964-9194 WEB SITE: **stjamescathedral.on.ca**
SUBWAY: Castle Frank and go west along Bloor Street East and south on Parliament Street.

Our oldest cemetery is the burial ground for many of the city's prominent historical figures. At the Parliament Street entrance is the Chapel of St James-the-Less, built in 1861. The heavily wooded burial ground, although not officially a park, is a favourite place for neighbourhood strolls.

SUNNYBROOK PARK
WHERE: Eglinton Avenue East at Leslie Street.
MAP: *City of Toronto*, area 12H, and in detail below. WHEN: Daily. ADMISSION: Free. TELE-PHONE: 416-392-8186 WEB SITE: **city.toronto.on.ca/parks**
SUBWAY: Eglinton and take any 34 bus to Leslie Street.

In the geographical centre of the city there's a series of inter-connected parks known collectively as the Central Don. Anchored by Edwards Gardens in the north, the Central Don includes the popular Sunnybrook Park together with Serena Gundy, Wilket Creek and Ernest Thompson Seton parks. Sunnybrook is home to the Central Don Stables, sporting fields and lots of picnic sites in a mature forest setting. You can drive through the park complex, but it's worth the experience to get out of your vehicle and stay awhile. In the winter, bring cross-country skis and a toboggan.

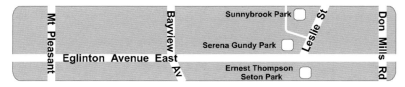

TORONTO MUSIC GARDEN
WHERE: Queen's Quay West at Lower Spadina Avenue. MAP: 3 WHEN: 24 hr.
ADMISSION: Free. WEB SITE: **city.toronto.on.ca/parks**

When it opened to the public in June, 1999 the garden was hailed as being one of the most creative uses of open space in the city. Internationally renowned cellist Yo-Yo Ma worked with landscape architects to interpret the six movements of Johann Sebastian Bach's *Suite #1 for Unaccompanied Cello* through various garden designs. Curved paths and signs encourage us to move through the various botanic 'movements' and enjoy features such as the maypole and music pavilion.

TORONTO ZOO

WHERE: Two kilometres north of Sheppard Avenue East on Meadowvale Road.
MAP: *City of Toronto*, area 21D, and in detail below.
WHEN: Daily, 9.00 AM – 5.00 PM. Closed Christmas Day. ADMISSION: $.
TELEPHONE: 416-392-5900 WEB SITE: **torontozoo.com**
SUBWAY: Kennedy and take the Zoo bus.

Since it opened in 1974 at a cost of $20,000,000, more than 30,000,000 people have visited what is considered to be one of the world's finest zoological parks. Over 6,000 animals, representing about 400 species, live in 287 ha of natural parks representing Africa, the Americas, Eurasia, Indo-Malaysia and Canada. It was one of the first zoos designed without a lot of bars, and many animals appear to be roaming freely. The zoo was built in a wilderness setting next to Rouge Park and its grounds support ponds, waterfalls and gardens.

VILLAGE OF YORKVILLE PARK

WHERE: Cumberland Street at Bellair Street. MAP: 24 WHEN: 24 hr. ADMISSION: Free.
TELEPHONE: 416-392-1111 (Toronto Parks Department). SUBWAY: Bay.

What you see is the result of an international design competition launched by the city in 1991. Several objectives were set for the project, including a desire "to provide a variety of spatial and sensory experiences..." In reality, it has 13 separate sections for plant life and a rock. And it's that 19 x 15 m slab of rock that caused all the controversy. It's over a billion years old, weighs 650 tonnes, and it took 20 flatbed trucks to haul it in pieces from the northern town of Gravenhurst. Once in place, the bits were flame treated around the edges to create almost invisible seams. It's not polite to ask how much all of this cost.

WOODBINE PARK

WHERE: Lake Shore Boulevard East at Kingston Road.
MAP: *City of Toronto*, area 13N and in detail below. WHEN: 24 hr. ADMISSION: Free. TELE-PHONE: 416-392-1111 (Toronto Parks Department).
SUBWAY: Coxwell and take the 22 bus.

When they tore down the old Greenwood Racetrack, the land was given over to housing and an ambitious new park that would cover the western half of the area. About $5,300,000 will be spent on developing the park over the next 15 years. Future amenities will include a band shell seating 22,000 people, an elaborate fountain display, over 600 trees, extensive walking trails, and a story book place for kids. Signs alone will cost $50,000

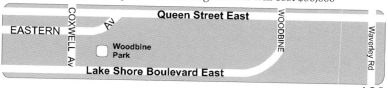

Worship

Every major religion is represented in the city. Places of worship range from cathedrals that have become landmarks to small neighbourhood gathering places. The following buildings are noted for their historic and architectural significance.

CHURCH OF ST STEPHEN-IN-THE-FIELDS
WHERE: College Street at Bellevue Avenue. MAP: 18 WHEN: During services.
ADMISSION: Free. TELEPHONE: 416-921-6350 WEB SITE: **saintstephens.on.ca**
SUBWAY: College and take the 506 bus west to Bellevue Avenue.

St Stephen's church was built in a field surrounded by dense forests in the late 1850s. The land was part of the old Bellevue Homestead that included much of what is today's Kensington Market. The building was destroyed by fire in 1865 and rebuilt exactly like the original. Twenty-five years later it was enlarged to its present dimensions. In 1927, St Stephens became the first Canadian church to broadcast its services via radio to Europe.

CHURCH OF THE HOLY TRINITY
WHERE: 10 Trinity Square, Eaton Centre. MAP: 14 WHEN: Daily, 11.00 AM – 3.00 PM. AD-
MISSION: Free. TELEPHONE: 416-598-4521
WEB SITE: **toronto.anglican.ca/parish/ht**

The church was north of the city when it was built in 1847 on land donated by John Simcoe Macauley. In those days it was common practice for the Church of England to charge pew fees. Mary Lambert Swale of Yorkshire, England, paid for the construction and stipulated that "it be free and unappropriated forever" so that working class parishioners would not be burdened with financial obligations. The building's bricks were made locally in the Don Valley, timbers were taken from the surrounding forest and the roof slate came from England as ballast in British sailing ships. When the Eaton Centre was being built, serious thought was given to demolishing the church and its two adjacent historic sites. Today, Holy Trinity continues its traditional work of supporting underprivileged people in the inner-city - and it serves a great lunch.

LITTLE TRINITY CHURCH
WHERE: 417 King Street East. MAP: 11 WHEN: During services. ADMISSION: Free.
TELEPHONE: 416-367-0272 WEB SITE: **littletrinity.on.ca**
SUBWAY: King and take the streetcar east to Trinity Street.

Little Trinity is situated in one of the most historic parts of the city. Built in 1842, it's the oldest church in Toronto and its community roots go back to the mid-1800s when it was a focal point for the first immigrant wave from Ireland. Like many of the old churches, it burned down and was rebuilt.

METROPOLITAN UNITED CHURCH
WHERE: 56 Queen Street East. MAP: 10 WHEN: During services. ADMISSION: Free. TELE-
PHONE: 416-363-0331 SUBWAY: Queen.

This is the grandest of the original Methodist churches in the city and the first church in North America to have a carillon. When it was built in 1870, it was looked upon as the denomination's 'Cathedral Church'. The respected

Casavant organ makers of Québec built over 8,000 pipes into the church's instrument in 1930. Organ and carillon recitals are held during the church's Music at the Metropolitan series from May through October. Today, the church is part of the United Church of Canada.

ST JAMES' CATHEDRAL

WHERE: Northeast corner of Church Street and King Street East. MAP: 10
WHEN: Daily, 7.30 AM – 5.30 PM; Saturdays, 9.00 AM – 3.00 PM. Sunday services.
ADMISSION: Free. TELEPHONE: 416-364-7865 WEB SITE: **stjamescathedral.on.ca** SUBWAY: King.

The city's Anglican cathedral, built in 1853, is the third church on this site since 1803. When the Royals are in town, this is where they usually worship on Sundays. The cathedral is set in one of the city's most attractive downtown parks. There are free music concerts every Tuesday at 1.00 PM, September through June.

St MICHAEL'S CATHOLIC CATHEDRAL

WHERE: Corner of Bond and Shuter streets. MAP: 15
WHEN: Monday through Saturday before 6.00 PM and for Sunday services.
ADMISSION: Free. TELEPHONE: 416-364-0234 SUBWAY: Dundas.

William Thomas adapted the cathedral's cruciform shape from a 14th century Gothic style. The Great Chancel Window, designed by French artist Etienne Theuenot, was installed ten years after the church was built and nine years before the tower spire was added. St Michael's was consecrated on September 29th, 1848 and is still known as the principal church of Canada's largest Catholic diocese.

St PAUL'S ANGLICAN CHURCH

WHERE: 227 Bloor Street East. MAP: 25
WHEN: Monday through Friday, 12 noon – 2.00 PM; Sunday services. ADMISSION: Free
TELEPHONE: 416-961-8116
SUBWAY: Bloor-Yonge and go one and a half blocks east on Bloor Street East.

St Paul's is one of the largest churches in Canada. It was originally designed by E J Lennox in 1913 after St Paul's in London to seat 2,500 people. Renovations in 1991 reduced this number to 1,700. The Rose Window is one of the largest in the world. Stone relics from British churches dating back to 563 AD are on display inside the main entrance. It's possibly the most interesting church in the city. Next door is the previous St Paul's Church, built in 1842, which is used now for administration.

St PAUL'S CATHOLIC BASILICA

WHERE: 83 Power Street at Queen Street East. MAP: 11
WHEN: Sundays 7.30 AM – 12 noon; Saturdays 4.00 PM – 6.00 PM. ADMISSION: Free.
TELEPHONE: 416-364-7588
SUBWAY: Queen. Take the Queen streetcar to Power Street.

The Roman Catholic cathedral built on this site in 1826 represented the first presence of formal Catholicism in Toronto. The present Italian Renaissance structure, based on Rome's St Paul-Against-the-Wall, opened in 1889. The city's first Catholic cemetery, which is now unmarked, was just to the east of this building. The *Pietà*, sitting to the left of the main entrance, is in memory of victims who died during the 1847 typhus epidemic that swept the city. St Paul's was elevated to minor basilica status in August, 1999 and is recognized as the Mother Church of the archdiocese.

TRINITY COLLEGE CHAPEL

WHERE: 6 Hoskin Avenue. MAP: 18 WHEN: Daily, 7.00 AM – 10.00 PM.
ADMISSION: Free. TELEPHONE: 416-978-3288 (Chaplain's office).
WEB SITE: **trinity.toronto.edu/divinity/chape**l SUBWAY: Museum.

Sir Gilbert Scott, architect of Liverpool's Gothic cathedral, created this chapel for the University of Toronto's Trinity College. He was also famous for designing the British Post Office's distinctive red telephone booths. The chapel is one of the finest examples of traditional architecture in the country and among the city's best acoustic spaces.

*City*Life & entertainment

There's so much going on in town throughout the year that it's impossible to get involved in everything. Regardless of the season, Toronto makes life interesting. Enjoy!

Major annual events

JANUARY
Chinese New Year
FEBRUARY
Canadian International Auto Show
Chinese New Year
MARCH
Toronto Sportsmen's Show
APRIL
National Home Show
JUNE
Downtown Jazz Festival
Gay Pride Week
Toronto Dragon Boat Race Festival
Toronto International Festival Caravan
JULY
Beaches Jazz Festival
Canada Day
Caribana
Celebrate Toronto Street Festival
CHIN Picnic
Corso Italia Toronto Fiesta

Downtown Jazz Festival
Great Salmon Hunt
The Fringe Theatre Festival
Toronto International Festival Caravan
Toronto Outdoor Art Exhibition
AUGUST
Canadian National Exhibition
Caribana
Great Salmon Hunt
Taste of the Danforth
SEPTEMBER
Cabbagetown Festival
Canadian International Air Show
Canadian National Exhibition
Computer Fest
Toronto International Film Festival
Word on the Street
NOVEMBER
Royal Agricultural Winter Fair
Santa Claus Parade

Visitors come to Toronto to see the sights. Those of us who live here go out in our millions to take part in hundreds of annual events. Here's a brief list of where we like to go.

BEACHES INTERNATIONAL JAZZ FESTIVAL
WHERE: Queen Street East between Woodbine and Beech avenues.
MAP: *City-wide Neighbourhoods*, area 13N, and in detail on the next page.
WHEN: Mid-July. ADMISSION: Free. TELEPHONE: 1 888 277-0796
WEB SITE: **beachesjazz.com** SUBWAY: Woodbine. Take a 92 bus to Queen Street East.

The Beach(es) is a trendy part of town, filled with old homes and occupied by a closely-knit community. Musicians, locals and tens of thousands of other people turn out to make the festival one of the city's top summer music attractions. They take over a two-kilometre section of Queen Street East during the four-day blowout, packing bistros, street corners, rooftops and Kew Gardens.

CABBAGETOWN FESTIVAL
WHERE: Parliament Street south of Wellesley Street East. MAP: 21
WHEN: Second weekend in September.
ADMISSION: Free for street activities. TELEPHONE: 416-921-0857
WEB SITE: **oldcabbagetown.com**
SUBWAY: Wellesley and take a 94 bus east to Parliament Street.

Become part of the neighbourhood as one of our most distinctive communities stages what it calls "the best Fall Festival in downtown." Pancake breakfasts, street dancing, a film festival, garage sales, plus a parade and restaurant/pub crawl are just some of the things you can enjoy. The festival also gives homeowners the opportunity to showcase their renovated Victorian houses to those of us who want to peep inside. It's a good idea to case the neighbourhood beforehand to make a list of houses displaying a small plaque indicating that the owners will be happy to welcome you at festival time.

CANADA DAY
WHERE: Various locations around the city. WHEN: July 1. ADMISSION: Free.

Most of the city closes for the national holiday. The biggest celebrations are at Ontario Place, Nathan Phillips Square, Centre Island, Mel Lastman Square and Queen's Park. Catch the Symphony of Fire at Ontario Place, or watch the Toronto Harbour Parade of Lights. Centre Island has the country's oldest and biggest canoeing and rowing regatta. Official greetings, good times and music abound in Nathan Phillips Square, or you can relax with your kids during activities at Queen's Park. The International CHIN Picnic kicks off for four days at Exhibition Place. In the evening, families turn out for local fireworks in parks across the city. The best uptown venue is Mel Lastman Square where there's a fireworks display and live Canadian talent. Both East York and Scarborough hold local community parades.

CANADIAN INTERNATIONAL AIR SHOW
WHERE: Exhibition Place. MAP: 1 WHEN: Labour Day weekend.
ADMISSION: Included with CNE ticket, but free everywhere else around the lake.
TELEPHONE: 416-393-6061 WEB SITE: **cias.org**
SUBWAY: Union and take the Harbourfront 509 streetcar to Exhibition Place.

The air show is entering its second half-century as the grand finale to the Canadian National Exhibition. Military and civilian aircraft from around the world take part, often including appearances by the American Stealth B-2 bomber. The Canadian Forces Snowbirds aerobatics team is the real crowd pleaser. It was formed in 1970 and consists of nine Canadair CT-114 Tutor aircraft.

CANADIAN NATIONAL EXHIBITION (CNE)
WHERE: Exhibition Place. MAP: 1 WHEN: Mid August through Labour Day.
ADMISSION: $. TELEPHONE: 416-393-6090 (Tickets). WEB SITE: **theex.com**
SUBWAY: Union and take the Harbourfront 509 streetcar to Exhibition Place.

'The Ex' has been a Toronto summer experience for well over 100 years and
has a place in most everyone's memory. The midway, candy floss, Food Hall
and exhibitors from more than 40 countries combine to make this a traditional family summer outing. The final weekend is topped-off with the Canadian International Air Show.

CARIBANA
WHERE: Various venues around the city. Parade starts from Exhibition Place and goes along
Lake Shore Boulevard West. Post-parade festivities are on Centre Island.
MAPS: 1, 2 and *Toronto Islands.*
WHEN: Last two weeks of July into August. Parade is held the final weekend.
ADMISSION: Free for the parade. TELEPHONE: 416-465-4884
WEB SITE: **toronto.com/caribana**
SUBWAY: Union and take the Harbourfront 509 streetcar to Exhibition Place for the parade;
or Union and take the 509 streetcar to Bay Street for the Centre Island ferry and the party.

This is North America's largest celebration of Caribbean culture. Two weeks
of events, food and festivities climax with the lavishly costumed parade that
attracts large crowds of people from all over the world. The next two days
are spent partying on Centre Island. Visitors are advised to book a hotel
well in advance.

CELEBRATE TORONTO STREET FESTIVAL
WHERE: Yonge Street at Lawrence Avenue, Eglinton Avenue, St Clair Avenue, Bloor Street
and Queen Street intersections. WHEN: Second weekend in July.
MAP: *City of Toronto* and *Downtown.*
ADMISSION: Free. TELEPHONE: 416-338-0338 WEB SITE: **city.toronto.on.ca**
SUBWAY: Lawrence, Eglinton, St Clair, Yonge-Bloor or Queen.

Big bands, jazz groups, dance, kids' stuff, family fun and star acts take over
five of the city's main Yonge Street intersections. The festival, which started
after Toronto amalgamated with its five surrounding municipalities, runs
from 11.00 AM – 11.00 PM Saturday, and 11.00 AM – 5.00 PM Sunday.
There's an official kick-off to the weekend on Friday night, usually at Eglinton Avenue. All intersections are closed to traffic.

CHIN PICNIC
WHERE: Exhibition Place. MAP: 1 WHEN: July 1 for four days. ADMISSION: Free.
TELEPHONE: 416-531-9991 (CHIN Radio). WEB SITE: **chinradio.com**
SUBWAY: Union and take the Harbourfront 509 streetcar to Exhibition Place.

For over 30 years CHIN Radio personality Johnny Lombardi has been host-
ing the world's biggest free international party for adults and kids. We turn
out in our thousands for stage performances, fun, games and food. But it's
the male and female bikini contests that hit the front pages. The picnic is one
of the city's most popular multicultural events.

CHINESE NEW YEAR
WHERE: In the city's three major Chinatowns:
Dundas at Spadina; Gerrard at Broadview; and around Sheppard at Midland – plus every
Chinese restaurant in town. WEB SITE: **toronto.com**
MAP: 13 (Dundas at Spadina). Also see *City of Toronto,* area 12M for Gerrard at Broadview
and area 17E for Sheppard at Midland. These two areas are detailed on the following page.
WHEN: End of January, or early February, depending on the date for Chinese New Year.
ADMISSION: $ for restaurant meals and free for street festivities.

115

TELEPHONE: 416-299-9092 (Chinese Business Promotion Centre).

This is the best time to go to a Chinese restaurant. Chefs pull out all the stops with lots of special dishes to make you drool during a two-week culinary extravaganza. Take in the noise and fun of dragon dances and fire crackers around the Dundas Street West and Spadina Avenue neighbourhood in the downtown core.

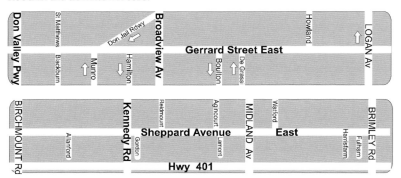

COMPUTER FEST
WHERE: Automotive Building, Exhibition Place. MAP: 1 WHEN: End of September.
ADMISSION: $. TELEPHONE: 416-925-1070 WEB SITE: **compfest.com**
SUBWAY: Bathurst and take the 511 streetcar to Exhibition Place.

Canada's largest computer show is a three-day event full of seminars, software demos, hardware, peripherals and exhibits. And it seems to get bigger and better every year. Representatives from about 100 companies are ready to answer any questions, or solve (hopefully) any problems you're likely to have. It's regarded as being the best of the city's five annual computer shows and a 'must attend' event for geeks and nerds.

CORSO ITALIA TORONTO FIESTA
WHERE: St Clair Avenue West between Dufferin Street and Lansdowne Avenue, or in Lansdowne Park. MAP: *City of Toronto*, area 8K, and in detail below.
WHEN: Second weekend in July. ADMISSION: Free.
TELEPHONE: 416-658-0901 WEB SITE: **toronto.com**
SUBWAY: Lansdowne and take a 47 bus north to St Clair; Dufferin and take a 29 bus north to St Clair.

The Italian community, which is our third largest ethnic group, puts on a two-day multi-cultural street experience in the middle of Corso Italia. It provides a good opportunity to really get into the Italian spirit, people-watch, take advantage of sidewalk sales, eat Italian food and relax with a cappuccino. If Italy should get to the final of the soccer World Cup again, this is where you should head for the festivities.

DOWNTOWN JAZZ FESTIVAL

WHERE: Various venues. WHEN: Last week in June for 11 days. ADMISSION: Varies.
TELEPHONE: 416-363-8717 WEB SITE: **tojazz.com**

More than 2,000 jazz artists play it up for devoted crowds during nine days of concerts at more than 30 locations. The festival has been a standard summer attraction for well over decade and draws top musicians from across the continent. Currently, Du Maurier tobacco sponsors the festival. As the federal government is likely to put severe restrictions on tobacco company participation in cultural events such as this one, the future of the festival in its present form is uncertain.

FASHION CARES

WHERE: Toronto Convention Centre. MAP: 9 WHEN: May. ADMISSION: $.
TELEPHONE: 416-340-2437 (AIDS Committee of Toronto). WEB SITE: **actoronto.org**
SUBWAY: Union and take the Skywalk.

It all started at a nightclub in 1985 when a group of people got together to raise awareness and money to fight HIV-AIDS. Since that humble beginning the event has moved to the Toronto Convention Centre and now raises about $800,000 for the one-night stand. It's the social highlight of the year for artists, designers, fashion gurus and corporate folk. The night is climaxed with the city's most glamorous and widely publicized fashion show. Two thousand people get those coveted gala tickets that include dinner and another 1,000 folk have to be satisfied with general admission.

GAY PRIDE PARADE

WHERE: Starts downtown at Bloor Street East and Church Street. Goes west along Bloor, south on Yonge, then east on Gould to Church.
MAPS: 25, 20 and 15 WHEN: Last Sunday in June. ADMISSION: Free.
TELEPHONE: 416-925-9872 (*Xtra!* Gay Infoline). WEB SITE: **pridetoronto.com**
SUBWAY: Bloor-Yonge, College or Wellesley.

The televised parade is the largest pride outing in Canada. Much lesser numbers turn out for the Dyke March the day before. These two events climax a week of gay and lesbian cultural activities centred in the Church and Wellesley neighbourhood. The immediate area is blocked to traffic from Friday night till early Monday morning for one non-stop street party. If you are coming to town for the celebrations, and want a nearby hotel, book well in advance.

GREAT SALMON HUNT

WHERE: Lake Ontario from Wellington to St Catharines.
WHEN: Mid-July to the end of August. ADMISSION: $. TELEPHONE: 416-695-0311
WEB SITE: **sportsmensshows.com**

It wasn't long ago that many people thought that the polluted waters of Lake Ontario would destroy the salmon stock. Those days are gone and now $1,000,000 in prize money awaits the angler who hauls in the specially tagged salmon. Otherwise ten prizes are awarded each week, with total cash amounting to $300,000. You have to register to be eligible for the riches, but don't get really excited until your catch weighs about 40 kg.

HARBOURFRONT

WHERE: Queen's Quay West. MAP: 3 and 4 WHEN: Year-round.
ADMISSION: Free, though some events could charge for tickets.
TELEPHONE: 416-973-3000 WEB SITE: **harbourfront.on.ca**

SUBWAY: Union and take the Harbourfront 509 streetcar.

A truly impressive number of events – about 4,000 in all - take place here every year with most around Harbourfront Park. Music, dance, stuff for kids, concerts, crafts, food and activities abound. It's a magnet for somewhere to go and do things for both us and the tourists. The area is generally regarded as being one of the most relaxing waterfront people places on the Great Lakes.

NATIONAL HOME SHOW
WHERE: Exhibition Place. MAP: 1 WHEN: Second week in April. ADMISSION: $.
TELEPHONE: 416-385-1880 WEB SITE: **toronto.com**
SUBWAY: Union and take the Harbourfront 509 streetcar to Exhibition Place.

The show is promoted as being a unique marketplace for homeowners to shop, compare and save. New ideas and expert advice draw crowds anxiously looking forward to spring. General categories include remodelling, gardening and decorating.

ROYAL AGRICULTURAL WINTER FAIR
WHERE: The Coliseum, Exhibition Place. MAP: 1 WHEN: First two weeks of November. ADMISSION: $. TELEPHONE: 416-393-6400 WEB SITE: **royalfair.org**
SUBWAY: Union and take the Harbourfront 509 streetcar to Exhibition Place.

Since 1922, the fair has been a celebration of Ontario's rural and agricultural traditions. Attractions include the Agricultural Show, the Royal Horse Show - which features top equestrians and attracts socialities and visitors from across Canada and around the world - and the Winter Garden Show. These three major components combine to make it the world's largest indoor annual fair.

SANTA CLAUS PARADE
WHERE: Route starts at Christie Street (MAP: 22), goes east along Bloor Street West, south on University, east on Queen Street West, south on Yonge, then east on Front Street East to Church. WHEN: November. ADMISSION: Free. TELEPHONE: 416-599-9090 #500
WEB SITE: **toronto.com** SUBWAY: Museum, Queen's Park, Osgoode, Queen, or King.

This city institution has been delighting families for nearly 100 years and the parade is believed to be the largest of its kind in North America. It attracts around 350,000 people along the route and is televised throughout the continent. Santa's float is usually last, but well worth waiting for. Don't forget to wear warm clothing.

TASTE OF THE DANFORTH
WHERE: Danforth Avenue between Hampton and Jones avenues.
MAP: *City Neighbourhoods* and in detail on the following page.
WHEN: Second August weekend.

118

ADMISSION: Free except for food. TELEPHONE: 416-469-5634
WEB SITE: **greektowntoronto.com** SUBWAY: Chester or Pape.

The largest Greektown in North America takes over 12 blocks of Danforth Avenue to put on a smorgasbord. They claim it's the "largest food festival in Canada." Take in the music, restaurants, kids' festival, fashion shows, people and possibly more food than you've ever seen before in one place. One or two dollars get you a taste and net proceeds go to charity.

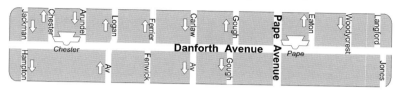

THE FRINGE : TORONTO'S THEATRE FESTIVAL
WHERE: Various stages throughout downtown. WHEN: First 11 days of July.
ADMISSION: $. TELEPHONE: 416-534-5919 WEB SITE: **fringetoronto.com**

The Fringe has been packing 'em in for the last dozen years. It puts on over 500 performances of short works on 10 stages by 90 theatre companies. Productions are mostly new efforts by promising playwrights. Tickets are usually under $10. The two-week theatrical *tour de force* is often called 'Toronto's biggest stage blowout.'

TORONTO DRAGON BOAT RACE FESTIVAL
WHERE: Centre Island. MAP: *Toronto Islands*. WHEN: Last weekend in June.
ADMISSION: Free. TELEPHONE: 416-598-8945 WEB SITE: **dragonboats.com**
SUBWAY: Union. Take the 509 streetcar to Bay Street and get a ferry to Centre Island.

This three-day re-enactment of an ancient Chinese legend pits competitive crews against each other to delight 100,000 cheering people. With 200 crews and 5,000 athletes, it rivals a similar annual festival held in Hong Kong. Next to the excitement of Chinese New Year, the festival is the biggest Chinese celebration in the city.

TORONTO'S CANADIAN INTERNATIONAL AUTO SHOW
WHERE: Toronto Convention Centre and SkyDome. MAP: 9 and 3
WHEN: Middle of February. ADMISSION: $. TELEPHONE: 416-585-3660
WEB SITE: **toronto.com** SUBWAY: Union.

One of the world's five official international auto shows. More than 46,500 sq m of floor space are given over to a dreamland of four-wheeled horse power. Promoted as the "total automotive experience", the Auto Show lets you see what nearly 150 exhibitors and manufacturers have to offer in the way of new, concept and vintage vehicles, plus lots of automotive gear.

TORONTO INTERNATIONAL FESTIVAL CARAVAN
WHERE: Over 20 locations throughout the city. WHEN: Last week of June into July.
ADMISSION: $. TELEPHONE: 416-977-0466 WEB SITE: **toronto.com**

This popular festival, involving more than 20 cities, countries and cultures, is over 30 years old. The annual bash celebrates Toronto's international diversity with pavilions showcasing national food, culture and heritage. You can get a 'passport' to visit all the pavilions as many times as you want. There's also an unlimited single day pass.

TORONTO INTERNATIONAL FILM FESTIVAL
WHERE: Various downtown cinemas. WHEN: Second week in September. ADMISSION: $.
TELEPHONE: 416-967-7371 WEB SITE: **bell.ca/filmfest**

Over 250,000 stars and lesser folk come from all over to see more than 300 movies and generally strut their way from gala to gala. It's the largest film festival in North America - and it's media frenzy time in town. The glitzy parade started in 1976 with the unassuming title, 'Festival of Festivals'. Readers of the *Los Angeles Times* have voted this the number one film festival in the world.

TORONTO OUTDOOR ART EXHIBITION
WHERE: Nathan Phillips Square. MAP: 9 WHEN: Second weekend in July.
ADMISSION: Free. WEB SITE: **toronto.com** SUBWAY: Queen, or Osgoode.

This popular exhibition has been a city fixture for nearly 40 years and is one of the biggest free outdoor art exhibitions on the continent. A professional jury selects participants to ensure a high standard of competing artists. Prize money is estimated at over $20,000. Set aside a few hours to see the variety of works in 15 media categories.

TORONTO SPORTSMEN'S SHOW
WHERE: National Trade Centre. MAP: 1 WHEN: Second week in March. ADMISSION: $.
TELEPHONE: 416-695-0311 WEB SITE: **sportsmensshows.com** SUBWAY: Union.

Since its inception just over 50 years ago, the show has attracted more than 10,000,000 visitors. This is where you'll find everything to do with hunting, camping, hiking, boating and fishing. More than 6 ha of exhibition space are now used for the annual event.

WORD ON THE STREET
WHERE: Queen Street West between University and Spadina avenues. MAP: 8 and 9 WHEN: Last Sunday in September, 11.00 AM – 6.00 PM. WEB SITE: **canada.com/wots**
ADMISSION: Free. TELEPHONE: 416-504-7241 SUBWAY: Osgoode.

A day to celebrate the joy of reading with authors, publishers and thousands of other like-minded spirits. A seven-block section of Queen Street West is closed to traffic and lined with close to 200 booths full of books and magazines, lots of places for author readings, general literary activities and family fun spots. This is the country's biggest public book bash.

Ballet & dance

 When summer activities come to a close, three renowned companies start to unveil their new productions. And visiting artists arrive to join them on the city's stages.

DANCEMAKERS
WHERE: Premier Dance Theatre, Harbourfront. MAP: 4 WHEN: October through May.
ADMISSION: $. TELEPHONE: 416-535-8880 (Administration); 416-973-4000 (Tickets).
WEB SITE: **dancemakers.org** SUBWAY: Union and take the Harbourfront 509 streetcar.

Dance magazine has called Dancemakers "Toronto's pre-eminent contemporary troupe." The company has travelled extensively throughout Canada, the United States, South America and Europe, winning acclaim wherever it performed. During its home seasons it has been nominated several times for the prestigious Dora Mavor Moore Award.

DANNY GROSSMAN DANCE COMPANY

WHERE: Premier Dance Theatre. MAP: 4 WHEN: October through May. ADMISSION: $.
Telephone: 416-531-8350 WEB SITE: **dgdance.org**
SUBWAY: Union and take the Harbourfront 509 streetcar.

During the last 25 years, Danny Grossman has moulded his troupe into a Toronto institution that's noted for its *avant-garde* interpretations of social themes through dance. The unique style of his choreography, maintained throughout about 30 works, has found its way into the repertoires of companies around the world.

NATIONAL BALLET OF CANADA

WHERE: Hummingbird Centre, 1 Front Street East. MAP: 10 WHEN: Fall through spring.
ADMISSION: $. TELEPHONE: 416-345-9686 (Administration); 416-345-9595 (Tickets).
WEB SITE: **national.ballet.ca** SUBWAY: Union.

Celia Franca founded the company in 1951 and, as it enters its second half-century, it's planning a joint venture with the Canadian Opera Company to build a ballet-opera house downtown on University Avenue at Queen Street West. Until that tentative vision materializes, performances continue at the 3,200-seat Hummingbird Centre. Critics have been generous to the company over the years, giving rave reviews to dancers, choreographers and set designers. The company concentrates on a solid repertoire of classical works while encouraging new ballets and Canadian choreographers. The season highlight is *The Nutcracker*, which is traditionally performed during the festive season to sold-out audiences.

Cinema

 Toronto is known as 'Hollywood North'. We're the third largest film and television production centre in North America after Los Angeles and New York. And the industry employs over 20,000 people. On top of that, we have the largest number of people, per capita, in North America who go to the movies.

Toronto gave Hollywood its first great movie star. Mary Pickford was born here near the corner of University Avenue and Elm Street in 1893. Despite this stupendous gift, Hollywood moguls now say that we're threatening Tinseltown's economy by making it 25% cheaper to shoot movies here than in California. Our crews and production companies smile and boost their bank accounts by over $1,320,000,000 annually. We might be big on making movies, and we're certainly big on going to Imax® theatres, but the independent movie houses are almost extinct. Three major and highly competitive, cash-strapped cinema exhibition chains have replaced them: AMC, Cineplex Odeon and Famous Players.

AMC

WHERE: See newspapers or Web site. WHEN: See newspapers or Web site.
WEB SITE: **amctheatres.com**

Although AMC is the newest kid on the block in Toronto, it's history goes back to 1920 when American Edward D Durwood opened his Durwood Theatre. This humble beginning evolved into AMC, which credits itself with inventing the multiple-theatre concept in 1963 in Kansas City. It also touts its introduction of the coffee cup holder arm rest and advance ticket sales. AMC closed its Canadian headquarters in 1999, but is planning an expansion into a new Dundas Square location with a 24-screen complex.

CINEPLEX ODEON
WHERE: See newspapers or Web site. WHEN: See newspapers or Web site.
WEB SITE: **cineplex.com**

Loews Cineplex Entertainment was founded in 1998 with the merger of Loews Theatres and Cineplex Odeon Corporation. Loews was the oldest motion picture exhibitor in North America, having been started in 1904 by Marcus Loew. He then joined with Louis B Mayer and Samuel Goldwyn in 1924 to launch MGM. Cineplex Odeon was once a Canadian company, created by Garth Drabinsky. It opened Canada's first multi-screen cinema complex in April, 1979 at the Eaton Centre. On March 13, 2001 this historic site closed due to financial reasons.

FAMOUS PLAYERS
WHERE: See newspapers or Web site. WHEN: See newspapers or Web site.
WEB SITE: **famousplayers.com**

N L Nathanson owned the now long-gone Majestic Theatre on Adelaide Street and used it to begin the Regent chain. In 1929 he installed the country's first movie sound system in Montreal's Palace Theatre. Famous Players is the oldest movie exhibition company in the country and has more screens here than any of its competitors. But it's Canadian no longer. Viacom, the American entertainment mega-giant, has taken over.

TORONTO INTERNATIONAL FILM FESTIVAL
WHERE: Various downtown cinemas. WHEN: Second week in September.
ADMISSION: $. TELEPHONE: 416-967-7371
WEB SITE: **bell.ca/filmfest**

Over 250,000 stars and lesser folk come from all over to see about 300 movies and generally strut their way from gala to gala. It's the largest film festival in North America - and it's media frenzy time in town. The glitzy parade started in 1976 with the unassuming title, Festival of Festivals. Readers of the *Los Angeles Times* once voted this the number one film festival in the world.

Classical & choral music

 The city has three major orchestras, two internationally famous ensembles and four honoured choirs. By adding a formidable list of visiting soloists from around the world, we have become a significant centre for classical and choral music.

CANADIAN CHILDREN'S OPERA CHORUS
WHERE: Various locations. WHEN: November through May. ADMISSION: $.
TELEPHONE: 416-366-0467

For over 30 years the 75 members of this highly acclaimed group of youngsters have appeared in productions by the Canadian Opera Company, the Toronto Symphony Orchestra and the National Ballet of Canada. The chorus is engaged in about 40 of these productions during the year, as well as staging their own concerts.

ELMER ISELER SINGERS
WHERE: Various locations. WHEN: October through May. ADMISSION: $.
TELEPHONE: 416-971-4839 WEB SITE: **elmeriselersingers.com**

The late Elmer Iseler, known as 'the Dean of choral conductors' by his peers across Canada, founded the choir in 1979. It is one of the few professional choirs in the world. The 20-voice ensemble, known for its purity of tone and vocal colour, is the choir-in-residence at the University of Toronto's Faculty of Music. It travels extensively, giving around 100 concerts annually in North America and Europe.

SCARBOROUGH PHILHARMONIC ORCHESTRA
WHERE: Birchmount Park Collegiate. WHEN: November through May. ADMISSION: $.
TELEPHONE: 416-261-0380 WEB SITE: **total.net/~spo**
SUBWAY: Warden and take the 17 bus.

The community orchestra was formed in the late 1970s to serve those of us living in the east end with local classical orchestral music. It gives about a dozen concerts each year, dividing its repertoire among classical, pop, opera and children's programs. Each concert features at least one Canadian composition.

TAFELMUSIK
WHERE: Trinity-Saint Paul's United Church. MAP 23 WHEN: September through May.
ADMISSION: $. TELEPHONE: 416-964-9562 WEB SITE: **tafelmisik.org**
SUBWAY: Spadina.

More properly named the Tafelmusik Baroque Orchestra, this internationally acclaimed ensemble of 19 players performs with Baroque and classical instruments. The season schedule usually offers 40 concerts in town and numerous appearances overseas. The award-winning group was founded in 1979.

TORONTO CHILDREN'S CHORUS
WHERE: Various churches. WHEN: September through June. ADMISSION: $.
TELEPHONE: 416-932-8666 WEB SITE: **torontochildrenschorus.com**

Places like New York's Carnegie Hall and London's Barbican Centre are no strangers to this group of young choristers whose ages range from six to 17. Although the chorus consists of 320 voices, most performances usually rely on about a third of the total company. The repertoire is taken from works written between the Renaissance and the 20th century and contains Canadian compositions.

TORONTO CONSORT
WHERE: Trinity-Saint Paul's United Church. MAP 23 WHEN: November through May.
ADMISSION: $. TELEPHONE: 416-966-1045 (Administration); 416-964-6337 (Tickets).
WEB SITE: **toronto.com** SUBWAY: Spadina.

The ensemble's six members are noted for their repertoire of music written from the 12th through 17th centuries, even though their performances often include some contemporary music by Canadian composers. The group was founded in 1972 and its playing of Middle Ages and Renaissance music has garnered critical acclaim across Canada and in cities throughout the United States and Europe.

TORONTO MENDELSSOHN CHOIR
WHERE: Roy Thomson Hall. MAP: 9 WHEN: September through May. ADMISSION: $.
TELEPHONE: 416-598-0422 WEB SITE: **tmchoir.org** SUBWAY: St Andrew.

This is one of the oldest and most respected performing arts groups in Canada. The choir was formed in 1894 and today has a membership of 160 volunteer choristers. Apart from its four annual concerts in Roy Thomson Hall, The Mendelssohn joins with the Toronto Symphony Orchestra during the performance of major choral works. The choir's annual highlight is a sold-out performance of Handel's *Messiah*.

TORONTO PHILHARMONIA ORCHESTRA
WHERE: George Weston Recital Hall, Toronto Centre for the Arts.
MAP: *North York Centre*. WHEN: September through May. ADMISSION: $.
TELEPHONE: 416-499-2204 WEB SITE: **torontophil.on.ca** SUBWAY: North York Centre.

Before changing its name to the Toronto Philharmonia, the orchestra was known as the North York Symphony Orchestra. It was founded in 1971 and is the orchestra-in-residence at the highly acclaimed George Weston Recital Hall, where it gives about a dozen concerts annually. The repertoire, under the direction of conductor Kerry Stratton, is based on the classics and contemporary Canadian works.

TORONTO SYMPHONY ORCHESTRA
WHERE: Roy Thomson Hall. MAP: 9 WHEN: September through May. ADMISSION: $. TELEPHONE: 416-593-7769 (Administration); 416-593-4828 (Tickets).
WEB SITE: **tso.on.ca** SUBWAY: St Andrew.

Some of the renowned conductors who have led the TSO during its 75-year residency in Toronto have included Sir Ernest MacMillan and Seiji Ozawa. The orchestra gives about 125 concerts each season that often include outstanding international soloists. The TSO has toured extensively to cities across Canada, the United States, Europe, Japan and Australia.

Clubs and bars

 There are probably more than 6,000 clubs, bars and places featuring live music scattered from one end of the city to the other. But no one really knows for sure.

The club, live music, bar and jazz scenes change almost daily. However, here's the best way to keep abreast of what's happening and where: Get a copy of either **eye** or NOW weekly newspapers. They're free, come out every Thursday, and you can get a copy from street boxes, coffee shops, bars, convenience stores and restaurants anywhere downtown. The most popular areas around the inner-city are on maps 8 and 9. If you're wired, the following two Internet sites will have most of the information you need:

torontobars.com
A complete listing of nightclubs, jazz spots, dance bars, bar grills, sports and wine bars, pubs/taverns, karaoke bars, Latino/ethnic, cigar haunts, gay and lesbian places, venues with pop groups and pool/billiards halls. If the magnitude of all this overwhelms you then stay home, click the *Bartender's*

Guide, and learn how to mix yourself a stiff drink. The other feature of this Web site is *Cool Toronto Links*. It lists most of the city's general interest sites.

xtra.ca

Pink Triangle Press, publishers of the gay and lesbian bi-weekly newspaper, *XTRA!*, has put this site together. Use search for *Bars and Clubs*. If you're not on-line, you can get a copy of the paper just about anywhere around the intersection of Church Street and Wellesley Street East in the gay neighbourhood. Woody's on Church Street is reputed to sell more beer than any other bar in the city.

Opera

The Grand Opera House they built on Adelaide Street in 1874 was demolished a long time ago to make way for a bank. Now, opera buffs hope that banks will help them build a new one.

The Canadian Opera Company and the National Ballet of Canada tried to induce the provincial government to set aside the southeast corner of Bay and Wellesley streets for a ballet-opera house. Plans fell through when the government was defeated. By 1999 the company, with a depleted bank balance and less than thunderous continuing support from the National Ballet, went ahead and unveiled an artist's concept for a ballet-opera house on University Avenue between Queen and Richmond streets. The dream is waiting for the start of Act 2.

CANADIAN OPERA COMPANY (COC)
WHERE: Hummingbird Centre. MAP: 10 WHEN: November through May.
ADMISSION: $. TELEPHONE: 416-363-6671 (Administration); 416-872-2262 (Tickets).
WEB SITE: **coc.ca** SUBWAY: Union.

Canada's premier opera company is now entering its second half-century. Before 1961, when it moved into the O'Keefe Centre (now the Hummingbird Centre), the COC performed at the University of Toronto's Hart House, the Royal Conservatory of Music - with which it was associated - and the Royal Alexandra Theatre. Since the 1990-91 season, some productions are staged at the Elgin Theatre. The company's administrative, workshop and rehearsal space is housed in the Joey and Toby Tanenbaum Opera Centre, which includes the 450-seat Imperial Oil Theatre. The building was constructed in 1885 for the Consumers Gas Company in the style of an early Christian basilica.

OPERA ATELIER
WHERE: Various locations. WHEN: Season varies. ADMISSION: $.
TELEPHONE: 416-925-3767 (Information); 416-872-1212 (Tickets).
WEB SITE: **toronto.com**
The internationally acclaimed Opera Atelier fits no particular mould. The company specializes in historically precise performances of opera, ballet and drama in a mix that invites a unique theatrical experience. Exquisite costumes and stylistic gesturing are trademarks that have been researched at the Bibliothèque Nationale and the Paris Opéra, the Juilliard School and London's Royal Academy of Dancing. The company tours worldwide to

give its audiences an enjoyable and entertaining experience rooted in Baroque traditions.

TORONTO OPERETTA THEATRE
WHERE: Jane Mallett Theatre, St Lawrence Centre. MAP: 10
WHEN: October through June. ADMISSION: $. TELEPHONE: 416-465-2147
WEB SITE: **torontooperetta.com** SUBWAY: Union

Although the company headed by Guillermo Silva-Marin is just over 15 years old, it has established itself as the city's foremost performer of operetta. During its long season, it presents two fully staged classic operettas featuring Canadian artists and a series of Sunday concert matinees.

Professional sports

 The city is no stranger to winning the Stanley Cup, the Grey Cup, or even the World Series. In fact, we've won them all more than once.

AMERICAN LEAGUE BASEBALL – TORONTO BLUE JAYS
WHERE: SkyDome. MAP: 3 WHEN: Baseball season ADMISSION: $.
TELEPHONE: 416-341-1111 (Ticket information); 416-341-1234 (Ticket order by credit card); 416-341-1000 (Administration).
WEB SITE: **bluejays.com** SUBWAY: Union and take the Skywalk.

The city's twice World Series champions slug it out for yet another try at the big prize. Gone are the 45,000+ crowds at SkyDome since the long-gone but not forgotten baseball strike, so good tickets are usually available for each game. Fans are enthusiastic about the stadium's good food and bargain-priced hotdogs.

CANADIAN FOOTBALL LEAGUE – TORONTO ARGONAUTS
WHERE: SkyDome. MAP: 3 WHEN: Football season. ADMISSION: $.
TELEPHONE: 416-341-5151 (Tickets and administration). WEB SITE: **argonauts.on.ca**
SUBWAY: Union and take the Skywalk.

The Argos are the oldest professional sports team in North America. Over recent years their die-hard fans have dwindled, but as soon as the club looks like making it to the Grey Cup final, the city comes alive with football fever.

CANADIAN OPEN TENNIS – MASTERS SERIES
WHERE: National Tennis Centre. MAP: *City of Toronto.* WHEN: First week in August.
ADMISSION: $. TELEPHONE: 416-665-9777 WEB SITE: **tenniscanada.com**
SUBWAY: Keele and take the 41 bus north to Steeles Avenue West.

This is Canada's top international tennis event. It's shared with Montréal, so that men's matches in Toronto are held on even-numbered years and the women's program on odd-numbered years. This is a Masters Series event on the world professional circuit and is sandwiched between Wimbledon and the US Open. Consequently, it attracts big names. Total prize money is $US 3,000,000. American M. Farnum won the first men's singles in 1883.

MOLSON INDY
WHERE: Exhibition Place & Lakeshore Boulevard West. MAP: 1 WHEN: Mid-July.
ADMISSION: $. TELEPHONE: 416-966-6213 (Administration); or 416-872-INDY (Tickets).
WEB SITE: **molson.com/motorsport**

SUBWAY: Union and take the Harbourfront 509 streetcar to Exhibition Place.

Top racing drivers from around the world compete with Canadian champions in a one-week event that offers lots more than just the roar of engines. The Indy is part of the 20-race FedEx championship that includes events in Australia, Brazil, Japan and the United States. Michael Andretti won this event for the sixth time in July, 2000.

NATIONAL BASKETBALL ASSOCIATION – TORONTO RAPTORS

WHERE: Air Canada Centre. MAP: 4 WHEN: Basketball season. ADMISSION: $.
TELEPHONE: 416-366-3865 WEB SITE: **nba.com/raptors**
SUBWAY: Union and take the PATH walkway south.

The young club is still intent on winning the championship and we're filling the stadium. Lots of hoopla both on and off the court. In the first game played at the Air Canada Centre on Sunday, February 21, 1999 the Raptors defeated the Vancouver Grizzlies 102-87.

NATIONAL HOCKEY LEAGUE – TORONTO MAPLE LEAFS

WHERE: Air Canada Centre. MAP: 4 WHEN: Hockey season. ADMISSION: $.
TELEPHONE: 416-977-1641 WEB SITE: **torontomapleleafs.com**
SUBWAY: Union and take the PATH walkway south.

The old Maple Leaf Gardens has seen its last NHL game, but fans are just as excited about the Air Canada Centre. And no fan can compete with a Leaf's fan. The team mightn't have won the Stanley Cup since May 2, 1967, but the Leafs know how to fill a stadium. For trivia fans, the Leafs defeated the Montréal Canadiens 3-2 in overtime on Saturday, February 20, 1999 during the first game played at the Air Canada Centre.

THOROUGHBRED HORSE RACING:
QUEEN'S PLATE AND BREEDERS' STAKES

WHERE: Woodbine Racetrack. MAP: *City of Toronto*
WHEN: Queen's Plate during the last weekend in June; Breeders' Stakes in mid-August.
ADMISSION: $. TELEPHONE: 416-675-7223 WEB SITE: **ojc.com**
SUBWAY: Islington and take the 37A bus.

The Queen's Plate is the oldest continuously run thoroughbred race in North America. It's the first Triple Crown event and carries a purse of about $500,000 for the winner. The Breeders' Stakes, also run at Woodbine, and the Prince of Wales Stakes held at Fort Erie, round out the Triple Crown events.

Theatre

Toronto has often been promoted as the third largest live theatre centre in the English-speaking world after London and New York. This could be true, considering the city has 91 professional theatre companies performing on 79 stages.

The following are some of the highly acclaimed major theatre companies that provide us with a diversity of stage productions:

BUDDIES IN BAD TIMES

WHERE: 12 Alexander Street. MAP: 20 WHEN: Throughout the year. ADMISSION: $.
TELEPHONE: 416-975-9130 (Administration); 416-975-8555 (Tickets).
WEB SITE: **buddies.web.net** SUBWAY: Carlton.

Buddies has been characterized as the most controversial, influential and vital theatre in the country. It was founded in 1979 and had its modest beginnings in a dilapidated building on George Street. A few years ago it moved into a new space on Alexander Street, close to the gay community. The only full-time gay stage in North America, its productions cover a full spectrum of *avant-garde* material that has garnered over 30 national prizes, including three coveted Governor-General's Awards. The Chamber, which seats 300, and the much smaller Tallulah's Cabaret, have been the launching pads for dozens of now successful playwrights, directors, technicians, actors and designers.

CANADIAN STAGE COMPANY

WHERE: St Lawrence Centre. MAP: 10 WHEN: Year round. ADMISSION: $.
TELEPHONE: 416-367-8243 (Administration, 26 Berkeley Street); 416-368-3110 (Tickets).
WEB SITE: **canstage.com** SUBWAY: Union.

The Canadian Stage Company was created in 1987 as a not-for-profit, community supported organization through the merger of the Toronto Free Theatre and CentreStage. It earns over half its $7.2-million budget from seat sales. Using the St Lawrence Centre, the Berkeley Street Theatre and the thousand-seat amphitheater in High Park as its venues, Canadian Stage produces a full season of mainly Canadian works. Occasionally, they'll perform internationally contemporary plays such as the acclaimed *Angels in America*.

MIRVISH PRODUCTIONS

WHERE: Princess of Wales Theatre (MAP: 8); Royal Alexandra Theatre (MAP: 9).
WHEN: During performances year round. ADMISSION: $.
TELEPHONE: 416-593-0351 (Administration for both theatres);
416-872-1212 (Tickets for both theatres).
WEB SITE: **mirvish.com** (Includes on-line ticket sales). SUBWAY: St Andrew.

'Honest' Ed Mirvish and his son David are two theatrical entrepreneurs who have made one of the city's major theatre districts their own. Ed is more than a theatrical person known for his marketing genius. He's one of the city's icons. Literally rising from rags to riches, he has gone from working as a kid in his parents' modest shop to running his own flamboyant department store, London's Old Vic theatre and two of our most prestigious stages. The Mirvishes own both the historic Royal Alexandra and the modern Princess of Wales theatres on King Street West, and used to run most of the restaurants in between. Bus loads of patrons from western New York and cities throughout southern Ontario commute to Mirvish's stage offerings imported from Broadway and London's West End. The shows include everything from mega-musicals such as *Miss Saigon* and *The Lion King* to award-winning dramas like *Art*.

TARRAGON THEATRE

WHERE: 30 Bridgman Avenue. MAP: 26 WHEN: September through June. ADMISSION: $.
TELEPHONE: 416-536-5018 WEB SITE: **tarragontheatre.com**
SUBWAY: Dupont and take 4 bus to Howland Avenue.

Bill Glassco founded this critically acclaimed theatre in 1970 as "a playwright's theatre". Over the last 30 years it has undertaken hundreds of productions and established itself as a leading venue for the creation and development of new works. The theatre has two areas: the 205-seat MainSpace and the 100-seat ExtraSpace.

THEATRE PASSE MURAILLE

16 Ryerson Avenue. MAP: 7 WHEN: Usually September through May. ADMISSION: $.
TELEPHONE: 416-504-8988 (Administration); 416-504-7529 (Tickets).
WEB SITE: **passemuraille.on.ca** SUBWAY: Osgoode and take the 501 streetcar.

The theatre was founded on the radical intention of creating a distinctly Canadian voice in theatre. Now into its fourth decade, that voice has been heard. Passe Muraille has acted as mentor for emerging theatres across Canada, from Newfoundland's CODCO and Saskatoon's 25th Street Theatre to our own Buddies in Bad Times. There are two spaces: Mainstage and Backstage.

THE FRINGE: TORONTO'S THEATRE FESTIVAL

WHERE: Various stages throughout downtown. WHEN: First 11 days of July.
ADMISSION: $. TELEPHONE: 416-534-5919 WEB SITE: **fringetoronto.com**

The Fringe has been packing 'em in for the last dozen years. It puts on over 500 performances of short works on 10 stages by 90 theatre companies. Productions are mostly new efforts by promising playwrights. Tickets are usually under $10, or you can get a 10 show pass for $60. The two-week theatrical *tour de force* is often called 'Toronto's biggest stage blowout.'

YPT – YOUNG PEOPLE'S THEATRE

WHERE: 165 Front Street East. MAP: 10
WHEN: October through June. Weekends and holiday matinees (public); weekday matinees (school children). ADMISSION: $.
TELEPHONE: 416-363-5131 (Administration); 416-862-2222 (Tickets).
WEB SITE: **toronto.com** SUBWAY: Union or King.

YPT is Canada's largest professional theatre for young people and the city's first not-for-profit theatre. Its productions cater to a wide spectrum, running from classic to contemporary theatre and shows with a distinctly Canadian theme. The company has strong links to the educational system and remains an integral and important part of the artistic and cultural life of our changing and socially diverse city. There are two performing spaces: one with 468 seats, the other with 300.

*City*Food

There are about 18,000 places to eat in the city – including 1,500 sidewalk cafés. They represent the cuisines of 169 countries. When you dine out, the world is on your plate.

Eating out*InTheCity*

Only recently has Toronto seriously begun to rival Montréal as the gastronomic capital of Canada. Food connoisseurs from Québec, of course, scoff at such Torontonian pretence. Perhaps Toronto didn't put the *haute* into *haute cuisine*, but its leading edge over Montréal comes from the enticing diversity of dishes that can be found in this city's more numerous ethnic neighbourhoods.

Dining out around town ranges from very classy establishments and intimate patios to family-run neighbourhood eateries and trendy thirtysomething places. Fast food outlets and fashionable coffee shops abound. Restaurant competition is so intense in some areas that any momentary lapse in the kitchen could doom a place to extinction quicker than you could order a bottle of designer water.

RESTAURANT AREAS

The best concentrations of good, expensive restaurants are in Yorkville and on Yonge Street in midtown. Trendy folk hang out around the Entertainment District, or head for little places along Queen Street West. The Greek community dominates The Danforth, which exudes Mediterranean sights and aromas. The influential Bay Street élite don't stray far from their skyscrapers for power lunches. Baldwin Street, between McCaul and Beverley streets, is a small hidden treasure. Theatre crowds stay close to their seats around Yonge and Front streets, along King Street West near John Street and on Elm Street between Yonge and Bay streets. Italian restaurants are everywhere. Downtown's Chinatown looks more like Vietnam these days, but the old, established Chinese places are still hard to beat for atmosphere.

Bon appétit!

DRESS

A general rule is to dress for dinner in what's known as 'smart casual' attire. This ranges from Versace in Yorkville and midtown to Tommy Hilfiger and the Gap elsewhere. Business people dress conservatively when clients are around. A jacket and tie are encouraged for places with a $$$$$ rating.

TIPPING

Tips for waiters are generally about 15% of the food bill before taxes. A quick way to do the math is add the two taxes (7% + 8%) on the bill. If the service is bad, tip less or, in extreme cases, not at all. The maître d'hôtel should be offered $5.00 - $10.00, depending on the tone of the establishment. (Don't confuse this fellow with a person who just points you in the general direction of a table at Joe's Greasy Spoon.) The sommelier gets 10% of the before-tax price of wine.

PRICES

Here's a general pre-tax price guide for restaurants listed in City**Food**, based on an average dinner and one drink for two:

$$$$$	Over $150.00		$$	$50.00 - $75.00
$$$$	$100.00 - $150.00		$	Under $50.00
$$$	$75.00 - $100.00			

CREDIT CARDS

Make sure ahead of time that the restaurant you choose accepts traveller's cheques or your credit card. This saves possible embarrassment. On the following pages the term 'All major' is used. This refers to American Express, Mastercard and Visa credit cards. American visitors should be aware that Toronto restaurants do not accept the Discover Card.

> **HELPFUL TIPS:** Always keep in mind that restaurants are in an unpredictable business. Chefs and menus can change like the weather. Before you go out for dinner, check ahead to make sure the place you choose is still open. Even great *Michelin* star restaurants have been known to close without notice. In one case the chef committed suicide. Also check the green, yellow or red entrance sign rating the restaurant's cleanliness.

REVIEWS

All restaurants listed throughout City**Companion** enjoy popular neighbourhood support – and an official *green* sign outside confirms the support of the city health department. (Be cautious of *yellow* signs!) To read what influential columnists are saying, get a copy of the monthly *Toronto Life*. The reviews are a bit obscure at times, with style dominating substance, but affluent patrons and chefs alike read them. You'll also find the *Toronto Life* annual seal of approval on many restaurant doors around town. The weekly newspapers **eye** and NOW have pithy restaurant reviews designed primarily for the trendy set. The *Globe and Mail, National Post, Toronto Sun* and the *Toronto Star* usually have major restaurant reviews in their weekend editions. On the Internet, check out **toronto.com** and **torontolife.com**

Ten good restaurants

 These establishments have been tested by time, critics, fastidious folk and economic swings. They rank up there with the best in the city. Impartiality dictates an alphabetical list.

AUBERGE DU POMMIER
CUISINE: French contemporary. ADDRESS: 4150 Yonge Street. MAP: *City of Toronto*. TELE-PHONE: 416-222-2220 LUNCH: Monday – Friday. DINNER: Monday – Saturday. CHECK: $$$$. CREDIT CARDS: All major. RESERVATIONS: Recommended.

The *auberge* is almost hidden among trees on the west side of Yonge Street, just north of York Mills Road. It provides a rewarding dining experience in the competitive midtown area, while offering a unique location away from city noise. Two renovated century cottages form the basis of a relaxing 160-seat restaurant that's noted for its high-class cuisine, tasteful appointments, faultless presentation and professional service. Fireplaces add an intimate atmosphere in winter and the terrace is just right for summer dining. The wine list, which complements the menu superbly, relies on French and Californian vintages. In 2000, the room received a Four Diamond AAA rating

AVALON
CUISINE: Continental. ADDRESS: 270 Adelaide Street West. MAP: 8
TELEPHONE: 416-979-9918 LUNCH: Wednesday – Friday. DINNER: Monday – Saturday.
CHECK: $$$$. CREDIT CARDS: All major. RESERVATIONS: Recommended.

Avalon is situated in the middle of the Theatre District, which is known for good restaurants and keen competition. For those so inclined, there's a six-course gastronomic menu that sets this place apart from those nearby. Less challenged folk can select from a nicely balanced blend of well-executed dishes on the general menu. A good, 300+ wine cellar is matched to daily changes in the menu. The room has an island fireplace, soft minimalist décor and is staffed with sophistication. It earns the top vote of several media critics.

CANOE
CUISINE: Canadian. ADDRESS: 66 Wellington Street West, 54th floor. MAP: 9
TELEPHONE: 416-364-0054 WEB SITE: **oliverbonacini.com** LUNCH: Monday – Friday.
DINNER: Monday – Friday. CHECK: $$$$. CREDIT CARDS: All major.
RESERVATIONS: Recommended.

In such a multicultural city, defining Canadian cuisine becomes a challenge. Canoe literally rises above it all – to the 54th floor of the TD Bank tower – and boldly offers traditional fare such as Arctic char and roast of caribou. By using as many local and indigenous ingredients as possible in the kitchen, it refuses to appease fashionable fusion tastes. Many believe it's the best truly Canadian restaurant in the country. Renowned service, a praised wine list and great view. Little wonder that this is a favourite place for Bay Street tycoons to relax over lunch away from merger stress.

CENTRO GRILL AND WINE BAR
CUISINE: Canadian. ADDRESS: 2472 Yonge Street. MAP: 33 TELEPHONE: 416-483-2211
LUNCH: Closed. DINNER: Monday – Saturday. CHECK: $$$$. CREDIT CARDS: All major.
RESERVATIONS: Required. WEBSITE: **centrorestaurant.com**

This is a highly respected restaurant that has had a committed international following for years. You can choose the main room on the second floor, or the sushi and oyster bar on the main level. There are over 800 labels on the wine list and only Rosenthal china on the table. Foie gras is made from ducks organically raised in Québec. Roasted rack of Ontario lamb has a honey mustard crust. Service and attention to detail are both impeccably executed. It's the only place in town where a reservation is required for any evening. In 2000, the room received a Four Diamond AAA rating.

LAI WAH HEEN

CUISINE: Chinese. ADDRESS: 108 Chestnut Street. MAP: 14
TELEPHONE: 416-977-9899 LUNCH: Daily. DINNER: Daily. CHECK: $$$$.
CREDIT CARDS: All major. RESERVATIONS: Recommended.

When the *New York Times* says that the best dim sum in North America likely resides here, you get the impression that this is no ordinary Cantonese restaurant. And it isn't. The décor in beige and black is dramatically modern and betrays the influence of high Hong Kong style. The baked shark's fin soup comes to the table covered in puff pastry. Service is impeccable. If you judge a good Chinese restaurant by the number of Chinese businesspeople seen with out-of-town guests, go no further than here. *Gourmet Magazine* has elevated Lai Wah Heen to its Top Table list.

MERCER STREET GRILL

CUISINE: Continental. ADDRESS: 36 Mercer Street. MAP: 8 TELEPHONE: 416-599-3399
WEB SITE: **mercerstreetgrill.com** LUNCH: Closed. DINNER: Daily. CHECK: $$$.
CREDIT CARDS: All major. RESERVATIONS: Recommended.

Mercer is a small street in the Entertainment District and the Mercer Street Grill looks like a lonely bunker sitting next to a parking lot. Don't be fooled. Too many Top Ten lists include this establishment that's been a city favourite for fine, upscale dining over the years. The kitchen concentrates on an eclectic and wide-ranging menu influenced by Asian flavours. Seafood, chicken and duck highlight a fine dining experience that's topped with a fine array of desserts.

NORTH 44°

CUISINE: International. ADDRESS: 2537 Yonge Street. MAP: 33 WEB SITE: **toronto.com**
TELEPHONE: 416-487-4897 LUNCH: Closed. DINNER: Monday – Saturday.
CHECK: $$$$. CREDIT CARDS: All major. RESERVATIONS: Recommended.

When lists of favourite restaurants are published, it's unusual if North 44° is not one of the top two. This is an elegant, modern and stylish place with an enviable reputation for well-executed cuisine, creatively served by a professional and knowledgeable staff. Menu selections challenge a mostly upwardly mobile, well-heeled and well-dressed crowd. Sage braised rabbit and quail in sesame marinade are but a prelude to the indulgent desserts. North 44°, by the way, is Toronto's latitude.

PREGO DELLA PIAZZA

CUISINE: Italian. ADDRESS: 150 Bloor Street West. MAP: 24 TELEPHONE: 416-920-9900
LUNCH: Daily. DINNER: Daily. CHECK: $$$$. CREDIT CARDS: All major.
RESERVATIONS: Recommended.

In a city awash with good Italian restaurants, this one seems to rise above all others. Not surprisingly, it caters to a high-end Yorkville clientele including a constant smattering of recognizable personalities. The room has a lushly modern look, while the summertime patio is definitely a place on which to be seen. There's a prevailing air of professionalism and perfection. And there's praise for superb food that defines itself as a 'new Italian wave'. If you're looking to expand the selection further and explore some French cuisine, the Black and Blue restaurant, under the same management, is attached.

SCARAMOUCHE
CUISINE: French. ADDRESS: 1 Benvenuto Place. MAP: 28 TELEPHONE: 416-961-8011 LUNCH: Closed. DINNER: Monday – Saturday. CHECK: $$$$$. CREDIT CARDS: All major. RESERVATIONS: Recommended.

Scaramouche, housed in a tastefully decorated and muted room, has the distinction of being one of the most expensive restaurants in the city. This doesn't deter a conservative and, quite frankly, rich clientele. That said, Scaramouche also has one of the most extensive wine lists in town and includes several *grands crus*. Desserts have won acclaim from serious diners. Arguably, it has the city's most professional staff. This is a classic restaurant in every sense, including the prestigious South Hill address.

TRUFFLES
CUISINE: Continental. ADDRESS: 21 Avenue Road (Four Seasons Hotel). MAP: 24 TELEPHONE: 416-928-7331 LUNCH: Closed. DINNER: Monday – Saturday. CHECK: $$$$$. CREDIT CARDS: All major. RESERVATIONS: Accepted.

Truffles has been given three prized awards. It's the only restaurant in Toronto to have captured the 2000 CAA/AAA Five Diamond Award and *Gourmet* magazine's best overall restaurant citation. It has also been given *Hotel* magazine's nod as one of the ten best hotel restaurants in the world. The menu has some interesting Asian twists to traditional dishes that makes it one of the most creative kitchens in the city. Tables are well spaced around an under-stated room that is light, sophisticated and private.

Best value for money

 When you're on a limited budget, it's hard to find a place offering loads of good food and service. If this is your predicament, then here's the place you're looking for.

MANDARIN
CUISINE: Chinese and Canadian buffet. ADDRESSES: 2200 Yonge Street. MAP: 33 TELEPHONE: 416-486-2222; and 2206 Eglinton Avenue East. MAP: *City of Toronto*. TELEPHONE: 416-288-1177 LUNCH: Daily. DINNER: Daily. CHECK: $. CREDIT CARDS: All major. RESERVATIONS: Recommended for holiday and weekend dinners and Sunday lunch.

There are never any surprises at one of the large Mandarin restaurants. For 20 years this popular chain of expertly run family dining rooms has won numerous awards for the all-you-can-eat buffet, salad bar and Chinese food. The welcome and service are almost embarrassingly warm and polite. The food's quality and presentation never varies. Balancing a wide range of conventional Chinese dishes is a dinner menu of prime rib and fresh crab legs, or lobster in season. Desserts vary from traditional Chinese pastries to flans, cakes and fresh fruit. At least six ice cream flavours are on hand. The beverage list is limited, with average house wine, liqueur, creative cocktails and beer all usually under $5. Washrooms set a standard for cleanliness that could well be copied by more upscale establishments. Dress is as casual as you like. There are three other Mandarin locations in the city at 1027 Finch Avenue West; 200 Queen's Plate; and 1255 The Queensway. Reserve a table well in advance for weekend dinners, Mother's Day and Chinese New Year.

American

LEFT BANK
567 Queen Street West. MAP: 7 TELEPHONE: 416-504-1626
LUNCH: Closed. DINNER: Wednesday – Saturday. CHECK: $$$$.
CREDIT CARDS: All major. RESERVATIONS: Advisable at the weekend.

Twists and turns on the menu can suggest anything from French to fusion, but it's the American originality that brings people back time and again. There's a casual atmosphere in a candle-lit room that's rather soberly decorated in various shades of brown. This is a trendy Queen Street West retreat for people interested in fresh ingredients, an eclectic menu and a preference for joining other martini aficionados on Thursday evenings.

PLANET HOLLYWOOD
277 Front Street West at the corner of Blue Jays Way. MAP: 8 TELEPHONE: 416-596-7827
LUNCH: Daily. DINNER: Daily. CHECK: $$$. CREDIT CARDS: All major.
RESERVATIONS: Accepted for large parties.

It doesn't get any more American than this. If you want to munch next to Sharon Stone's ice pick, or slurp your soup near the motorcycle Richard Gere rode in *An Officer and a Gentleman*, then this is your place. The cuisine is called 'California new classic', including an apple pie supposedly invented by Arnold Schwarzenegger's mother. Despite all the hype, the worldwide chain has had its share of economic woe. However, spring 2001 arrived with Planet Hollywood still open in Toronto.

TORTILLA FLATS
429 Queen Street West. MAP: 8 TELEPHONE: 416-593-9870 LUNCH: Daily.
DINNER: Daily. CHECK: $$. CREDIT CARDS: All major. RESERVATIONS: Not necessary.

When you walk inside, there's a bit of Tex-Mex overkill amid all the paraphernalia on the walls. That aside, the place is usually crowded with people from all over who come here for spicy experiences discovered in items such as chimichang and queso fundito. There are veggie burgers for the feint of heart and a zillion other things to explore on the menu. This is the most popular spot along Queen West for dudes who want a Corona while they gaze at a longhorn's stuffed head above the bar.

UTOPIA CAFÉ AND GRILL
586 College Street. MAP: 17 TELEPHONE: 416-534-7751 LUNCH: Daily. DINNER: Daily.
CHECK: $$. CREDIT CARDS: All major. RESERVATIONS: Not required.

Don't let the name fool you, even though lots of the customers might seem to be looking for the political nirvana. At first glance the menu might appear to be burgers 'n sandwiches, but dig a little deeper and all sorts of interesting stuff appears. Onion rings done in an almost greaseless beer batter and a mushroom and watercress paté take their place alongside Atlantic salmon on focaccia, burritos and sprightly tzatziki. You can wash it all down with Ontario micro-brewery offerings on tap, or by the bottle. All this and a little light jazz to boot.

WAYNE GRETZKY'S
99 Blue Jays Way. MAP: 8 TELEPHONE: 416-979-PUCK. LUNCH: Daily. DINNER: Daily.
CHECK: $$$. CREDIT CARDS: All major. RESERVATIONS: Recommended for dinner.

Anyone who enters this *terre de Gretzky* will be submerged in hockey stuff. The address - #99 – was Wayne's jersey number. The telephone number is PUCK. Wayne, of course, is Canadian, but the food is American. As with Gretzky himself, this haunt is a bit larger than life. There's a 280 sq m patio on the roof and almost as much hockey history stashed around the room as you'll find in the Hockey Hall of Fame. The menu boasts Wayne's favourite meals, such as steak tenderloin. If you can't bear tearing yourself away from the Great One, at least you can take away a memory from the souvenir shop. And, if you don't know who Wayne Gretzky is, then you'd better climb back on board your space ship and go home to your planet.

Canadian

CANOE
66 Wellington Street West, 54th floor. MAP: 9 TELEPHONE: 416-364-0054
LUNCH: Monday – Friday. DINNER: Monday – Friday. CHECK: $$$$.
CREDIT CARDS: All major. RESERVATIONS: Recommended.

In such a multicultural city, defining Canadian cuisine becomes a challenge. Canoe literally rises above it all – to the 54th floor of the TD Bank tower – and boldly offers traditional fare such as Arctic char and roast of caribou. By using as many local and indigenous ingredients as possible in the kitchen, it refuses to appease fashionable fusion tastes. Many believe it's the best truly Canadian restaurant in the country. Renowned service, a praised wine list and great view. Little wonder that this is a favourite place for Bay Street tycoons to relax over lunch away from monitors and mouses.

CENTRO GRILL AND WINE BAR
2472 Yonge Street. MAP: 33 TELEPHONE: 416-483-2211 LUNCH: Closed.
DINNER: Monday – Saturday. CHECK: $$$$. CREDIT CARDS: All major.
RESERVATIONS: Required.

This is a highly respected restaurant that has had a committed international following for years. You can choose the main room on the second floor, or the sushi and oyster bar on the main level. There are over 800 labels on the wine list and only Rosenthal china on the table. Foie gras is made from ducks organically raised in Québec. Roasted rack of Ontario lamb has a honey mustard crust. Service, attention to detail and comforts are all impeccably executed. It's probably the only place in town where a reservation is required for any evening.

TRAPPER'S
3479 Yonge Street. MAP: *City of Toronto*. TELEPHONE: 416-482-6211
LUNCH: Monday – Friday. DINNER: Daily. CHECK: $$$$. CARDS: All major.
RESERVATIONS: Recommended for dinner.

When you go inside and see pictures of Muskoka cottage country, you know the room specializes in Canadian fare. Add to this some low decibel jazz and a dominance of vintages from British Columbia and Ontario on the multi-page wine list. Trapper's has been around this neighbourhood since 1985 and specializes in main course seafood, such as Atlantic salmon and Muskoka trout, poultry and pasta. You can also ask for vegetarian dishes, even though they might not appear on the menu. Service is typically Canadian: professional and polite.

Chinese

CHAMPION HOUSE
480 Dundas Street West. MAP: 13 TELEPHONE: 416-977-8282
LUNCH: Daily. DINNER: Daily. CHECK: $$. CREDIT CARDS: All major. RESERVATIONS: Recommended.

Go down a few steps into what has been one of Chinatown's culinary fixtures over the years. Street level bustle fades away in a room with subtle lighting and linen tablecloths. There's a full menu containing about 30 vegetarian dishes along with the usual fare. One of the strengths of this establishment is the Peking duck, spread over four courses and heralded with a gong. The cocktail list is better than what you'd normally expect in this part of town.

DRAGON DYNASTY
2301 Brimley Road. MAP: *City of Toronto*. TELEPHONE: 416-321-9000
LUNCH: Dim sum daily. DINNER: Daily. CHECK: $$$$. CREDIT CARDS: All major.
RESERVATIONS: Recommended for weekend dinner.

Those in the know will tell you that many of the best Chinese restaurants in town are in Scarborough. At the Huntingwood intersection of Brimley Road is a typical strip mall and a very untypical restaurant. So untypical, in fact, that people lining up to get in are more smartly dressed than the crowd you'd find downtown. This is a high-class room catering to a well-to-do Chinese community. Table servers are patient and polite with those of us who might be uninitiated into the finer points of Chinese cuisine. The food is so well prepared that Dragon Dynasty is one of the most sought-after fine dining restaurants in the city's prospering Chinese neighbourhoods of Scarborough.

DYNASTY
131 Bloor Street West, 2nd floor. MAP: 24 TELEPHONE: 416-923-3323 LUNCH: Daily.
DINNER: Daily. CHECK: $$$. CREDIT CARDS: All major.
RESERVATIONS: Accepted.

On the second floor of the old Colonnade you'll find one of the most respected Chinese restaurants in the Bloor-Yorkville area. It's certainly not an overly ornate place, but it does attract Asian visitors who seem to be in the know about where to go when they're in town. The cuisine is Cantonese and getting past the great array of starters is a challenge as you contemplate more substantial fare. The chicken wings here are boned and soaked in wine. This will give you an idea of how the chef's culinary mind wanders away from the ordinary. If you're one of those who appreciates the Hong Kong style, this is a welcome destination.

HAPPY SEVEN

358 Spadina Avenue. MAP: 13 TELEPHONE: 416-971-9820
OPEN: 11.00 AM – 5.00 AM daily. CHECK: $. CREDIT CARDS: Mastercard, Visa.
RESERVATIONS: No.

Virtually any time you get a craving for fish in black bean sauce, Happy Seven will be there to calm your addiction. After a daily late morning opening it goes all the way through till 5.00 AM. The place is constantly in motion with swift service, lots of customers and a super clean, brightly-lit environment. The only problem with the place is making up your mind. The menu lists well over 200 dishes, including 14 soups and 30 seafood concoctions.

LAI WAH HEEN

108 Chestnut Street, 2nd floor, Metropolitan Hotel,. MAP: 14
TELEPHONE: 416-977-9899 LUNCH: Daily. DINNER: Daily. CHECK: $$$$.
CREDIT CARDS: All major. RESERVATIONS: Recommended.

When the *New York Times* says that the best dim sum in North America likely resides here, you get the impression that this is no ordinary Chinese restaurant. And it isn't. The décor in beige and black is dramatically modern and betrays the influence of high Hong Kong style. One of ten shark's fin soups comes to the table covered in puff pastry. Service is impeccable. If you judge a good Chinese restaurant by the number of Chinese businesspeople seen with out-of-town guests, go no further than here. *Gourmet* magazine has elevated Lai Wah Heen to its Top Table list.

LEE GARDEN

331 Spadina Avenue. MAP: 13 TELEPHONE: 416-593-9524 LUNCH: Closed.
DINNER: Daily. CHECK: $$. CREDIT CARDS: All major. RESERVATIONS: Not accepted.

The only problem about this place is getting in. Lineups seem to be the order of the day, especially at weekends when droves of folk come for the lack of MSG and fat. The staff is well versed in a varied menu and you can dine in a smoke-free environment that is unusual for Chinatown. (It will probably become the norm when the city's no smoking bylaw comes into effect in 2002.) Lee Garden is an old timer on Spadina and has built a devoted following over the years.

LUCKY DRAGON

418 Spadina Avenue. MAP: 13 TELEPHONE: 416-598-7823 LUNCH: Daily.
DINNER: Daily. CHECK: $$. CREDIT CARDS: All major. RESERVATIONS: Not required.

You can find something on the menu from just about any province in China. Here's a good place for those oriental tidbits and more than generously proportioned main dishes. Just about everything on the menu comes in at under $10. The room is long and narrow, brightly lit with no nonsense tables and chairs. People have been coming this way for years just for the food.

MANDARIN

2200 Yonge Street. MAP: 33 TELEPHONE: 416-486-2222
2206 Eglinton Avenue East. MAP: *City of Toronto*. TELEPHONE: 416 288-1177
LUNCH: Daily. DINNER: Daily.
CHECK: $. CREDIT CARDS: All major.
RESERVATIONS: Recommended for holiday and weekend dinners and Sunday lunch.

There are never any surprises at one of the large Mandarin restaurants. For many years this popular chain of expertly run family dining rooms has won numerous awards for the all-you-can-eat buffet, salad bar and Chinese food. The welcome and service are almost embarrassingly warm and friendly. The food's quality and presentation never varies. Balancing a wide range of conventional Chinese dishes is a dinner menu of prime rib and fresh crab legs or lobster (in season). Desserts vary from traditional Chinese pastries to flans, cakes and fresh fruit. At least six ice cream flavours are on hand. The beverage list is limited, with average house wine, liqueur, creative cocktails and beer all usually under $5. Washrooms set a standard for cleanliness that could well be copied by more upscale establishments. Dress is as casual as you like. There are three other Mandarin locations in the city at 1027 Finch Avenue West; 200 Queen's Plate; and 1255 The Queensway. Book well in advance for Mother's Day and Chinese New Year.

WAH SING

47 Baldwin Street. MAP: 13 TELEPHONE: 416-599-8822 LUNCH: Monday – Friday. DINNER: Daily. CHECK: $$. CREDIT CARDS: All major. RESERVATIONS: Advisable for weekend dinner.

Although Chinese restaurants all feature seafood in one form or another, this one specializes in the art of its preparation. Wah Sing is regarded as being near the top of the crustacean heap. The room is modest, with pink tablecloths, comfortable sitting surfaces and small white lights. Seafood lovers can agonize over about 100 combinations before zeroing-in on their favourite section of the menu. See if the two-for-one lobster special is available the day you visit. Or try the sizzling grouper with ginger and scallions. Competition along this stretch of Baldwin Street is fierce. Wah Sing won't make you wish you went some place else.

XAM YU

339 Spadina Avenue. MAP: 13 TELEPHONE: 416-340-8603 LUNCH: Daily. DINNER: Daily. CHECK: $$. CREDIT CARDS: Mastercard, Visa. RESERVATIONS: Accepted.

One of the authentic things about Chinatown's restaurants is the seeming endless list of dishes detailed on the walls. Couple this with the menu and the decision-making process can exhaust the most decisive person on the planet. Xam Yu leans towards seafood, but that doesn't stop you from ordering mushroom soup, eggplant or tofu. The kitchen is inventive, the presentation is a cut above many of its neighbours and the staff is helpful and polite.

Continental

AVALON

270 Adelaide Street West. MAP: 8 TELEPHONE: 416-979-9918 LUNCH: Wednesday – Friday. DINNER: Monday – Saturday. CHECK: $$$$. CREDIT CARDS: All major. RESERVATIONS: Recommended.

Avalon is situated in the middle of the Theatre District, which is known for good restaurants and keen competition. For those so inclined, there's a six-course gastronomic menu that sets this place apart from those nearby. Less challenged folk can select from a nicely balanced blend of well-executed dishes on the general menu. A good, 300+ wine cellar is matched to daily changes in the menu. The room has an island fireplace, soft minimalist décor and is staffed with sophistication. It earns the top vote of several media critics.

BISTRO TOURNESOL
406 Dupont Street. MAP: 26 TELEPHONE: 416-921-7766 LUNCH: Tuesday – Friday.
DINNER: Daily. CHECK: $$. CREDIT CARDS: American Express, Visa.
RESERVATIONS: Recommended.

Here's a place that relies on mainly local ingredients, often of organic origin. You can choose from *prix fixe* and *à la carte* combinations, with the former giving a choice from about 10 appetizers and one main dish. Although 'continental' with its overall offerings, a distinctly French touch prevails. The bright sunny room truly reflects *un tournesol* and the staff reflects an additional sunny disposition. This is one of the most popular places in the East Annex.

CITIES BISTRO
859 Queen Street West. MAP: 7 TELEPHONE: 416-504-3762
LUNCH: Tuesday – Friday, except during the summer. DINNER: Daily. CHECK: $$.
CREDIT CARDS: All major. RESERVATIONS: Recommended on weekends.

Cities is small, seating about 30 people in an intimate and cosmopolitan setting. Market fresh food is used throughout a menu that ranges from calamari, through chicken to a scallop and tiger shrimp salad served on charred pineapple salsa. The wine list is sparse and offers brands that concentrate on lightness. Service is attentive and unobtrusive. Desserts, showing a basic French flair, are well worth considering.

MERCER STREET GRILL
36 Mercer Street. MAP: 8 TELEPHONE: 416-599-3399 LUNCH: Closed. DINNER: Daily.
CHECK: $$$. CREDIT CARDS: All major. RESERVATIONS: Recommended.

Mercer is a small street in the Entertainment District and the Mercer Street Grill looks like a lonely bunker sitting next to a parking lot. Don't be fooled. Too many Top Ten lists include this establishment that's been a city favourite for fine, upscale dining over the years. The kitchen concentrates on an eclectic and wide-ranging menu often influenced by Asian flavours. Seafood, chicken and duck highlight a fine dining experience that's topped with a fine array of desserts.

MÖVENPICK
165 York Street. MAP: 9 TELEPHONE: 416-366-5234
BREAKFAST: Daily. LUNCH: Daily. DINNER: Daily. CHECK: $$ (Dinner).
CREDIT CARDS: All major. RESERVATIONS: Accepted.

Critics seem to pass Mövenpick restaurants by with either a cursory glance or a blind eye. Not so with all those people who pack these unusual and innovative Swiss eateries, where service and good food abound. This one at York Street near Adelaide Street West ranks among the busiest Sunday brunch places downtown, with locals relaxing along the sidewalk patio, or inside among all the goodies that are freshly prepared by a battery of chefs. Long a favourite breakfast and lunch haunt of the business crowd, Mövenpick has also garnered loyal dinner patrons over the years. Some of the things that keep folk coming back for more include the unusual ambience, ultra-fresh food, innovative surroundings, pleasant attitude and prices that are affordable.

PRONTO

692 Mount Pleasant Road. MAP: *City of Toronto*. TELEPHONE: 416-486-1111
LUNCH: Closed. DINNER: Daily. CHECK: $$$$. CREDIT CARDS: All major.
RESERVATIONS: Recommended.

Freshly cut flowers highlight an already fine room, reflected onto itself from ceiling mirrors. Pronto has been a successful place since the day it opened. It was a culinary mainstay for the local upscale neighbourhood until the rest of town found out. There's always a wider than normal range of specials. And desserts defy choice with such spellbinders as a rhubarb and coconut Napoléon. A large wine rack offers more than the normal range of good Italian reds and several private imports.

STORK ON THE ROOF

2009 Yonge Street. MAP: 32 TELEPHONE: 416-483-3747 LUNCH: Closed.
DINNER: Tuesday – Saturday. CHECK: $$$. CREDIT CARDS: All major.
RESERVATIONS: Recommended.

This is what you call an upscale Dutch treat. Among the fine restaurants in midtown is this gem with culinary roots planted in the Netherlands. You'll find hints of Indonesian influences and exotic Asian herbs mixed with lemon and sesame flavours. Try the sautéed shrimp and scallops and finish the meal with some Dutch apple pie. There are more than a half dozen wines by the glass and an interesting and varied choice of bottles.

TOWN GRILL

243 Carlton Street. MAP: 16 TELEPHONE: 416-963-9433 LUNCH: Tuesday – Friday.
DINNER: Daily. CHECK: $$$. CREDIT CARDS: All major. RESERVATIONS: Advisable.

The Old Cabbagetown crowd needn't stray far from the neighbourhood to find some of the city's more interesting places to eat. The Town Grill positions itself towards the upper end of the nearby eateries and has won a faithful following from people much further afield than Parliament and Carlton. There's a distinct freshness about the menu, thanks to some subtle and creative spicing. A well-balanced assortment of about 40 wines is available for your pleasure, many of which can be ordered for under $20.

TRUFFLES

21 Avenue Road (Four Seasons Hotel). MAP: 24 TELEPHONE: 416-928-7331
LUNCH: Closed. DINNER: Monday – Saturday. CHECK: $$$$$. CREDIT CARDS: All major.
RESERVATIONS: Accepted.

This room holds promise that the grand Canadian hotel dining rooms of the past might be making a comeback. Certainly the Four Seasons chain of luxury hotels, which started in Toronto, is pushing Truffles in that direction. The room has been given three prized awards. It's the only restaurant in Toronto to have captured the 2000 CAA/AAA Five Diamond Award and *Gourmet* magazine's best overall restaurant citation. It has also been given *Hotel* magazine's nod as one of the ten best hotel restaurants in the world. The menu has some interesting Asian twists to traditional dishes that makes it one of the most creative kitchens in the city. Tables are well spaced around an under-stated room that is light, sophisticated and private on the hotel's second floor.

French

ARLEQUIN
134 Avenue Road. MAP: 24 TELEPHONE: 416-928-9521
LUNCH: Monday – Saturday. DINNER: Monday – Saturday. CHECK: $$$.
CREDIT CARDS: All major. RESERVATIONS: Recommended.

For over 15 years, Arlequin has been a welcome fixture at Avenue and Davenport roads. Here's a place that can juggle over 4,000 bottles in its wine cellar. Front counter take-out and a sit-down clientele consist mainly of the arty folk who abound in this part of town. There's even something on the menu for children. Despite its name, Arlequin doesn't clown around in the kitchen. This is a serious and pleasantly elegant room with time-honoured credentials. Expect items such as confit of duck, salad with grilled fennel, or a *prix fixe*, four-course meal for under $20.

AUBERGE DU POMMIER
4150 Yonge Street. MAP: *City of Toronto*. TELEPHONE: 416-222-2220
LUNCH: Monday – Friday. DINNER: Monday – Saturday. CHECK: $$$.
CREDIT CARDS: All major. RESERVATIONS: Recommended.

The auberge is almost hidden among trees on the west side of Yonge Street, just north of York Mills Road. It provides a rewarding dining experience in the competitive midtown area, while offering a unique location away from city noise. Two renovated century cottages form the basis of a relaxing 160-seat restaurant that's noted for its cuisine, tasteful appointments, faultless presentation and professional service. Fireplaces add an intimate atmosphere in winter, and the terrace is just right for summer dining. The wine list, which complements the menu superbly, relies on French and Californian vintages.

CORNER HOUSE
501 Davenport Road. MAP: 27 TELEPHONE: 416-923-2604 LUNCH: Closed.
DINNER: Tuesday – Saturday. CHECK: $$$$. CREDIT CARDS: All major.
RESERVATIONS: Recommended.

In the shadow of Casa Loma there's an unobtrusive little house that's become the favourite destination of Forest Hill's upper class when they go out for dinner. Five small rooms provide the privacy and ambience that's expected in this part of town. But it's the food that's really the big attraction. Here's where you can indulge in the rich traditions of French cooking from either the full menu, or a reasonable *prix fixe*. Even though it's out of the way for some city dwellers, the Corner House is a serious contender for membership in Toronto's top ten places to dine.

HERBS
3187 Yonge Street. MAP: *City of Toronto*. TELEPHONE: 416-322-0487
LUNCH: Monday – Friday. DINNER: Daily. CHECK: $$$$. CREDIT CARDS: All major. RESERVATIONS: Recommended.

Herbs pioneered an *haute* form of cuisine and presentation in midtown before others moved into the neighbourhood. It still ranks among the preferred places to go for finicky folk who need a fix of French food with a continental twist. Duck, seafood and sweetbreads are given special care in the kitchen. If you're considering dessert, make sure not to get your blood checked for a few days. The wine selection is above average and there's a small sidewalk patio where you can graze.

LE PAPILLON

16 Church Street. MAP: 10 TELEPHONE: 416-363-3773 LUNCH: Tuesday – Sunday. DINNER: Tuesday – Sunday. CHECK; $$$. CREDIT CARDS: All major. RESERVATIONS: Advisable.

Toronto has surprisingly few French restaurants specializing in dishes from Québec. Le Papillon bases its menu on *la belle province* in airy and pleasant surroundings. Situated close to both the St Lawrence and Hummingbird centres, the room has become a favourite place to go for the theatre crowd. There's an abundance of choices among *hors d'oeuvres*, salads and soups, but keep an appetite for the over-sized Breton-styled crêpes. The wine list is adequate, but diners often opt instead for the hard Granny Smith apple cider.

PROVENCE

12 Amelia Street. MAP: 21 TELEPHONE: 416-924-9901 LUNCH: Daily. DINNER: Daily. CHECK: $$$$. CREDIT CARDS: All major. RESERVATIONS: Recommended.

In the cosmopolitan area around Parliament and Carlton streets, several little restaurants have opened to cater to the diverse cultural mix of neighbourhood people. Some, like Provence, have earned a reputation that has spread far beyond Old Cabbagetown. The bright room spreads out on to the sidewalk during summer and lures folk into the pleasures of its highly regarded kitchen. Southern France is evident in the décor, service and selection of fine foods. You can choose from an extensive *à la carte* menu, or an accommodating *prix fixe*. The wine cellar represents several countries, though favours the regions of France.

QUARTIER

2112 Yonge Street. MAP: 32 TELEPHONE: 416-545-0505 LUNCH: Monday – Friday. DINNER: Daily. CHECK: $$$. CREDIT CARDS: All major. RESERVATIONS: Advised.

The Davisville crowd has some good restaurants along Yonge Street that have captured a lot of attention. Quartier is among the best with a traditional French menu that includes duck confit with pomme salardaise, five spice pickerel with organic risotto, and a hearty filet mignon. Modestly priced wines are selected from France, Ontario and California with most available by the glass.

SCARAMOUCHE

1 Benvenuto Place. MAP: 28 TELEPHONE: 416-961-8011 LUNCH: Closed. DINNER: Monday – Saturday. CHECK: $$$$$. CREDIT CARDS: All major. RESERVATIONS: Recommended.

Scaramouche, housed in a tastefully decorated and muted room, has the distinction of being among the most expensive restaurants in the city. This doesn't deter a conservative and, quite frankly, rich clientele. That said, Scaramouche also has one of the most extensive wine lists in town and includes several *grands crus*. Desserts are mostly splendid and have won acclaim from serious diners. Arguably, it has the city's most professional staff. This is a classic restaurant in every sense, including the prestigious sobriety of a South Hill address.

Greek

AVLI
401 Danforth Avenue.
MAP: *City of Toronto*, area 12L and in detail on the next page.
TELEPHONE: 416-461-9577 LUNCH: Daily. DINNER: Daily. CHECK: $$$.
CREDIT CARDS: All major. RESERVATIONS: Advisable at weekends.

The owners like to talk about their "2,000 year-old lusty, saucy, satisfying tradition" of well-prepared Greek food. They even refer to the "specialties of their foremothers" that include lamb pie kleftiko, vegetarian moussaka, and boneless chicken stuffed with a combination of cashews, dates, apples and rice. There's a bright entrance past the sidewalk tables into a quiet, white and sparsely decorated room filled with dark tables. The wine list isn't extensive, but it complements the menu in grand fashion. Avli is less boisterous than most along The Danforth and it won't disappoint anyone serious about their Greek food.

FRIENDLY GREEK
551 Danforth Avenue. MAP: *City of Toronto*, area 12L and in detail on the next page.
TELEPHONE: 416-469-8422 LUNCH: Daily. DINNER: Daily. CHECK: $$.
CREDIT CARDS: All major. RESERVATIONS: Recommended at weekends.

Everything on the Danforth is friendly, but the Friendly Greek has earned his stripes. That's why this establishment is a magnet for tourists and locals alike. One is the reasons is the comparatively attractive prices, and another is the barrage of comfort food that arrives at your table. It's advisable to eat lightly during the day if you intend coming here for dinner. Wine – including many Greek labels - will set you back less than $20 a bottle. If the congenial atmosphere moves you, there's nothing to stop you from staying here most of the night. The Greek remains friendly until 4.00 AM. *Opa*!

OUZERI
500A Danforth Avenue. MAP: *City of Toronto*, area 12L and in detail on the next page.
TELEPHONE: 416-778-0500 LUNCH: Daily. DINNER: Daily. CHECK: $$$.
CREDIT CARDS: All major. RESERVATIONS: Best considered for the weekend.

If longevity is one of the criteria for success, then Ouzeri has arrived. This is a cheery place, with conversation challenging the piped-in music even to the second floor rafters. The menu mixes traditional fare with some new creations, but the chicken rosemary pie and mushrooms in a light, flaky pastry is an item few can refuse. Despite some confusion at times, the staff manages to get the right dishes to the right tables in a professional fashion. This is a venue to celebrate an occasion in a truly Greek manner.

PAPPAS GRILL
440 Danforth Avenue. MAP: *City of Toronto*, area 12L and in detail on the next page.
TELEPHONE: 416-469-9595 LUNCH: Daily. DINNER: Daily. CHECK: $$.
CREDIT CARDS: All major.
RESERVATIONS: Accepted.

The Danforth is the centre of North America's largest Greek neighbourhood. So it's no surprise that the street is filled with good restaurants and a Mediterranean atmosphere. Pappas is a big, noisy, friendly place and the outdoor patio is a magnet during the summer, bringing in folks from all over town. Lots of vegetarian stuff and pizzas fresh from clay ovens are on the luncheon menu. When the sun sets, out come all the traditional Greek dishes served by a large, friendly staff. If you're thinking of bringing along up to 100 close friends, Pappas can accommodate you. Just let them know ahead of time that you're coming. You might even get your very own floor.

Indian

ANNAPURNA
1085 Bathurst Street. MAP: 26 TELEPHONE: 416-537-8513
LUNCH: Monday – Saturday.
DINNER: Monday – Saturday (Wednesday till 6.30 PM). CHECK: $. CREDIT CARDS: Not accepted.
RESERVATIONS: Recommended for more than four people.

This unassuming room is nearing its quarter century in the West Annex, which makes it the oldest vegetarian restaurant in Canada. The menu mixes western touches with a basic southern Indian tradition to produce such apparent contradictions as French onion soup alongside masala dosai. This is a place for people serious about vegetarian food that packs a delicious punch at a very affordable price.

BOMBAY PALACE
71 Jarvis Street. MAP: 10 TELEPHONE: 416-368-8048
LUNCH: Daily. DINNER: Daily. CHECK: $. CREDIT CARDS: All major.
RESERVATIONS: Advisable on weekends and during Hindu festivals.

Lots of folk in the know will tell you that this is one of their favourite Indian restaurants downtown. Menu items are influenced by the flavours of southern India, which means a good assortment of chili sensations and coconut sauces. The atmosphere is informal and it's becoming a good, inexpensive place to go for families and their kids. The daily 25-item all-you-can-eat lunch buffet, for example, sets you back about $10.

CUISINE OF INDIA
5222 Yonge Street. MAP: *North York Centre*. TELEPHONE: 416-229-0377 LUNCH: Daily.
DINNER: Daily. CHECK: $$. CREDIT CARDS: All major. RESERVATIONS: Recommended.

The papadums arrive before you can get comfortably seated and this kind of service continues throughout your stay. The same kind of attention is evident in the kitchen where chefs grind their own spices to make sure that flavour is always at an optimum level. One of the things you'll notice here is a cultural mix of people and a near absence of traditional Indian décor. If you're inquisitive, you can always peep into the glassed-in kitchen to check out the tandoori ovens. Don't forget the mango or saffron ice cream.

HOST
14 Prince Arthur Avenue. MAP: 24 TELEPHONE: 416-962-9224
LUNCH: Daily. DINNER: Daily. CHECK: $$$. CREDIT CARDS: All Major.
RESERVATIONS: Recommended.

This Prince Arthur address has seen reputable kitchens come and go over the years. The Host is the latest occupant and its faithful client base assures it of a long and happy life here. The pleasant surprise is not so much the excellent Indian food, or comfortable surroundings and fine service, but the relatively modest price – a rarity in Yorkville. The menu is top notch with virtually everything portraying culinary authenticity.

INDIAN FLAVOUR
595 Bay Street. MAP: 14 TELEPHONE: 416-408-2799 LUNCH: Daily. DINNER: Daily. CHECK: $$. CREDIT CARDS: All major. RESERVATIONS: Advisable for dinner.

Samosas, tandoori chicken, lamb tikka and chicken kesar malai are available on a menu that has proven to be successful with lunch hour business types and evening family groups. Although you can order from a menu, it's the regular buffet here that has made the room a permanent favourite with people interested in Indian food that's a cut above the ordinary. There's minimal traditional décor in this split-level room and it can get a bit crowded at times, due mainly to the busy location in the Atrium.

INDIAN RICE FACTORY
414 Dupont Street. MAP: 26 TELEPHONE: 416-961-3472 LUNCH: Monday – Friday.
DINNER: Daily. CHECK: $$. CREDIT CARDS: All major.
RESERVATIONS: Recommended for dinner.

This room has been a fixture in the West Annex for over three decades, which is a testament to its high rating among patrons who come here from across the city. One severe critic said "almost everything here is delicious" and went on to describe "formidable pakoras." All of the dishes are well worth exploring including the lamb masalader, which is marinated, grilled and garnished with mint. Making a reservation for dinner is recommended because the restaurant has only 45 seats and these are usually spoken for early in the evening.

International

360
301 Front Street West in the CN Tower. MAP: 3
TELEPHONE: 416-362-5411 LUNCH: Daily. DINNER: Daily.
CHECK: $$$$. CREDIT CARDS: All major. RESERVATIONS: Required.

Many of the world's restaurants set atop towers manage to let the food take second place to the view. Such is not the case with 360. It's higher off the ground than any other restaurant in the world. And food is taken very seriously up here. A change took place around the mid-1990s when the revolving room decided to stop packing the tourists in and become an upscale place for Torontonians. There's a varied menu from Arctic char to paté and from pasta dishes to memorable desserts – and more than a hint of Canadian fusion. The wine list is extensive. Tourists, of course, are still more than welcome to come up and dine with the locals.

BOBA
90 Avenue Road. MAP: 24 TELEPHONE: 416-961-2622
LUNCH: Closed. DINNER: Monday – Saturday.
CHECK: $$$$. CREDIT CARDS: All major.
RESERVATIONS: Essential on the weekend.

The menu here can skip from Asian to the shores of the Mediterranean without losing a beat. Grilled quail, roasted sea bass and chicken breast wrapped in rice paper are only some of the items to challenge your ability to make decisive judgements. A solid wine cellar – mandatory in this part of town – has about 120 labels, making it one of the best around. It goes all the way from New Zealand and France to California. This is a decidedly upscale place for upscale people.

JUMP CAFÉ & BAR

Melinda Street in Commerce Court East. MAP: 9 TELEPHONE: 416-363-3400
LUNCH: Monday – Friday. DINNER: Monday – Saturday. CHECK: $$$$.
CREDIT CARDS: All major. RESERVATIONS: Recommended.

Jump is buried in the heart of the country's most influential business and financial district and its patrons ooze everything that's successful. The bar is packed when the market rises. The lunch crowd shows its appreciation for one of the most discussed kitchens in town. The room is bright and cheerful, overlooking the inner concrete plaza of Commerce Court. Venison, salmon, rack of Australian lamb and grilled portobello mushrooms adorn plates brought to the table by experienced and friendly servers. As befits the new century, the wine list is almost exclusively New World.

LA MAQUETTE

111 King Street East. MAP: 10 TELEPHONE: 416-366-8191 LUNCH: Monday – Friday. DIN-
NER: Monday – Saturday. CHECK: $$$. CREDIT CARDS: All major.
RESERVATIONS: Recommended.

This establishment has a fine reputation for elegant surroundings, memorable food, artistic presentation and a varied menu. There's a relaxing and intimate atmosphere with muted jazz usually permeating the place at dinner. Choose seating on the patio, in a solarium, or next to a cozy winter fire. A popular early *prix fixe* meal for theatre patrons costs around $20 per person.

LATITUDE WINE BAR & GRILL

89 Harbord Street. MAP: 18 TELEPHONE: 416-928-0926 LUNCH: Daily. DINNER: Daily.
CHECK: $$$. CREDIT CARDS: Diners, Mastercard, Visa.
RESERVATIONS: Recommended for dinner.

Scented candles set a tone for what has become one of the city's favourite places to dine. The menu offers an array of flavours ranging from Latin to Asian with unexpected hints of other national origins. An oyster and mango combination contrasts with lemongrass salmon and chicken with roasted pumpkin seeds. This is quite a cozy establishment with limited seating, so make sure of your reservation.

LE CONTINENTAL

Prince Hotel, 900 York Mills Road. MAP: *City of Toronto*, area 13F.
TELEPHONE: 416-444-2511 LUNCH: Tuesday – Friday. DINNER: Tuesday – Saturday.
CHECK: $$$$. CARDS: All major. RESERVATIONS: Advisable.

Toronto is fortunate to have some fine hotel dining rooms. Le Continental at the Prince Hotel is the star performer in this category in the east end of town. The room has a spacious feeling with tables arranged discreetly apart amid subtle screens in muted colours. The menu seems to be influenced by French sauces, perfect textures and top-notch ingredients. The wine list concentrates on French and American labels. Table service befits the room with professionalism and attention to detail.

MERCER STREET GRILL
36 Mercer Street. MAP: 8 TELEPHONE: 416-599-3399 LUNCH: Closed. DINNER: Daily.
CHECK: $$$$. CREDIT CARDS: All major. RESERVATIONS: Recommended.

Mercer is a small street in the Entertainment District and the Mercer Street Grill looks like a lonely bunker sitting next to a parking lot. Don't be fooled. Too many Top Ten lists include this establishment that's been a city favourite with upwardly mobile types over the years. The kitchen concentrates on an eclectic and wide-ranging menu influenced by Asian flavours. Seafood, chicken and duck highlight a fine dining experience that's topped with a fine array of desserts.

MÖVENPICK MARCHÉ
161 Bay Street inside Heritage Square. MAP: 9 TELEPHONE: 416-366-8986
DAILY: 7.30AM – 2.00AM. CHECK: $. CREDIT CARDS: All major.
RESERVATIONS: Not accepted.

Mövenpick has a knack for being different. And from the moment Marché opened just inside the Yonge Street entrance to Heritage Square, it became an instant hit. It's worth waiting in line to get in and then wandering around the market atmosphere getting a bevy of chefs to prepare your food just the way you like it. If you opt for a seat outside in the Galleria, then you've got the best indoor view in the city. Not bad when you consider that this experience won't break the bank.

NORTH 44°
2537 Yonge Street. MAP: 33 TELEPHONE: 416-487-4897 LUNCH: Closed.
DINNER: Monday – Saturday. CHECK: $$$$. CREDIT CARDS: All major.
RESERVATIONS: Recommended.

When lists of favourite restaurants are published, it's unusual if North 44° is not one of the top two. This is an elegant, modern and stylish place with an enviable reputation for well-executed cuisine, creatively served by a professional and knowledgeable staff. Menu selections challenge a mostly upwardly mobile, well-heeled Versace kind of crowd. Sage braised rabbit and quail in sesame marinade are but a prelude to the indulgent desserts. North 44°, by the way, is Toronto's latitude.

PANGAEA
1221 Bay Street. MAP: 24 TELEPHONE: 416-920-2323
LUNCH: Monday – Saturday. DINNER: Monday – Saturday.
CHECK: $$$$$. CREDIT CARDS: All major.
RESERVATIONS: Recommended.

Over recent years this spot on Bay Street, just north of Bloor Street West, has seen several optimistic restaurants open to fanfare and close in silence. Inside, the present occupant espouses the term 'cuisine vitale'. It's a high-priced name for fusion. And most everything here comes at a price, including the afternoon tea at $15 a head. Pangaea attracts the Bloor West shopping crowd, tired from browsing around Hermès and Chanel. The décor has a feeling of Zen about it. As one critic noted: "There are few wall pieces to distract from the $200 haircuts". Despite the seeming pretension of the place, the kitchen is one of the best in Yorkville and the menu changes monthly. There are even 19 wines by the glass, which is a blessed event in this part of town.

ROSETTA
924 Kingston Road. MAP: *City of Toronto*. TELEPHONE: 416-690-6081
LUNCH: Closed. DINNER: Tuesday – Saturday. CHECK: $$$$. CARDS: All major.
RESERVATIONS: Advisable at weekends.

Foreigners – and that includes anyone not living in The Beach area of town – might pass this little place by as they walk along Kingston Road. Small is better in the case of Rosetta. There's a funky retro feeling about the place, with its old soda fountain and dated counter stools, but this is the place's charm. The menu is crafted with ingenious combinations of flavours among seafood and meat dishes, while the wine list relies on a rewarding selection of vintages. The friendly staff knows the regulars well and stands waiting to welcome newcomers, however 'foreign' they might be.

ROSEWATER SUPPER CLUB
19 Toronto Street. MAP: 10 TELEPHONE: 416-214-5888 LUNCH: Monday – Friday.
DINNER: Monday – Saturday. CHECK: $$$$. CARDS: All major.
RESERVATIONS: Recommended.

In an area where serious competition is only a few steps away, the Rosewater has opted for pleasure bordering on decadence. Persian carpets and a marble dance floor start to give you some idea. It's a spot for the well-heeled Bay Street crowd to strut their stuff in syncopation with live dinnertime music. Some menu items embrace the trendy fusion style while others stick to more traditional offerings. Either way, there's a refined consistency born from a well-educated kitchen staff. The wine list is noteworthy.

Italian

ACQUA
10 Front Street West. MAP: 9 TELEPHONE: 416-368-7171
LUNCH: Monday – Friday. DINNER: Monday – Saturday. CHECK: $$$.
CREDIT CARDS: All major. RESERVATIONS: Recommended.

There's a certain style about this room that's attracting business tycoons and ordinary folk alike to the corner of Front and Yonge streets. Operating under a culinary premise somewhere in between *nouvelle cuisine* and New Age, the menu has a tempting array of selections that even cater to diabetics and vegetarians. There are seasonal changes in a menu that sometimes includes masterful classic Italian dishes using seafood and chicken. This is one place where you should pay special attention to the dessert menu. A long bar inside is usually crowded after work and tables along the galleria side of the restaurant can get a bit noisy due to passing pedestrian traffic.

ANGELINI'S
504 Jarvis Street. MAP: 20 TELEPHONE: 416-922-5811 LUNCH: Monday – Friday.
DINNER: Monday – Saturday. CHECK: $$$$. CREDIT CARDS: All major.
RESERVATIONS: Recommended.

Angelini's is one of a handful of upscale restaurants that are housed in historic homes. In this case, it's a former residence of Toronto's once-richest man, Charles Gooderham. True to this pedigree, the menu bespeaks tradition and the service sometimes borders on Old World. During the summer, you can relax outside on a large patio under tall shade trees. Despite all these attributes, paying the check might not require your bank manager's approval. The dress code suggests that you wear something appropriate, such as a jacket and tie for men. As a critic once remarked: "It's a good place to take your grandparents once a year."

BIAGIO
155 King Street East. MAP: 10 TELEPHONE: 416-366-4040
LUNCH: Monday – Saturday. DINNER: Monday – Saturday. CHECK: $$$$.
CARDS: All major. RESERVATIONS: Recommended.

This establishment has more than held its own for well over a decade in an area where competition is often fierce. There's a nice patio for summer business lunches and a comprehensive wine list with half bottles available. The setting in St Lawrence Hall couldn't be more 'Toronto' and the theme of the old city is reflected on walled photographs. The menu is influenced by Northern Italian traditions and meals are executed with welcome professionalism.

COPPI
3363 Yonge Street. MAP: *City of Toronto*. TELEPHONE: 416-484-4464
LUNCH: Monday – Friday. DINNER: Monday – Saturday. CHECK: $$$$. CARDS: All major.
RESERVATIONS: Advisable for dinner.

A lot of care is taken in this kitchen, with special attention given to seafood. There's a noticeable freshness to the ingredients and a regard for the traditions of coastal Italian cuisine. The wine list is comprehensive with a dominance of Italian vintages and a smattering of bottles from other countries. In this upscale area of town there are lots of good places to choose and Coppi will not turn into a disappointment.

GALILEO
193 King Street East. MAP: 10 TELEPHONE: 416-363-6888 LUNCH: Monday – Friday. DINNER: Monday – Saturday. CHECK: $$$$. CARDS: All major.
RESERVATIONS: Recommended for Friday and Saturday.

There's a nice, quiet ambience to this place that's recognized for its service and civility. Its modern décor, including a white floor, sets the room and its noticeable bar off to distinction. The menu ranges from calamari, through duck to a to-die-for crème brûlée. Wines favour Italian reds and you have a wide selection of good vintages. It's one of the neighbourhood's most respected Italian rooms.

IL POSTO NUOVO
148 Yorkville Avenue in York Square. MAP: 24 TELEPHONE: 416 968-0469
LUNCH: Monday – Saturday. DINNER: Monday – Saturday. CHECK: $$$$$.
CREDIT CARDS: All major. RESERVATIONS: Recommended.

The well-to-do who inhabit Yorkville have made this room their favourite for two decades. It's where you can get a perfectly prepared magret of duck positioned over a ragoût of wild mushrooms and savory cabbage. Even the ravioli is a thing to be remembered. A well-chosen cellar highlights a changing assortment of bottles from France, Italy and California. Expect those at the next table to be ladies lunching, or influential business people lingering over an after dinner cognac.

MAMMINA'S
6B Wellesley Street West. MAP: 19 TELEPHONE: 416-967-7199
LUNCH: Monday – Friday. DINNER: Monday – Saturday. CHECK: $$$.
CREDIT CARDS: All major. RESERVATIONS: Recommended at week's end.

When select Hollywood folk come here for the Toronto International Film Festival, they call into Mammina's to get away from the crowd. For one thing, it's a small place and easy to miss. That means you can usually escape the foreign press. Second, word has spread around Tinseltown that Mammina's surrounds itself with a quiet professionalism. The food, rooted in northern Italy, is always memorable; the service is smooth and low-key; the room is sparsely decorated and the lighting low. What's more, a bottle of Italian wine will cost you less here than anywhere else. Everything considered, you can't do much better.

OLD SPAGHETTI FACTORY
54 The Esplanade. MAP: 10 TELEPHONE: 416-864-9761 LUNCH: Daily.
DINNER: Daily. CHECK: $. CARDS: All major.
RESERVATIONS: Not necessary, except for large groups.

There was a whisper around town at the time that a psychiatrist devised the concept for this restaurant. Consequently, when it opened over a quarter century ago, people never expected it to last very long. It was kinda weird inside and people weren't acting pretentiously. There were even lots of kids there enjoying themselves. And, as any psychiatrist will tell you: that's crazy. Nothing has changed and you can still feed the family downtown without robbing the kids' piggy banks, or lying on a couch expressing guilt about your frugal traits. The Factory even looks after folk with special dietary needs. What more could you want?

PAESE
3827 Bathurst Street. MAP: *City of Toronto*. TELEPHONE: 416-631-6585
LUNCH: Monday – Friday. DINNER: Daily. CHECK: $$$. CARDS: All major.
RESERVATIONS: Advisable at weekends.

Paese seems to hold the mortgage on fine southern Italian cuisine north of the 401, much to the chagrin of those who think everything that's good is south of the expressway. The room has an upscale environment without formality and attracts regular patrons from the affluent north Bathurst area. Appetizers range from bruschetta to smoked salmon and there are about a dozen pasta dishes. Mains concentrate on traditional chicken and veal. A varied wine list highlights Italian labels.

PREGO DELLA PIAZZA
150 Bloor Street West. MAP: 24 TELEPHONE: 416-920-9900 LUNCH: Daily.
DINNER: Daily. CHECK: $$$$. CARDS: All major. RESERVATIONS: Recommended.

In a city awash with good Italian restaurants, this one seems to rise above all others. Not surprisingly, it caters to a high-end Yorkville clientele including a constant smattering of recognizable personalities. The room has a lushly modern look, while the summertime patio is definitely a place on which to be seen. There's a prevailing air of professionalism and perfection. And there's praise for superb food that defines itself as a 'new Italian wave'. If you're looking to expand the menu further and explore a food court concept, the Black and Blue and Enoteca are connected under the same management.

TOULÀ

1 Harbour Square, Westin Harbour Castle Hotel, 38th floor. MAP: 4
TELEPHONE: 416-777-2002 LUNCH: Daily. DINNER: Daily. CHECK: $$$$$
CREDIT CARDS: All major. RESERVATIONS: Recommended.

This is the first excursion into North America for the respected Milan-based Italian restaurant chain, Gruppo Toulà SPA. The official opening (inside the now not revolving 38th floor of the Harbour Castle Hotel) was during the second last week of March, 2001. There are great expectations for both diners and the company itself. If successful, plans are to expand the chain into selected cities throughout North America. So far, so good. The service is impeccable, the menu well balanced and expertly executed, and the ambience is designed to satisfy fastidious and well-heeled folk. Whether or not the odd location down on the waterfront away from the city's established restaurant districts proves successful remains to be seen. Toulà has arrived on this side of the Atlantic and Torontonians will be the first to vote.

Japanese

AKANE-YA
2214a Queen Street East. MAP: *City of Toronto*.
TELEPHONE: 416-699-0377 LUNCH: Closed.
DINNER: Tuesday – Sunday. CHECK: $$$. CARDS: All major.
RESERVATIONS: Recommended.

In this case, small is better. No more than two dozen people can fit into this room at the corner of Beech Avenue - and that includes a half dozen seated along the sushi bar. It could be the best restaurant in the Beach neighbourhood. What the place might lack in predictable Japanese adornments, it certainly makes up for with food that knows few peers anywhere else in town. If you enjoy teriyaki and tempura, be prepared to adjust your taste buds up a notch.

HIRO SUSHI

171 King Street East. MAP: 10 TELEPHONE: 416-304-0550 LUNCH: Monday – Friday. DINNER: Monday – Saturday. CHECK: $$$. CREDIT CARDS: All major.
RESERVATIONS: Recommended.

In a city where sushi has become a fad, Hiro Sushi has elevated it to an art form. Surprising little innovations blend with more traditional tricks to make your meal something to remember. There's little doubt that here is a place for connoisseurs of subtle and meticulous tastes to enjoy the foremost in freshness and execution. The room is low-key and minimalist so as not to distract from presentation. For added authenticity, it's worth your while to dine here omakase-style.

NAMI

55 Adelaide Street East. MAP: 10 TELEPHONE: 416-362-7373
LUNCH: Monday – Friday. DINNER: Monday - Saturday. CHECK: $$$$. CARDS: All major.
RESERVATIONS: Recommended.

The starkly modern black on white exterior gives way to a more restful interior orchestrated by kimino-clad attendants. The sushi bar is on the right, traditional seating straight ahead and privately screened rooms immediately on the left. Choose from the familiar greaseless tempura or beef teriyaki, or proceed on to an adventure from the main menu. The overall food quality, artistry of presentation and serene service out-score most of the similar places in town. An established place with a solid reputation.

TAKESUSHI

22 Front Street West. MAP: 9 TELEPHONE: 416-862-1891 LUNCH: Monday – Friday. DINNER: Tuesday – Saturday. CHECK: $$$. CREDIT CARDS: All major. RESERVATIONS: Recommended.

There's nothing pretentious about Takesushi. The décor won't win prizes, but an interesting array of finely executed items makes the room worth a visit. The list of appetizers ranges close to 50, while main courses are substantial and rely usually on udon and soba noodle bases. Keep a lookout for the friendly waiters: they tend to deliver upcoming courses at an unmeasured rate of speed. There's a wide range of beers, but less than a half-dozen sakes available. The sushi bar gives you a glimpse of folk scurrying past along the sidewalk.

Korean

IL BUN JI

668 Bloor Street West. MAP: 22 TELEPHONE: 416-534-7223 LUNCH: Daily. DINNER: Daily. CHECK: $$. CREDIT CARDS: All major. RESERVATIONS: Not required.

An interesting Korean-Japanese mix of dishes has made Il Bun Ji one of Koreatown's favourite places. A pleasant staff makes you feel right at home and an inexhaustible supply of roasted rice tea is always on the table. Apart from the standard sushi, sake and Japanese beer, it's worth exploring the elegantly prepared wakame salad, donburi and sunomono. To make the experience more authentic, try to get a private booth. Well worth the trip to this section of Bloor West.

KOREA HOUSE

666 Bloor Street West. MAP: 22 TELEPHONE: 416-536-8666 LUNCH: Daily. DINNER: Daily. CHECK: $$. CREDIT CARDS: Mastercard, Visa. RESERVATIONS: Not necessary.

Korea House has been honing its reputation in this neighbourhood for a long time. If you're a neophyte when it comes to Korean food, the complete dinner for $25 relieves you from making a whole lot of uninformed decisions. The meal includes rice, loads of barley-flavoured green tea and fresh dessert fruits. The waitresses are aware that too much spice could upset your comfort level, so let them know whether the chef should "turn it down a notch." If you want to wander further afield, try hakmool changol, which is a seafood and vegetable hotpot.

SE JONG

658 Bloor Street West. MAP: 22 TELEPHONE: 416-535-5918 LUNCH: Daily. DINNER: Daily. CHECK: $$. CREDIT CARDS: All major. RESERVATIONS: Not required.

Understandably, there are quite a few Korean restaurants in this part of town. But not all of them are exclusively Korean when it comes down to the menu. Often Japanese dishes alternate with Korean and this gives rise to a Korean-Japanese hybrid. Not so at Se Jong. Here is a small, affordable and friendly place where you can feast on gunmandu, kimchi and japchae bap till your tummy's content. Look into the kalbi dinner of short ribs and beef, or the minau tang fish stew. U jok tang (ox leg) is for those who appreciate something different.

Malaysian

MATA HARI
39 Baldwin Street. MAP: 13 TELEPHONE: 416-596-2832
LUNCH: Tuesday – Friday. DINNER: Tuesday – Sunday. CHECK: $$$. CREDIT CARDS: All major. RESERVATIONS: Advisable at weekends.

There's a tempting historic blend of Chinese and Malay cuisines rippling through a menu that offers about two dozen main dishes. The service could well have been rooted in the legendary Raffles: it's discreet and polite to a fault. There are little touches like a lowered public telephone, barrier-free access for disabled persons and dietary considerations that take into account most needs. The wine list, usually meagre in south Asian restaurants, is even a pleasant surprise. Although competitive neighbours along Baldwin Street surround Mata Hari, they have to try hard to make a squeeze play.

Moroccan

BOUJADI
220 Eglinton Avenue East. MAP: *City of Toronto*.
TELEPHONE: 416-440-0258 LUNCH: Closed.
DINNER: Wednesday – Saturday. CHECK: $$. CARDS: All major.
RESERVATIONS: Not accepted.

The Boujadi Café is set in the trendy Yonge-Eglinton section of midtown where restaurant competition is keen. However, the Moroccan culinary delights in this room have won over a faithful following in the neighbourhood. It's a small, family-run place and menu items are prepared in the traditional tagine slaoui. If you've wanted to venture into Moroccan food, but didn't quite know what to ask for, try the marhaba. It's a collection of all sorts of different food samples and a good introduction to the well-run kitchen. Don't be surprised if you think about a second visit.

Peruvian

BOULEVARD CAFÉ
161 Harbord Street. MAP: 17 TELEPHONE: 416-961-7676 LUNCH: Daily.
DINNER: Daily. CHECK: $$$. CREDIT CARDS: All Major.
RESERVATIONS: Advisable for weekends.

This café on the corner of Borden Street is one of the most likeable places around. The menu is chock full of tantalizing Peruvian fare that takes its genesis from African, Spanish and Incan flavours. The room is charming and the patio is a delight during the summer, even though there's usually a wait to go there. Never mind, the staff will let you nibble on free cornbread and sip sangria until your table is ready. The spicy seafood stew is worth investigating, as is the rack of lamb with zucchini and eggplant. Peruvian wines are well represented.

EL BODEGON
537 College Street. MAP: 17 TELEPHONE: 416-944-8297 LUNCH: Wednesday – Sunday. DINNER: Wednesday – Sunday. CHECK: $$$S. CREDIT CARDS: All major. RESERVATIONS: Advisable for dinner.

There's a distinct feeling that you've landed in South America the moment you walk through the door. The décor and music are both unashamedly Latin and the service is just as sunny. But do be patient with your server when the room gets crowded. Menu portions are almost too generous. Favourite dishes include seafood, chicken and red meats served with available salads and bean concoctions. The wine list is modest with vintages well suited to the cuisine. The summer patio is a local attraction, alive with good-natured folk.

LA COCINA DE DOÑA LUZ
807 St Clair Avenue West. MAP: *City of Toronto*. TELEPHONE: 416-652-7430 LUNCH: Daily. DINNER: Daily. CHECK: $$. CARDS: American Express, Mastercard. RESERVATIONS: Recommended at weekends.

Diners in search of something different are exploring the taste sensations of Peruvian cuisine. La Cocina de Doña Luz is one of a half dozen restaurants that takes pride in giving first-timers a memorable evening at the table. And it has the advantage of being away from the downtown hustle. The menu re-assures with familiar fare such as paella, then goes on to challenge the adventurous with dishes like tripe casserole. Even doughnuts get a new lease on life when wrapped in fennel pumpkin flour. Wines favour influences from Spain and Chile.

XANGO
106 John Street. MAP: 8 TELEPHONE: 416-593-4407 LUNCH: Closed. DINNER: Tuesday – Sunday. CHECK: $$$$. CREDIT CARDS: All major. RESERVATIONS: Recommended.

Strictly speaking, Xango describes itself as Latin rather than Peruvian. This means that the chef embraces just about every cuisine found in South America. This old house has seen many fine restaurants, the former being Orso. These days, crowds come to Xango with equal respect. This is the place for people who've become jaded and want to put something unexpected and exciting back into their culinary lives. How often have you had to consider empanadas juiced with onions, or oxtail served in a thick wine and chili sauce? Or been confronted with desserts created by a dietitian's worst enemy? Just a thought.

Portuguese

ADEGA
33 Elm Street. MAP: 14 TELEPHONE: 416-977-4338 LUNCH: Monday – Friday. DINNER: Monday – Saturday.

CHECK: $$$$. CREDIT CARDS: All major. RESERVATIONS: Advisable.

The appearance of Adega has brought fine Portuguese cuisine to this busy part of town. For years Elm Street has been known as one of downtown's most varied restaurant districts and this room adds yet another choice. Fish and seafood dominate the menu, as might be expected, and the servers are polite, professional and willing to help folk in the pleasantries of Portuguese food and a fine selection of wine. There's a wine cellar, an upstairs bar, lots of ports and Madeiras, and a cigar room available until the city says otherwise.

CHIADO
864 College Street. MAP: *City of Toronto*. TELEPHONE: 416-538-1910
LUNCH: Monday – Saturday. DINNER: Monday – Saturday. CHECK: $$$$.
CARDS: All major. RESERVATIONS: Advised.

The Portuguese community is the fourth largest cultural group in Toronto. Therefore, it comes as no surprise that Portuguese cuisine is treated with respect in the city. Never a year passes without Chiado being listed among the city's best restaurants, regardless of the type of cuisine. The room has a relaxing and elegant atmosphere with service provided by some of the finest waiters in town. Food tends to concentrate on the lighter side with no heavy overtones. There's no hiding the fact that many of the wines hail from Portugal and servers are pleased to help you with any vintages that could be unfamiliar. If you could choose only one Portuguese restaurant, this is likely the place.

Seafood

FISH HOUSE
144 Front Street West. MAP: 9 TELEPHONE: 416-595-5051
LUNCH: Monday – Friday. DINNER: Daily. CHECK: $$$.
CREDIT CARDS: All major. RESERVATIONS: Accepted.

Location is everything and the Fish House is situated where the financial and entertainment districts meet at University Avenue. The kitchen brings in seafood from all over, including Ontario trout, Florida mahi and Chilean sea bass. One of the special treats is to order salmon cooked on a cedar plank. King crab is another favourite. Sometimes the service can get a bit behind schedule, so arrive early if you want to catch a show.

LA PÊCHERIE
133 Yorkville Avenue. MAP: 24 TELEPHONE: 416-926-9545 LUNCH: Monday – Friday. Buffet Saturday & Sunday. DINNER: Daily. CHECK: $$$$. CREDIT CARDS: All Major. RESERVATIONS: Advisable for weekend dinner.

For some strange reason, Toronto isn't overly supplied with good, traditional seafood places. Perhaps it's because so many of the ethnic restaurants specialize in seafood dishes. But La Pêcherie, housed within its Mövenpick parent, offers the Yorkville crowd an old fashioned place to go without being embarrassed. The kitchen respects freshness and subtlety and it shows. The menu gives diners a wide scope, including Arctic char, oysters in various guises, moist swordfish steaks and perfectly prepared salmon. Wine comes by the glass, half-litre, half bottle and usual full bottle selections.

RODNEY'S OYSTER HOUSE
209 Adelaide Street East. MAP: 10 TELEPHONE: 416-363-8105
LUNCH: Monday – Saturday. DINNER: Monday – Saturday. CHECK: $$$.
CARDS: All major. RESERVATIONS: Recommended.

Regulars will tell you that this is their favourite seafood place in town. And it's not just the oysters that keep them coming back. Here's one of those relaxed basement places that doesn't give a damn about trendy décor. Painted brick walls, drain pipes and lots of ducting will do just fine. Act like the locals and sit up at the long granite bar where you can watch the endless shucking going on. Revel in the best oysters, mussels, quahogs and periwinkles in town, three kinds of chowder and wonderful fries. Throw in seasonal lobster and crab and a limited selection of good beers and wine. And relax. On July 22, 2001 Rodney's opens its new digs at 469 King Street West.

Spanish

SEGOVIA
5 St Nicholas Street. MAP: 19 TELEPHONE: 416-960-1010
LUNCH: Monday – Friday. DINNER: Monday – Saturday. CHECK: $$$.
CREDIT CARDS: All major. RESERVATIONS: Recommended at weekends.

When you look north along St Nicholas Street from the Wellesley Street corner you can't help noticing a splash of colour on Segovia's exterior walls. That kind of attention extends inside, where you're afforded old-world service by senior attendants well versed with the day's offerings. This is a traditional Spanish room with dark woods and muted strains of a classical guitar. Many regulars opt for what the chef is preparing that evening and never seem to be disappointed. Over the years Segovia has earned a reputation for fine Spanish food and wines at reasonable prices.

TAPAS
226 Carlton Street. MAP: 16 TELEPHONE: 416-323-9651 LUNCH: Friday & Saturday.
DINNER: Tuesday – Sunday. CHECK: $$$. CREDIT CARDS: All major.
RESERVATIONS: Advisable at weekends.

Tapas has been here for quite a few years, bringing a touch of Iberia to Old Cabbagetown. It's in one of those pleasant old neighbourhood houses and has a touch of authenticity, void of Spanish clichés like matador pictures on the walls. The establishment comes by its name honestly. There are over 40 tapas on the menu, which doesn't leave much room for main dishes such as the traditional paella. Service is low-key and the clientele appreciates the pleasant tone of the place. Spanish wines dominate an average-sized list.

Steakhouses

TOM JONES
17 Leader Lane. Map: 10 TELEPHONE: 416-366-6583
LUNCH: Monday – Friday. DINNER: Daily. CHECK: $$$$.
CREDIT CARDS: All major. RESERVATIONS: Recommended.

Upscale steakhouses have come and gone, but this restaurant has been around for a long time and consistently offers predictable, though expensive, steak, seafood and lamb. The wine list is well regarded and you shouldn't have a problem selecting just the right bottle for your dinner. Service is attentive and the staff is well versed in the ways of the kitchen. Décor tends to recall earlier days with gaslight lamps, lots of wood panelling and stained glass. There are three levels, including a third floor salon and second tier piano bar.

RUTH'S CHRIS STEAKHOUSE
Toronto Hilton Hotel, 145 Richmond Street West. MAP: 9 TELEPHONE: 416-955-1455
LUNCH: Thursday & Friday. DINNER: Daily. CHECK: $$$$$. CREDIT CARDS: All major.
RESERVATIONS: Recommended.

It's possible for 200 carnivores to pack into the five rooms here and sample US prime steaks brought to the table sizzling in butter. There are ten choices of potato. You can partake of a popular bread pudding with whiskey sauce, or smoke a cigar in a special lounge – at least until the city disapproves of anyone smoking almost anywhere. It all comes at a price, of course: this establishment vies with some other expensive purveyors of steak in town to set you back at least $150 for a good night out.

THE KEG MANSION
515 Jarvis Street. MAP: 20 TELEPHONE: 416-964-6609
LUNCH: Closed. DINNER: Daily. CHECK: $$$. CREDIT CARDS: All major.
RESERVATIONS: Advisable.

No other steakhouse in town offers its customers the real thing more than the Keg Mansion. It's housed in the impressive old McMaster mansion, one of the last great houses south of the Rosedale Ravine. One customer describes it this way: "It's the only restaurant I've been in where there's a fireplace in the women's washroom." The Keg chain is also noted for good steaks and friendly service at a reasonable price. And the wine list, though not nearly as thorough as many of its competitors, is well within reason. You won't find too many food critics wandering around, but that's their loss. Developers are eyeing this property, so check to see if it's still open.

Thai

BANGKOK GARDEN
18 Elm Street. MAP: 14 TELEPHONE: 416-977-6748
LUNCH: Monday – Friday. DINNER: Daily. CHECK: $$$$.
CREDIT CARDS: All major. RESERVATIONS: Recommended.

It's been a long time since Thai restaurants first made their appearance in Toronto. And the Bangkok Garden was one of the country's first. Today, it retains its upscale appearance and menu, catering to moneyed folk who still know their way around the subtle and spiced delicacies of southeast Asia. It's also the only restaurant in the city that has a fake river running through lush tropical gardens. If Thai is your thing – and you want to spend a bit more than usual on ambience and discreet service – Bangkok Garden is just your cup of green tea.

GOLDEN THAI
105 Church Street. MAP: 10 TELEPHONE: 416-868-6668 LUNCH: Monday – Friday.
DINNER: Daily. CHECK: $$. CARDS: All major. RESERVATIONS: Not required.

It's hard to find a Thai restaurant that's not up to par and this one generally exceeds most people's expectations. For many years it has been a magnet for those in the know around this part of town. It's housed in one of downtown's older buildings and offers a toned-down décor. The menu is balanced and varied, catering to local, business and tourist clienteles. Service is friendly and polite.

VANIPHA FINE CUISINE
Northwest corner of Denison Avenue and Dundas Street West. MAP: 13
TELEPHONE: 416 340-0491 LUNCH: Monday – Saturday. DINNER: Monday – Saturday.
CHECK: $$$. CREDIT CARDS: Visa. RESERVATIONS: Not required.

These are the new digs for this highly respected kitchen – just down the street from where it stood for years at 193 Augusta Avenue. The place is now larger and a bit more upscale than it was before, but the Laotian-Thai cuisine made the journey successfully in March of 2001. The new place still has no pretensions and newcomers might think they've landed in the wrong part of town. Make no mistake, Vanipha has an unusually creative and dedicated kitchen that weaves magic with soups, appetizers and main dishes. For those who delight in devouring intense spices, try the chicken in coconut curry.

VANIPHA LANNA
471 Eglinton Avenue West. MAP: *City of Toronto*. TELEPHONE: 416-484-0895
LUNCH: Monday – Saturday. DINNER: Monday – Saturday. CHECK: $$.
CARDS: All major. RESERVATIONS: Recommended for late week dinners.

Over the years, the restaurant has never strayed far from being the city's top Thai establishment. Perhaps it's the grease-free fare, the no smoking environment, or just the seduction of tastes from the Chiang Mai region. Spices range from subtle to ouch. Seafood, soups and a daunting array of appetizers make this one place that demands a return visit. And the price is right.

YOUNG THAILAND
81 Church Street. MAP: 10 TELEPHONE: 416-368-1368 LUNCH: Monday – Friday.
DINNER: Daily. CHECK: $$. CARDS: All majors.
RESERVATIONS: Recommended.

Many folk say that this is one of the top two Thai places in town. The room goes a bit overboard with plants, but it's what turns up on the plate that counts. Here, you certainly won't be disappointed and the customary zing to Thai cuisine is just right. The atmosphere is casual and staff practise the art of politeness.

There are three other locations: 111 Gerrard Street East; Yonge Street at Lola Road; and 165 John Street.

Vietnamese

INDOCHINE
4 Collier Street. MAP: 25 TELEPHONE: 416-922-5840
LUNCH: Monday – Saturday. DINNER: Monday – Saturday.
CHECK: $$$. CREDIT CARDS: All major. RESERVATIONS: Accepted.

Just across the street from the northern end of the Toronto Reference Library is a little restaurant that you could easily pass by. If you enjoy superior Vietnamese food, try not to miss it. The menu obviously inherits dishes from the days when Vietnam was French Indochina. There are also hints of Chinese and Thai influences. This is a room with sophistication and fine food for those weary of the stripped-down Vietnamese eateries elsewhere in town. Don't forget to end the evening with some homemade coconut or mango ice cream.

PHO HU'NG
350 Spadina Avenue. MAP: 13 TELEPHONE: 416-593-4274 LUNCH: Daily. DINNER: Daily. CHECK: $$ CREDIT CARDS: Not accepted. RESERVATIONS: Not necessary.

In Chinatown, where mediocre Vietnamese restaurants seem to be opening on every corner, it's good to know where to find Pho Hu'ng. As its name suggests, this is a great place for soups. But this is only a start to a legion of well-prepared and creative delicacies enhanced by Asian aromas. Strengths are directed towards beef and chicken dishes that come topped off with crunchy bean sprouts, lime and basil. This is not a place where alcohol dominates the drinks list, so go local and enjoy the tangy tropical juice. This is a cash only place, but the check is a pleasant surprise.

Visiting *TheCity*

First-time visitors usually notice two things straight away: polite and culturally diverse people, plus a relaxed and tolerant atmosphere.

Half the city's 16,500,000 annual visitors come by car, 40% by plane and 10% by either train or bus. Over 40% arrive from other parts of Canada, a third from the United States and the remainder from overseas. Chances are better than 70% that you'll return to the city after your first visit. This is due mainly to a variety of things to do, the diverse cultures, inexpensive shopping, interesting attractions, safe streets and an open-minded society.

*Canada*Customs & immigration

CUSTOMS

Although many people tell little white lies when they go through customs, it's best to answer questions directly and honestly when you meet the customs officer. This will save you time, possible embarrassment, a hefty fine, or even imprisonment.

You are allowed to bring into the country all the personal effects needed for your visit. If you are at least 19 years old you can bring with you, duty-free, 200 cigarettes and 50 cigars; 1.1 litres (40 oz) of wine *or* liquor *or* 24 x 355 ml (24 x 12 oz) cans of beer *or* ale. Coolers with an alcohol content of 0.5% or less are not considered to be alcoholic beverages for customs purposes. If you bring more than these amounts of tobacco or alcohol you will have to pay high taxes to both Canada Customs and the government of Ontario. You can also bring, duty-free, unlimited gifts valued at less than $CA 60.00 each, providing they are not tobacco or alcohol products.

> **HELPFUL TIP:** Don't be too generous with the number of gifts you bring into the country. There can be a fine line between all your "birthday gifts" and commercial quantities – which are taxable.

It is a very serious criminal offence, carrying heavy penalties, to bring illegal drugs or undeclared firearms into Canada. If you are bringing firearms into the country for sport or hunting, for use in competitions, or for in-transit movement through Canada, you must declare them to customs at the border. Weapons that are totally prohibited from entering the country include 'mufflers' and 'silencers' for guns, 'switchblade' knives, fully automatic firearms, sawed-off rifles and shotguns. It is a criminal offence for foreigners to carry their hand guns in Canada.

If you have any questions, give Canada Customs a call at 416-973-8022, Monday to Friday, 8.30 AM - 4.30 PM. You'll find them very helpful, particularly by keeping Americans up to date on the latest customs benefits under the North American Free Trade Agreement (NAFTA).

IMMIGRATION

You'll meet Canadian immigration officials when you land at the airport or when you cross over the border in your vehicle. You'll be on Canadian territory and under Canadian law. If you're an American you can be asked for proof of citizenship, so carry a passport or your birth certificate. Naturalized Americans should carry their naturalization papers. All other nationals must have a valid passport and, in some cases, a visa. Check with your travel agent to see if the visa requirement applies to you. It is a serious offence to enter Canada to work unless you have the required documentation.

Arrival by road

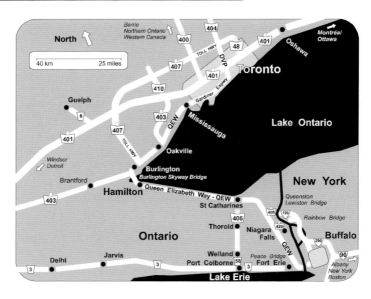

QUEEN ELIZABETH WAY *(The QEW)* and the **GARDINER EXPRESSWAY** (*The Gardiner*).

The QEW runs from the Ontario-New York border at Fort Erie, Ontario to Toronto. Be careful during the winter as the highway passes through a 'micro-climate' for a 15 km (10 mile) stretch on the Canadian side of the border. This phenomenon, brought about by the close proximity of Lake Erie to Lake Ontario, often causes sudden blinding snow squalls or dense fog. As the QEW approaches downtown Toronto it becomes the Gardiner Expressway. The Gardiner cuts through the downtown core dividing business and commercial areas from the waterfront. You have exits to all the major north-south downtown streets, the lakefront entertainment complexes, SkyDome and the CN Tower. The Gardiner can become very congested during rush hour. Speed limits: QEW is 100 km/h (62 mph) and the Gardiner is 90 km/h (56 mph).

HIGHWAY 400

This is the major highway that connects Toronto with northern Ontario and western Canada. As it approaches Toronto it expands to eight, then 12 lanes. Use extra caution during winter because this highway is renowned for its whiteouts just north of Toronto. It's also known as a 'boring' highway, so keep your wits about you and watch out for drivers who are speeding. Speed limit: 100 km/h (62 mph).

HIGHWAY 401 *(The 401)*

This is a major four lane provincial highway running from the Ontario-Québec border to Windsor on the Ontario-Michigan border. As it goes through Toronto it expands to 16 lanes and becomes the second busiest highway in North America. There are eight core express lanes with four collector lanes on either side. If you are unfamiliar with the 401 keep in the collector lanes to avoid missing your exit. Despite its size it can come to a standstill in bad weather, because of an accident, or during rush hour. If possible avoid using it from 6.30 AM - 10.00 AM and from 3.00 PM - 7.00 PM weekdays, as well as evenings on the first and last days of a holiday weekend when traffic is especially heavy. Speed limit: 100 km/h (62 mph).

HIGHWAY 403

If you're heading along the QEW coming into Toronto and want to get to Pearson International Airport, or the middle of Toronto, take highway 403 north from the QEW. The 403/QEW interchange is just before you get to Mississauga. The 403 connects with the 401 and the 407 ETR. This way you'll avoid having to go through downtown. Speed limit: 100 km/h (62 mph).

HIGHWAY 404 and the DON VALLEY PARKWAY (*The Parkway,* or *The DVP*)

Highway 404 runs south from the Town of Newmarket to the 401 in the middle of Toronto. As it continues southwest to downtown it becomes the six-lane Don Valley Parkway. Avoid the DVP during the morning rush hour into town (6.30 AM – 10.00 AM) and the afternoon rush hour going out of town (3.00 PM - 7.00 PM). During these times it's known locally as 'The Don Valley Parking Lot'. It's not at all unusual to experience congestion just south of the 401 any time due to volume. From the DVP you have access to many of Toronto's main east-west streets including interchanges at Lawrence Avenue, Eglinton Avenue, Don Mills Road, Bloor Street, Richmond Street and Lakeshore Boulevard. Speed limits: the 404 is 100 km/h (62 mph) and the DVP is 90 km/h (56 mph).

HIGHWAY 407 ETR

Highway 407 ETR (Electronic Toll Route) was the world's first electronically controlled toll highway without toll booths. It operates by photographing and recording your licence plate when you enter and exit. You get a bill through the mail. The system is capable of photographing 14,000 licence plates per hour. The 407's six lanes are designed primarily for drivers who want to bypass Toronto quickly. It runs for 69 km (43 miles) in an east-west direction just north of the city from highway 48 in the east to highway 403 in the west. There are proposals to extend it in both directions from highway 115 in the east to the QEW west of Burlington.

Inter-governmental agreements are in place to make sure that drivers with licence plates from all Canadian provinces and territories and from New York, Pennsylvania, Ohio, Michigan and Florida will be billed for tolls. The speed limit is 100 km/h (62 mph).

> **HELPFUL TIP:** A trip along the 407 is expensive. Prime-time tolls are 11 cents/km, which works out to about 18 cents/mile.

HIGHWAY 427 (*The 427*)

The 427 is the major north-south expressway linking Pearson International Airport with the QEW. It can get very busy in the morning going south into town and again in the afternoon, starting around 3.00 PM, going north. If you are using the 427 to get to or from Pearson during these periods make sure you leave yourself plenty of time. Remember that the Gardiner/QEW combination leading from downtown to the 427 is always busy.

HIGHWAY SIGNS

In keeping with Canada's metric system, distances and speeds are given in kilometres (km) and metres (m) only. There's no posted conversion into miles and yards.

 All provincial highways show their number inside a crown logo. This tradition goes back many years to when a provincial highway was known as 'The King's Highway'. All highway signs are clearly marked and the information is posted well in advance. Some signs provide basic information in French.

Always keep alert for signs indicating that your lane is about to end. This is especially important when you are using the 401.

There are special overhead electronic signs on the 401, the Gardiner and DVP that give you the current traffic conditions ahead. You can also find out about any problems by phoning 416-599-9090, 24hr.

DRIVING TIMES TO / FROM TORONTO

 The following are approximate driving times from downtown to downtown, based on daytime summer driving conditions and an average wait at Canada Customs where applicable:

Albany, NY: 6½ hours
Boston, MA: 9½ hours

Buffalo, NY: 1¾ hours
Detroit, MI: 4 hours

Montréal, PQ: 6 hours
New York City, NY: 9½ hours
Niagara Falls, ON: 1½ hours

Ottawa, ON: 5 hours
Pittsburgh, PA: 5½ hours
Stratford, ON: 1½ hours

Airports

LESTER B PEARSON INTERNATIONAL AIRPORT (YYZ)

 It's named after Canada's 19th prime minister, who won the 1957 Nobel Peace Prize.

Mostly referred to simply as 'Pearson', the airport is located about 25 km (17 miles) northwest of downtown. It's the busiest airport in the country, handling over 380,000 planes and 25,000,000 passengers a year from 60 domestic and international airlines. It has direct service to 140 destinations in 45 countries. Overall, Pearson ranks among the world's top 25 airports in terms of passenger volumes, aircraft movements and cargo handling.

Surrounding Pearson is what's known as the 'Airport Strip', a combination of hotels, restaurants and conference and exhibition facilities. It's also renowned for its lively nightlife. Together with the airport, the Strip generates about $10-billion in annual revenues and employs 100,000 people. It's one of the most important economic districts in the region.

PEARSON AIRPORT TERMINALS

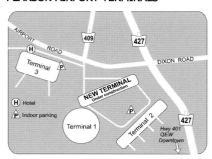

The airport has three terminals, so make sure you know which one your airline uses by checking your ticket, or phoning ahead. All of them are busy from before 5.00 AM until after midnight.

The map at the left gives you a general overview of the complex and connecting highways.

A free shuttle bus connects the buildings. The terminals have duty-free shopping, rental car offices, banks, restaurants, bookstores, bars, indoor parking and personal services. The 496 room Sheraton Gateway Hotel is linked directly to Terminal 3.

During the next few years Pearson will be undergoing a $4.4-billion renovation. A major new terminal, capable of handling 50-million passengers annually, is under construction to replace Terminal 1 and Terminal 2. This means you might experience some temporary inconveniences as airlines juggle terminal positions. The airport will also be upgrading and extending its parking and runway systems. Get virtual reality tours of the new terminal and shots of the construction site on the airport's Web site: **gtaa.com**

BAGGAGE HANDLING

 Baggage carts are available in the arrival and departure areas of each terminal. You have to either insert a dollar coin into the cart, or swipe your credit card to release it from the stack. Your dollar coin will pop back out after you insert the cart into the stack. Customer Service Representatives should be present to reimburse your credit card payment when you return the cart.

> **HELPFUL TIP:** Save yourself any aggravation by getting the services of a Skycap. The usual tip is $2 per bag.

PEARSON TAXI AND LIMOUSINE SERVICE

 There are taxi and limousine stands outside the arrivals level at each terminal building and a sidewalk dispatcher will organize your ride. The trip to downtown averages about 40 minutes but can take a lot longer in heavy traffic or bad weather. It's a good idea to organize your schedule around a one-hour trip during rush hours.

It's customary to tip the driver between 10% - 15% of the fare depending on the level of service provided. The dispatcher does not expect to be tipped. Always remember that tipping a taxi driver in Toronto is in appreciation of the service rendered. Although taxi drivers expect to be tipped, an amount less than that noted above will indicate your displeasure if the service is not professional. There are 3,320 taxis and limousines licensed to operate out of Pearson.

> **HELPFUL TIP:** There's only about a $5.00 difference in the fares charged by taxis and limousines to downtown. A limo is your better buy.

PEARSON BUS SERVICE

 The Pacific Western Airport Express bus service operates a 20 minute schedule from around 5.00 AM till midnight from each terminal building to most of the major downtown hotels and the Toronto Coach Terminal. The bus driver will give you all the details. The trip takes around 45 minutes depending on weather and traffic conditions. It costs about $14.00 for a one-way fare and $20.00 for the round trip. There are discounts for Seniors. For further information, phone 905-564-6333.

PEARSON SUBWAY CONNECTION

 The TTC operates a bus service to and from terminals 2 and 3 and the subway from around 5.30 AM weekdays till just after midnight. Bus 58A Malton runs every three-quarters of an hour from Terminal 2 arrivals level to Lawrence West subway station. The trip takes about 45 minutes. Bus 192 Airport Rocket connects the arrivals and departure levels of terminals 2 and 3 with the Kipling subway station. That trip takes only 20 minutes and service is a bit more frequent. The fare for either ride is $2.25. When leaving the airport, make sure you ask the bus driver for a free transfer that gets you on to the subway. The transfer also lets you travel to wherever you want to go in the city without having to pay any more money. For more information, call 416-393-4636. Web: **ttc.ca**

DRIVING FROM PEARSON

For downtown take Highway 427 south to the QEW, then east to downtown. As you leave the airport you'll find the highways are all very well marked. The QEW becomes the Gardiner Expressway and there are exits to all major north-south streets in the downtown area. If you are going to places in the middle of the city, take the 401 east to the north-south exit you want. It's a good idea to stay in the collector lanes if you are not familiar with the 401; otherwise you could miss your exit.

> **HELPFUL TIP:** Be careful if you are entering the 401 eastbound from the airport. Your lane merges quickly into fast-moving traffic. Slow down and make sure the traffic to your left is clear.

PARKING

The terminal areas have nearly 10,000 parking spaces. Terminal 2 has the largest free-standing parking lot in Canada, holding 4,500 vehicles. In 2003 it will be replaced with a 12,600 vehicle facility.

Despite the sizes of the parking lots, most of the lower level space is usually full. This means a drive to the upper levels before you find a spot. If you are driving a rental vehicle you'll notice there are special stalls for you to use in each terminal. If you have a disability there are specially marked parking spaces close to each terminal's entry and exit points. Other drivers cannot use these spaces.

> **HELPFUL TIP:** If you're going to be out of town for a few days, there's a cheaper above ground long-term parking facility. Just look for the signs. A shuttle bus gets you to and from the terminal.

PEARSON AIRPORT HOTEL SHUTTLE

Pearson International Airport supports a huge infrastructure that includes about 30 hotels, all within only a few kilometres of the terminal buildings. Many have a courtesy shuttle bus service for guests and you'll find free direct line telephones to these hotels near the arrivals exit in each terminal building. You might have to wait a few minutes for the shuttle to arrive, but it will save the cost of a taxi.

PEARSON ARRIVAL AND DEPARTURE INFORMATION

It's best to call your airline first as it usually has the most up to date information. Otherwise, you can phone 905-676-3506 between 7.00 AM - 10.00 PM daily for airlines using Terminal 1 and Terminal 2, or 905-612-5100 for flights operating out of Terminal 3. If you have a problem with either of these numbers, contact public relations. Their phone number is 905-676-3580. If you are within about 8 km (5 miles) of the airport you can tune your radio to AM 1280 for airline and airport traffic information. The airport is open to aircraft from 6.00 AM till midnight, although planes that have been held up for mechanical, security or weather reasons can take off and land outside these hours. However, the noisier an aircraft's engines the less likely it will be given permission to use the airport after midnight. Pearson has a highly sophisticated aircraft noise monitoring system and by the year 2002 only the quietest jets will be allowed to use the airport. The airport general information number is 905-676-3000. The Web site is **gtaa.com**

TORONTO CITY CENTRE AIRPORT (YTZ)
Better known locally as 'The Island Airport', it's on Centre Island in Toronto's Inner Harbour right next to downtown. It's used, on average, by about 400 passengers a day who travel on short-haul regional airlines. It's also a popular airport for private pilots. A 122 m (133 yds) ferry ride from the foot of Bathurst Street gets you across to the island.

However, there's always the possibility that a promised bridge or tunnel will replace the ferry. A free shuttle bus operates between the airport and the downtown Royal York Hotel. For more information, phone 416-203-6942.

TORONTO BUTTONVILLE MUNICIPAL AIRPORT (YKZ)
This ranks as the tenth busiest airport in Canada, handling about 190,000 takeoffs and landings a year. It's used mainly by private and corporate aircraft. Access to downtown is south on highway 404 and the DVP. For more information, phone 905-477-8100.

*Inter-city*Trains

 Union Station is downtown on Front Street West between Bay and York streets. It is the city's major rail terminal for Via Rail inter-city trains, GO Transit's regional rail commuter system, the TTC subway and Harbourfront LRT streetcar service along the waterfront. It's also right across the street from the Financial District. See Map 9.

Union Station is linked directly to the PATH underground walkway system and to the Air Canada Centre. Outside the main entrance on Front Street you'll find a major taxi stand. Opposite, outside the Royal York Hotel on the northeast corner of Front and York streets, you can board the Airport Express bus for Pearson Airport, or catch the shuttle bus to the Toronto City Centre Airport.

The station has bars, restaurants, coffee shops, ATMs, newsstands and personal services. It's linked to the Toronto Convention Centre next to the CN Tower along the elevated Skywalk. For more information, phone 416-365-1220 for Via Rail arrivals and departures; 416-869-3200 for GO Transit; or 416-393-4636 for the TTC.

It's worth seeing inside Union Station because of its widely acclaimed architecture. The Great Hall was modelled after the spectacular halls of ancient Rome and the elongated exterior is one of the city's best examples of architecture in the *beaux-arts* tradition. Three architects worked on the project before its opening in 1927. However, it was John M Lyle, who also designed Toronto's Royal Alexandra Theatre and hundreds of other buildings across Canada, who got most of the praise.

GO Transit

 GO Transit is a regional transit system that began modestly in September, 1970 as a limited bus service. Today, it connects Toronto and its surrounding communities with a fleet of distinctive green and white triple-decker GO trains and GO buses. It serves an 8,000 square kilometre (3,100 square mile) area bounded by Hamilton in the west, Barrie to the north and Bowmanville in the east. GO connects with most regional public transit systems within this area, including Toronto. The Toronto hub for GO trains is Union Station (Map 9) and GO buses operate from the Toronto Coach Terminal at Bay and Edward streets (Map 14). The system will carry an estimated 42,000,000 passengers during 2001.

The GO system is used mainly by commuters and is packed to and from Toronto during the morning and evening rush hours. To avoid the crowds, use GO trains after 9.00 AM and before 4.00 PM weekdays and any time on weekends and public holidays. The green and white logo above is shown on all GO trains, GO buses, GO train stations and bus stops. GO Transit is a public system funded by the provincial government and is North America's third busiest rail commuter service after New York and Chicago.

FARES
Fares are charged according to zones and whether you are an adult, senior, kid under 12, child under 5, or a student with a valid GO Transit ID card. The only way to find out how much a single trip will cost is to phone GO Transit at the numbers listed under *General Information*, or ask the attendant at any GO wicket. Regular commuters can get a monthly pass.

For a combined fare that covers both GO Transit and public transit (TTC) in Toronto, ask for an adult 'Twin Pass' which is sold at a discount and is only available from GO Transit. Get your tickets from the wicket attendant at GO train stations and GO bus stations, or from agencies. You can use Visa, Mastercard or a debit card at most stations, but you must pay a bus driver the exact cash fare. If you want to use the system extensively, buy a day pass.

GO trains work on the honour system. This means you don't have to show your ticket to an attendant before you board the train. But you must be able to show proof of payment during any on-board spot inspection. On GO buses, you must show your ticket to the driver when you get on the vehicle.

LOST AND FOUND
The office is located at Union Station, 140 Bay Street, around the corner from the main station entrance. They're open weekdays from 7.00 AM - 7.00 PM. Phone 416-327-9444.

BICYCLES ON THE TRAINS
Bicycles cannot be brought on to trains weekdays between 6.30 AM - 9.30 AM or between 3.30 PM - 6.30 PM. They are also prohibited inside Union Station. At other times, and at any time during the weekend and public holidays, you can stow your bike just inside the doors.

PEOPLE WITH DISABILITIES AND SENIORS

Many stations are accessible to passengers who use wheelchairs, or other mobility devices. Phone 416-869-3200 for a list of those that can accommodate your requirements. GO buses are not wheelchair accessible. Seniors, 65 years of age and over living in Ontario, get a discount on all fares.

MAPS AND TIMETABLES

You can get a full set of maps and timetables for all train and bus routes from the wickets at any GO station.

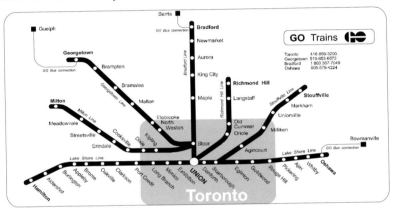

GENERAL INFORMATION

For anything you need to know, phone GO Transit weekdays 7.00 AM - 10 PM, or weekends and public holidays 9.00 AM - 7.00 PM at 416-869-3200. The free long distance number is 1 888 438-6646 and the free TTY line is 1 800 387-3652. The Web site is **gotransit.com**

*Inter-city*Buses

The bus station is called the 'Toronto Coach Terminal'. See Map 14.

The terminal handles about 2,500 people a day. It's the hub for all inter-city and regional buses. Inside, there's a coffee shop, storage lockers, bar, restaurant and newsstand. Just outside the door there are lots of shops, restaurants and ATMs. You're also right on the doorstep of Chinatown, city hall and Dundas Square. The terminal is connected through the Atrium Mall directly to the downtown PATH underground walkway and to Dundas subway station. For more information, phone 416-393-7911.

Public transit – The TTC

Toronto's public transit system is called 'The TTC' (Toronto Transit Commission). It's a fully integrated rapid transit system that uses 2,500 bus, streetcar, subway and RT (Rapid Transit) cars to move about 392,000,000 people every year over 6,300 km

(3,900 miles) of routes. The RT cars run above ground on elevated monorail-type structures.

FARES

One ticket, token or exact $2.25 cash fare takes you to any point in the system, regardless of the distance travelled. It's cheaper to buy a pack of tickets or tokens than to pay single cash fares. It's better still to get a daily, weekly, or monthly pass. If you are paying cash you must have the exact change when boarding a bus or streetcar. Bus and streetcar drivers don't make change or sell tokens and tickets. However, subway booth attendants have change, tokens and tickets. Over 1,600 agents in stores showing the TTC sign also sell tokens and tickets. Phone 416-393-4636.

There are discounted fares for seniors, students and children 12 years old and under. Kids under two travel free. Seniors must live in Ontario and students must be no more than 19 years old and be in full daytime attendance at school. A day pass for one person is good for unlimited travel weekdays after 9.30 AM and any time during the weekend. You can also get a pass to cover up to six people (no more than two adults) for unlimited travel on a Sunday or statutory holiday.

There's also a GTA (Greater Toronto Area) weekly pass that lets you take as many rides as you want on the TTC, Mississauga, Brampton, Vaughan, Richmond Hill and Markham transit systems as well as some GO Transit lines. This pass is good from Monday through Sunday and you can get more information by calling 416-393-4636.

> **HELPFUL TIP:** It's best to buy tokens because you can use them at unattended subway entrances and all turnstiles. This saves you lining-up.

TRANSFERS

It's often necessary to use more than one vehicle to get to your destination. To get from downtown to the Toronto Zoo, for example, you have to take the subway to Kennedy station and then transfer to the Toronto Zoo bus. When you get on the subway (the first vehicle you'll use), make sure you get a free transfer from one of the automatic dispensers. Save it and give it to the bus driver. If you don't get a transfer, you'll have to pay an extra fare on the bus. If you have to take more than two vehicles - such as a bus, a streetcar and the subway - get your transfer from the bus driver, show it to the streetcar driver, then keep it to give to the attendant in the subway booth (the last vehicle). You must make connections between vehicles as soon as possible. For example, you can't get off the bus and go shopping for an hour before getting on the streetcar.

SIGNS YOU SHOULD KNOW

 The top logo is red and white and it's the TTC's main identifying logo. The sign is also used to mark entrances to subway and RT stations. The sign in the middle is used on maps throughout *City***Companion** to show the name and location of subway stations. The bottom sign is a red and white bus or streetcar stop. On it there's a 'TimeLine' telephone number you can call to find out when the next couple of vehicles are due to arrive. Some stops show a disability sign. This means that ramp-equipped buses are used on this route. If there's a blue band on the sign it means the stop receives overnight service at least every 30 minutes.

ROUTE MAPS

All subway cars have system route maps, usually located above the doors. All subway stations display large maps of the area with bus and streetcar routes clearly shown. Most stops at intersecting bus and streetcar routes, where you can transfer from one vehicle to another, show route maps and timetables. See the map on page nine.

TTC RULES AND ETIQUETTE

On buses and streetcars you must stand behind the white line if you can't get a seat. Move to the rear and stay clear of the doors. To tell the driver you want to get off at the next stop, pull the overhead cord or push the button as soon as the vehicle leaves the previous stop. Get off the vehicle through the back doors. To open the doors, simply stand on the step. The doors will open automatically. Please reserve the seats just behind the bus driver for seniors and others who might need them.

On the subway platform, stand behind the yellow line away from the edge. When the train arrives let people off the car first, then move inside away from the doors. Three chimes will sound and an exterior amber light will blink just before the doors close. Stations are announced in advance.

SAFETY

The TTC is a safe transit system. Phone 416-393-4000 and ask them to send you a free copy of the booklet *Safety and Security on the TTC*. Here are some brief examples of what it contains:

- All subway stations and the RT line have public telephones for quick access to 911 emergencies. Coins aren't required.

- Subway and RT platforms have Designated Waiting Areas (DWAs) that are brightly lit and equipped with an intercom and closed circuit television. On the subway the DWA is located where the guard's car stops and on the RT where the driver's car stops.

- Subway and RT cars also have Passenger Assistance Alarms (PAAs). These are black and yellow strips located above the windows. Press them when a serious incident or emergency happens.

- There's a telephone number listed on each bus and streetcar stop. Call this TimeLine number to find out when the next vehicle is due. This saves you waiting unnecessarily on a dark night. If you can't read the number, phone 416-393-4636. The TimeLine service is available 24 hr.

- Between 9.00 PM and 5.00 AM women can ask the bus driver to let them off between stops so they can be closer to where they are going.

- When getting on subway and RT cars, listen for the door chimes and watch for the flashing amber door light. These are warnings that the doors are about to close. Do not try to force open the doors to board a vehicle. You could get seriously hurt.

- Never go on subway or RT tracks. If you drop anything, get help from the station attendant or any uniformed TTC employee.

PARKING

Parking is available at the Ellesmere, Lawrence East, Kennedy, Warden, Victoria Park, Keele, Islington, Kipling, Wilson, Yorkdale, Eglinton West, York Mills and Finch subway stations. Some of these lots provide free parking to drivers with a Metropass. Bicycle parking facilities are available at most subway stations. Be sure to lock or immobilize your bike after you park and don't leave it until too late at night before you return to collect it. For more information, phone 416-393-4636.

> **HELPFUL TIP:** Regular commuters fill most parking lots by 7.30 AM weekdays. The best idea is to take a bus or streetcar to the nearest subway station.

ALL NIGHT SERVICES

The 'Blue Night Network' service is provided from around 1.30 AM - 5.00 AM on a basic selection of bus and streetcar routes throughout Toronto. The red and white stop signs are marked with an additional reflective blue band. You can expect a vehicle at least once every 30 minutes.

The Blue Night Network routes are outlined on a special map in the *Ride Guide* available at all subway station ticket booths. The subway doesn't run between 1.30 AM - 6.00 AM, or before 9.00 AM Sundays.

LOST AND FOUND

The Lost and Found office is at the Bay subway station. It's open Monday through Friday, 8.00 AM - 5.00 PM, except public holidays. You can give them a call at 416-393-4100 from 9.00 AM - 5.00 PM.

PEOPLE WITH PHYSICAL DISABILITIES

The regular TTC system is not designed for people with physical disabilities. All stations are equipped with both stairs and escalators. For a list of the few stations that have elevators, phone 416-393-4636. However, the TTC does run a highly recommended service called 'Wheel-Trans' that provides a fleet of specially equipped wheelchair accessible buses for people with physical disabilities. Door to door service can be arranged by phoning 416-393-4111. The fare is the same as you'd pay on the regular system. People with a hearing impairment should phone the TDD service at 416-481-2523.

SMOKING

It's an offence to smoke anywhere on TTC property, including stations, vehicles and waiting rooms. Violating this City of Toronto by-law carries a stiff fine.

GENERAL INFORMATION

Call the TTC daily from 8.00 AM - 5.00 PM at 416-393-4636 for virtually anything you need to know. This is mainly a pre-recorded information service, so press 'zero' at any time if you want to speak with a live person. Be prepared to wait a few minutes for them to come on the line. You can ask for service in any one of 140 languages. However, you must identify the language in English. On statutory holidays only pre-recorded information is available.

> **HELPFUL TIP:** If you don't like listening to recorded messages or waiting on the phone, call the TTC's Customer Service weekdays at 416-393-3030. This will put you in touch straight away with a live person who can answer your questions, pass along your complaints, or thank you for compliments. The service available 8.30 AM - 4.30 PM, except holidays.

It's a good idea to get a free *Ride Guide* at any subway ticket booth. It provides a complete public transit guide for Toronto and its surrounding communities. Included are subway, bus and RT route maps, the Blue Network and GO Transit maps, as well as route maps for communities surrounding Toronto. If you'd like a copy, write to the Toronto Transit Commission at 1900 Yonge Street, Toronto, Ontario M4S 1Z2. You'll find the TTC Web site at **city.toronto.on.ca**

Driving

Toronto, like other large cities, has its share of traffic congestion and frustrating delays caused by weather, road repairs and accidents. Here are some general rules and tips to help you get around town more easily:

- You can turn right on most red lights providing you come to a full stop first, make sure the way is clear, and then proceed with caution.

- When a school bus has its lights flashing, all vehicles in both directions must come to a complete stop.

- All traffic must come to a complete stop to allow people to cross the street at clearly marked pedestrian crossings. It's customary for pedestrians to raise their arm to signal that they're about to step off the curb.

- Traffic must come to a full stop behind streetcars that are loading or unloading passengers. Do not overtake the streetcar until it has begun to move forward.

- Underground parking in the central downtown core is expensive during the day. Try to get a space before 9.00 AM when all-day rates are much cheaper.

- Gas prices are virtually identical, regardless of the gas station. The exception to this is a cash only gas bar at the corner of Carlaw Avenue and Dundas Street East, where prices are usually a couple of cents a litre cheaper than anywhere else.

- If you park on the street, obey the parking signs and plug the meter, or get a ticket from the nearby solar-powered dispenser and *put it on your dashboard*. If your car is missing, phone the police at 416-808-2222. It might have been stolen or towed to the pound.

- Be sensible about safety. Lock your vehicle and don't leave stuff in obvious view inside. You might feel more secure by using a steering lock. Radar detecting devices are illegal and will be seized if discovered.

Cycling

You might be surprised to see so many people on bicycles around the city on summer weekends. During the week heavy traffic on most main streets makes them too congested for safe cycling.

There's an average of more than 1,300 collisions between bikes and vehicles every year, most resulting in some kind of injury. More than half the people in Toronto believe that cycling in traffic is dangerous. It's best to reserve that bike ride for a weekend excursion and stick to the city's many bike paths, parks and ravines.

Despite all this, Toronto has been voted North America's best major city for cyclists. One of the many reasons is that there are 50 km (31 miles) of bike lanes along the city's 5,000 km (3,100 miles) of streets, including some in the downtown area. Another reason is that Torontonians love their bikes. Amazing statistics have been published in the local press stating that about nine kids out of ten have a bike and half of all adults own one.

And don't leave your bike lying around unattended. About 12,000 bicycles are stolen each year and police find only about five per cent of them. Make sure they're immobilized when you leave them some place.

Please be aware that it's against the law in Toronto to ride a bicycle without wearing a helmet.

Walking

Summer and fall are the best times to join the locals out for a stroll. Late September and October are particularly rewarding if you enjoy the fall colours. You'll find that city streets are safe any time of the day or night and the tremendous variety of neighbourhoods will give you a sense of discovery. Here are some tips to increase your enjoyment of exploring Toronto at street level:

- Look through *The***City** section and find out what local neighbourhoods interest you most. Think of combining your walk with visits to some unusual *City***Places.** Plan ahead by reading *City***Food** so you'll know where to stop for a meal.

- If you enjoy nature more than concrete, take a look through the *Parks, gardens, zoos and squares* section of *City***Places.**

- Don't forget the PATH underground walkway shown on page 11. It's a 10 km (6 miles) labyrinth of climate-controlled pedestrian passages under the city core that are filled with over 1,000 shops, restaurants and services. It's a fascinating place to spend a day walking around, regardless of the weather.

- Two places that offer quiet pleasures for the walker are the University of Toronto campus (Map 18) and Rosedale (Maps 29-30). Strangely, neither is well known to visitors or residents in other parts of the city.

- When walking around town, cross the street at intersections and obey the pedestrian walk signals. Jaywalking on main streets is not the local thing to do. Besides, it's dangerous. And keep an eye open for bicycle couriers in the city core – especially on sidewalks!

People with disabilities

 Toronto has demonstrated that it's a very manageable city for wheelchair users and people with disabilities. For example, there's 24 hr access to the Centre for Independent Living which can help solve any problems you might encounter.

If you arrive at Pearson International Airport, you'll find the terminals designed to assist you. To get downtown from Pearson, use an accessible limousine like Air Cab, or Airline Limousine, or take the airport bus. Each bus has room for two wheelchairs. If you prefer to drive, vehicles with hand controls are available from most of the rental car companies at the airport.

The major downtown hotels served by the airport bus have rooms specially adapted for people with disabilities. When you get into the city, you'll find all sidewalks slope to the street at intersections and public buildings are wheelchair accessible. However, the public transit system (TTC) is not universally accessible to wheelchair users. To compensate for this, the TTC operates a special 'Wheel-Trans' service of adapted buses. Wheel-Trans vehicles give you door-to-door service and you pay the same fare as you would on a regular bus. However, you need to book this service four days in advance.

If you usually have difficulty communicating with people, Wheel-Trans can supply you with a special *Accessible Service Flashcard*. Just show this card to the driver when you want special assistance. Visitors can get a temporary pass to use Wheel-Trans, or an *Accessible Service Flashcard*, by calling the TTC's administration office weekdays between 8.00 AM - 4.00 PM.

Celebrity Taxi and Royal Taxi each have vehicles equipped to handle wheelchairs. Call Royal in the morning for afternoon service on weekdays and 24 hr in advance for weekends. Celebrity asks you to book 24 hr in advance.

Here are some telephone numbers you'll find useful:

- Wheel-Trans   416-393-4111
- TTC disability information   416-393-4636
- Celebrity Taxi   416-398-2222
- Royal Taxi   416-785-3322

- Air Cab   416-225-1555
- Airline Limousine   905-676-3210
- Centre for Independent Living 416-599-2458 (24 hr)
                                    416-599-5077 (TTD)

*City*Information

  Toronto is recognized as being one of the world's most 'connected' cities. This section is designed to help you cut through Information Age clutter so you can find basic, practical city information quickly and easily.

EMERGENCY   Police – Fire – Ambulance   **Tel: 911**

ACCOMMODATION

You can choose anything from four-star hotels to modest bed and breakfast (B&B) establishments. Hundreds of hotels and B&Bs are listed on the **toronto.com** Web site including rates and seasonal packages. Many entries have their own Web sites and on-line booking services. You can also check the Web sites of major hotel chains, or take a few moments to browse through **torontotourism.com**

ALCOHOL & BARS

The legal drinking age is 19. Regular bar hours are 11.00 AM – 2.00 AM daily. Wine, spirits and some imported beers are available from government operated Liquor Stores. Look under *Liquor Control Board of Ontario* in the phone book for a list of outlets. Regular beer is sold at government operated Beer Stores. You'll find them in the telephone book under *Beer Store*. If a restaurant is 'licensed under the LLBO' (or AGCO), it means that alcohol is served. Drivers with a blood alcohol level of 0.08 or higher will be charged under the *Criminal Code of Canada* with impaired driving.

CITY INFORMATION SITES

Drop by the tourist office on Front Street West next to the Toronto Convention Centre for free brochures. The staff will answer any questions you might have. The following Internet Web sites are worth surfing:

city.toronto.on.ca

The city's non-commercial, official Web site. View camera shots of current highway traffic conditions throughout the city, public transit (TTC) information, maps, city statistics, and information about city government and services.

toronto.com

This is a large commercial Web site covering hotels, entertainment, restaurants, shopping and "all you need to know about T.O."

torontolife.com

A commercial Web site that offers a self-proclaimed upscale view of the city, an events guide and arts reviews. The restaurant guide is cryptic, though influential.

torontotourism.com

The best Web site for organizing a convention. However, if you're not in a group you'll find lots of information, value packages, hotel reservations and what to do and where to go when you get here. This is the official site of the Toronto Convention and Visitors Association.

CLOTHING

People dress casually all year round. Business attire is recommended for formal meetings. Wear 'smart casual' for dinner out and the theatre, or something more formal if you prefer. Check *City***Food** listings for the few top restaurants that might require a jacket and tie.

CRIME

Toronto has the lowest crime rate of any major city in North America. It ranks 25th in Canada in terms of per capita criminal offences. Crime has decreased each year for the last five years.

DENTAL EMERGENCY

The dental emergency service at 1650 Yonge Street is open daily from 8.00 AM – midnight. Phone 416-485-7121.

DIRECTIONS

People will give you directions by the compass. Instead of saying "Go up Yonge and turn right on Carlton…" they'll say "Go north on Yonge and east on Carlton…"

DISTRESS CENTRES

The following services are free:

Drug/Alcohol Addiction:
416-397-4636
Children's Aid Society:
416-924-4646
Community Services:
416-397-4636
Kid's Help Line:
1 800 668-6868

Sexual Assault:
416-597-8808
Suicide:
416-598-1121

DRUG STORES/PHARMACIES

All drug stores and pharmacies in the city have a pharmacist on duty. Most Shopper's Drug Mart stores are open till midnight daily. Phone 1 800 363-1020 for locations and 24 hr services, or look under the business section of the *White Pages* phone book.

ELECTRICAL CURRENT

Toronto operates on the standard North American 110-volt system. Overseas visitors should bring adapters for their electrical appliances.

HEALTH INFORMATION

Canada's Medicare system is available without cost only to Canadian residents with a valid Health Card. If you are visiting from outside the country it is advisable to get health insurance before you leave home.

Emergencies: Go straight to the nearest hospital. If your condition is not of an urgent nature, go to a walk-in clinic. Choose one listed under 'Physicians' in the *Yellow Pages* phone book.

HIV-AIDS: Phone 416-392-2437 (Toronto Health Department), or look in the phone book under *AIDS and HIV Services.*

Sexually Transmitted Diseases (STD): Phone 416-392-2437 for the nearest treatment centre. Gays and lesbians might prefer to contact the Hassle-Free Clinic, 556 Church Street (Map 20) for anonymous treatment and counselling. Men: 416-922-0603. Women: 416-922-0566.

HOLIDAYS

New Years Day
January 1
Good Friday
March/April, date varies.
Easter Monday
March/April, date varies.
Victoria Day
May, third Monday.
Canada Day
July 1
Simcoe Day
August, first Monday.
Labour Day
September, first Monday.
Thanksgiving
October, second Monday.
Remembrance Day
November 11
Christmas Day
December 25
Boxing Day
December 26

NEWSPAPERS

Corriere Canadese
Italian. Published Monday through Saturday.
Phone 416-785-4300
Web site: **corriere.com**

El Popular
Spanish. Published Monday through Saturday.
Phone 416-531-2495
Web site: **diarioelpopular.com**

Globe and Mail
English. Published Monday through Saturday.
Phone 416-585-5000
Web site: **theglobeandmail.com**

Korea Times
Korean. Published Monday through Friday.
Phone 416-787-1111
Web site: **koreatimes.net**

Ming Pao
Chinese. Published daily.
Phone 416-321-0088

National Post
English. Published Monday through Saturday.
Phone 416-383-2500
Web site: **nationalpost.com**

Sing Tao
Chinese. Published daily.
Phone 416-861-8168
Web site: **singtaotor.com**

Toronto Star
English. Published daily.
Phone 416-367-2000
Web site: **thestar.com**

Toronto Sun
English. Published daily.
Phone 416-947-2222
Web site: **canoe.ca**

POISON CONTROL

If you believe that you or your child has been poisoned by something that was swallowed, contact the Poison Control Centre at the Hospital for Sick Children immediately. It's open 24 hr. (See Map 14 for its downtown location on University Avenue at Gerrard Street West.)
Phone: 416-813-6621

POSTAL SERVICES

Regular post offices are open Monday through Friday, 8.00 AM – 5.00 PM, with some open Saturday till 1.00 PM. There are postal outlets throughout the city - mainly in drug stores - that can handle most postal needs. These outlets often operate daily during the store's regular hours.

When you buy stamps, you'll be charged an extra 7% (GST) tax.

SMOKING

The city has banned smoking in all indoor public places and common areas of apartment buildings. The exceptions are businesses, restaurants, bars and other commercial venues that provide a specially ventilated smoking area that is no more than 25% of the total business space.

There are no cigarette vending machines in the city and the sale of tobacco products to minors is illegal.

TAXES

Taxes totalling 15% are added to virtually all purchases, with some weird and illogical exceptions. The Provincial Sales Tax (PST) is 8% and the federal Goods and Services Tax (GST) is 7%. The PST on hotel bills is reduced to 5%.

The receipt you receive will have these taxes itemized.

TELEPHONES

Local public telephone calls cost 25 cents. Long distance can be paid for by American Express, Mastercard and Visa credit cards, telephone company cards, or telephone cash cards available at most convenience and drug stores. Follow the instructions on the phone's digital electronic display. You can choose either English or French.

Toronto has two local area codes: 416 and 647. You must dial the area code as part of all local calls made within the city – a total of 10 digits.

Do not dial 1 first.

TELEPHONE BOOK

The *White Pages* phone book lists residential numbers in the front and business numbers at the back.

The separate *Yellow Pages* list commercial and professional entries.

WASHROOMS/TOILETS

Use facilities in restaurants, bars, hotel lobbies, coffee shops, public buildings, shopping malls and department stores. Some have changing facilities for babies in both the male and female sections.

One of the rare public toilets is on King Street West opposite the Royal Alexandra Theatre.

*City*Weather

Nothing pre-occupies Torontonians more than the weather. It's possible for temperatures to range from 38.3C during August to −31.3C in January. It's not uncommon in spring to see the mercury fall overnight from 22C (72°F) to −9C (16°F).

Generally, summer is warm and often humid with thunder storms. Fall is usually clear and cool and considered by many to be the nicest time of the year. Winter can be very cold, but usually there aren't too many snow storms. Spring is mostly wet with temperatures ranging all over the place.

If you're already in town, tune in to *CablePulse24* on cable channel 24. This hip local television station has the weather and live highway cameras on screen almost 24 hours a day. Radio AM680 gives weather and road conditions every 10 minutes. All English-language newspapers have a weather section inside. For out-of-towners, log on to either **weather.ec.gc.ca** or **theweathernetwork.com** for present, short- and long-term forecasts.

| MONTH | TEMPERATURE | | | | HUMIDITY |
| | Celsius | | Fahrenheit | | |
	Hi	Lo	Hi	Lo	%
January	-1	-8	30	18	75
February	0	-7	31	19	72
March	4	3	40	27	68
April	12	3	53	38	57
May	18	8	64	47	54
June	24	14	76	57	55
July	27	16	80	62	53
August	26	16	79	61	56
September	22	12	71	54	60
October	15	7	60	45	63
November	8	2	46	35	73
December 1	-5	34	23		77

*City*Trivia

TORONTO CITY HALL is the result of an international competition that involved 520 architects from 42 countries. Viljo Revell from Helsinki, Finland submitted the winning entry. Construction began on November 7, 1961 and was completed on September 13, 1965. The building cost $31,000,000

INFORMATION FOR TORONTO MOTOR DRIVERS IN 1929 stated that: "The driver of an automobile is regarded by the law as in charge of a dangerous machine...the pedestrian has rights on a highway equal to those of the driver of an automobile, and notwithstanding the negligence of the pedestrian, the driver of the automobile is liable for damages if he could have avoided an accident by the exercise of proper care after becoming aware of the negligence of the pedestrian."

MEN LIVE LONGER IN TORONTO than in any of the country's 25 major cities. Women here have the second highest life expectancy. Despite pollution, smoking and job stress, people living in the city have the lowest overall urban death rate from heart disease and lung cancer. Incidentally, Canada ranks among the world's top five countries for prolonged life expectancy.

PARKING TICKETS to the value of $2,300,000 had to be trashed in 1998 because of mistakes made by parking control officers. Almost 5.5% of all tickets issued that year – 123,000 – were discarded for reasons "classified as officer controllable", including illegible handwriting, officer error and failure to complete the tag. It costs the city $21,500,000 annually to operate parking enforcement. About 2,500,000 tickets are handed out every year, generating about $45,000,000 in revenues.

THE POPULATION IN 2021 is estimated to show that 1.06-million people in Greater Toronto – about 15.5% of the total – will be 65, or older. That's more than double the 1996 census figure.

ETHNIC COMMUNITY LIVING CHOICES show that the majority of natural-born Canadian, English and Italian residents of the Greater Toronto Area prefer to live outside the city limits. The city is a heavy favourite with Chinese, Portuguese, Jamaican, Jewish, Filipino and Greek residents.

LIGHTS, CAMERA, MONEY! Foreign movies and television shows pumped over $1.4-billion into the city's economy in 2000. A total of 3,799 filming permits were issued by the city that year accounting for 1,211 projects and 7,532 shooting days. An additional $1.75 billion was spent by local companies on movies, commercials, television and special effects projects. The busiest day ever was October 1, 1999 when 30 crews invaded city streets.

THE TORONTO ISLAND FERRY *McBride* – named after Sam McBride, an old island summer resident and former mayor – has made more than 155,000 crossings of the Toronto Inner Harbour during the last 60 years. The 385-tonne ferry is licensed to carry 1,000 passengers.

HOMICIDES in Toronto decreased to 48 during 1999. This represents about 2.4 murders per 100,000 of population, compared with 10.8 in New York, 27.3 in Chicago and 60.0 in Washington DC - where there were more homicides during one long weekend than there were in Toronto for an entire year.

GREATER TORONTO'S POPULATION is larger than that of Newfoundland, Prince Edward Island, Nova Scotia, New Brunswick, Manitoba, Saskatchewan and the Yukon combined. It has 40% of Ontario's population and 17% of everyone who lives in Canada. Yet, its government cannot collect sales taxes, gasoline taxes, tobacco taxes, or control its highways and schools. All these come under the jurisdiction of either the provincial or federal government.

BICYCLE RIDERS are most likely to come to grief with open deck trucks. Frequency of collisions with other vehicles include, in order, TTC buses, emergency vehicles, closed trucks and motorcycles. While on the subject of bicycles, there are more than 12,000 stolen in the city each year.

SEX IN THE CITY. A survey of the city's bedroom habits has revealed the following: Gays (57%) are more likely to carry a condom in their pocket than straights (51%). During a selected week a third of straight couples had sex once or twice, 26% didn't have any and 8% didn't know. Half of all men (gay and straight) and 15% of females think about having sex several times a day. Just over 91% of all people surveyed said they were straight and 12% of all men surveyed said they were either gay or bisexual. Most people (53%) said they began fantasizing at 15 and lost their virginity between the ages of 16–20. Half the folk surveyed said they were happy with their sex lives and 6% didn't know. Another survey suggested that 44% of men and 63% of women in Toronto would prefer a good night's sleep to having sex.

CRUNCHING NUMBERS. Toronto's Gross Domestic Product (GDP) is almost $70-billion. The city has retail sales approaching $35-billion and is home for half the country's *Fortune 500* companies. The world's fourth highest concentration of commercial software companies is found here. It costs close to

$6-billion to run Toronto for a year. The city contributes just over 47% of the province's revenues, yet receives only 40% of provincial benefits and expenditures in return.

HEAD COUNTING. The three most popular festivals are Caribana (650,000 people attending), with Taste of the Danforth and the Celebrate Toronto Street Festival tying with 600,000 each. The most popular single-day events are the Santa Claus Parade (350,000) and the Gay Pride Day Parade (250,000). Organizers usually double these figures to out-hype each other.

ROAD HAZARD. The City of Toronto operates about 4,900 vehicles. A 1998 survey revealed that about one-third of these were involved in an accident during the previous year. This is five times higher than the average accident rate for privately owned vehicles. Regarding overall road accident rates, there are about 60,000 accidents each year in the city. Recent annual statistics showed that 58,235 accidents occurred among the city's 1,087,907 privately owned vehicles. This means that your chances are one in eighteen of getting at least one 'fender bender' annually.

***PHANTOM* FACTS.** Toronto's longest running stage musical was *Phantom of the Opera*. It opened at the Pantages Theatre on September 20, 1989 and closed after 4,226 performances on October 31, 1999. During that time more than 7-million tickets, valued at $465,000,000, were sold. Eight men played the role of the Phantom. The first was Colm Wilkinson and the last was Paul Stanley. Eight women played the part of Christine Daaés. During the ten-year run, 1,057 tonnes of dry ice were used on stage.

TAKE THE STAIRS. Each year the CN Tower hosts two charity stair climbs that attract around 7,000 participants. There are 1,760 inside stairs used for the climb and in 1989 Brendan Keenoy entered the *Guinness Book of Records* by racing up them in 7 minutes and 52 seconds. The oldest climber during the 20th century was 77-year-old Miklos Emheet, who took on the challenge in 1998 after practising on the stairs in his apartment building. If you're an average, fit person you should be able to do it in 30 minutes. It takes 58 seconds by elevator.

THE TORONTO PUBLIC LIBRARY is the largest in Canada. Its 98 branches serve 2,300,000 people and its collections consist of about 9,000,000 items in more than 100 languages. The library has 1,500,000 registered users (65% of the population), answers 8,000,000 questions every year, and welcomes 17,000,000 million visitors annually.

SUPERMAN has Toronto connections. In the comic strip, Metropolis was based on Toronto and the *Toronto Star* newspaper inspired the *Daily Planet.*

PLAY BALL! Long before the Blue Jays threw their first pitch inside SkyDome, Torontonians flocked to the Toronto Baseball Grounds bounded by the Don River, Queen Street East and Broadview and Eastern avenues. The facility, sporting a 2,200-seat grandstand, opened in 1886 at a cost of $7,000. Many years later, Babe Ruth hit his first professional out of the park homer at the now defunct Hanlan's Point baseball stadium.

A TAXING PROBLEM. Taxes owed to the city by businesses and residents in 1999 totaled $414,964,907.68. The top 20 delinquent taxpayers were all businesses and they owed the city a combined amount of $61,925,365.26. According to the local media, the biggest single offender on February 29, 2000 was Deal Makers of Canada Inc., which owed $9,635,332. The second highest debtor was the City of Toronto Economic Development Corporation, which was $3,513,332 in arrears. National Defence Canada owed $3,271,894.

THE ODDS OF GETTING KILLED. You're almost twice as likely to be killed in a traffic accident than being murdered. In 1999, there were 91 traffic fatalities and 48 homicides in the city. "People have lost respect for the rules of the road," Police Chief Julian Fantino said when the statistics were released.

TAKING STOCK. The Toronto Stock Exchange (TSE) main index was the world's fourth best performer in 2000. It recorded a gain of 4.2% over 1999. The top three exchanges were China's Shanghai B Index (136.6%), Ireland's Bourse (11.7%) and the Swiss Market with 5.5%. The New York Stock Exchange (NYSE) lost 6.16% and the NASDAQ lost just over 39% of its value. The TSE was the world's seventh largest stock exchange in 2000 based on market capitalization.

TRASHY FACTS. Toronto allocated $39.5-million for garbage collection in 2000. The money was spent by using 183 garbage trucks and 98 recycling trucks to haul away 3,011 tonnes of stuff every business day. The city has 25 female garbage collectors.

FILM GLAMOUR. During September, 2000 the 25th Toronto International Film Festival screened 329 movies - representing 56 countries - for more than 800 members of the international press and about 250,000 movie-goers. An estimated 2,500 stars, producers, directors and other important film folk from around the world attended. The lowest priced ticket was $2.00 when the festival opened in 1976. The same ticket cost $4.60 in 2000. The event has a $35-million positive impact on the city's economy.

PLACES TO AVOID. Here are Toronto's nine most dangerous intersections for drivers and pedestrians: Markham and Lawrence East, Warden and Lawrence East, Jane and Finch, Leslie and Sheppard East, Warden and Steeles East, Dufferin and Finch West, Black Creek Drive and Lawrence West, Don Mills and Eglinton East, and downtown's Jarvis at Lake Shore Boulevard East.

IMMIGRANT WEALTH. The city's immigrant population seems to be flushed with cash. In a single year, the Chinese community spent $5.2-billion, followed by the Italians with $4.4-billion and $2-billion for the Portuguese. Chinese spending habits included health clubs, cameras and restaurants, while the Italians splurged on clothing, food and household items.

RELAX! On April 1, 2001, there were 17 spas in Yorkville. Stillwater, at the Park Hyatt Hotel, is the largest. It occupies 3,048 square metres and is staffed by 70 professionals who can give 300 pamperings a day. The facility cost $5-million in furnishings and fixtures.

*City*Streets

Toronto has 5,250 km of streets – enough to stretch to London, England. There are 1,842 traffic lights to keep most of us from smashing into each other. Walking the city's 8,200 km of sidewalks is the same as walking to Rio de Janeiro.

Origins of *City*Street names

ADMIRAL ROAD
Admiral Augustus Baldwin was the younger brother of William Baldwin who built Spadina House. Admiral Road was part of Augustus' original estate and his house was on present-day Glen Edyth Place.

ALEXANDER STREET
Alexander Wood was a Scottish retailer who later became a controversial magistrate. For more information, see page 55

ARMOURY STREET
A huge armoury, built in 1893, occupied the area near the present court house. The drill hall measured 85 m by 38 m with a 22 m ceiling. Its basement was so large that it was used as a rifle range.

BATHURST STREET
The third Earl of Bathurst was Secretary of War for the Colonies from 1812-1827 under George IV. He never visited Canada.

BERKELEY STREET
This was the original Parliament Street. 'Berkeley' is derived from the name of the first house built on the corner of King Street.

BLOOR STREET
Joseph Bloore, despite his strong Methodist leanings, built one of York's first breweries near Sherbourne Street. The 'e' is now missing from the street.

CARLTON STREET
Guy Carleton, Lord of Dorchester, fought the French in Québec in 1759 and later became Lt-Gov of Québec from 1766-1768

CHURCH STREET
So named because the first church in the Town of York was built on the corner of King Street in 1807

CUMBERLAND STREET
One of Yorkville's first councilors, James Wallis, was born in the former county of Cumberland, England.

185

DANFORTH AVENUE
Asa Danforth was the American contractor who built the road from the Town of York to Kingston.

DAVENPORT ROAD
'Davenport' was the name of a house built on the hill by John McGill in 1797. See page 67

DUFFERIN STREET
This formed the early western side of the city and was known as the Side Line. It was re-named in 1876 after Governor-General Lord Dufferin, who opened the first Canadian National Exhibition here in 1878

DUNDAS STREET
John Graves Simcoe had this built as a military road in case the Americans attacked York. It was named after the Right Honourable Henry Dundas, who was Home Secretary at the time.

FINCH AVENUE
John Finch bought a property at the corner of Yonge Street in 1847 that was previously owned by John Montgomery. It was known as the Bird-in-the-Hand Tavern.

FRONT STREET
The eastern part of the street was originally named King Street after George III and later Palace Street, because it led to the parliament buildings at the foot of Berkeley Street. The present name comes from the fact that it once ran along the shore line of the lake. See page 37

GARDINER EXPRESSWAY
Frederick Goldwin Gardiner became the first chairman of Metropolitan Toronto when it was formed in 1953. He pressed vigorously for construction of the expressway in 1955

GEORGE STREET
The name came about in 1793 to honour the Prince of Wales, who later became George IV.

GLADSTONE AVENUE
William Ewart Gladstone was a four-term prime minister of Britain. Earlier in his career he was Under-Secretary to the Colonies.

HOMEWOOD AVENUE
George William Allen built an estate in 1846 in a thickly wooded forest near present-day Sherbourne and Wellesley. He named it 'Home Wood'. This area was later renowned for its fine mansions. See page 55

HURON STREET
The Huron First Nations lived in the Orillia and Midland areas until 1649. They made military and trading alliances with the French and soon took charge of the fur trade throughout Ontario and most of Quebéc.

INKERMAN STREET
A decisive battle during the Crimean War was fought in 1854 at Inkerman, where French and British forces defeated the Russians.

JARVIS STREET
The family of William Jarvis, provincial secretary from 1782–1817, owned a large tract of land here. The street was once the most fashionable address in the city.

LAWRENCE AVENUE
Peter Lawrence came from Yorkshire in 1829 and settled on lands that stretched down the present Don Valley.

LIPPINCOTT STREET
Captain Richard Lippincott was an American who came here via New Brunswick, where he fought with pro-British guerrillas in the American Revolution.

LONGBOAT AVENUE
Thomas Charles Longboat was born on the Six Nations Reserve near Brantford. He won the Boston Marathon in 1907, the Toronto Ward's Marathon three times (1906-08), and the World's Professional Marathon Championship in 1909

MAITLAND STREET
Sir Peregrine Maitland was Lt-Gov of Upper Canada (1818-1828) and Lt-Gov of Nova Scotia (1824-1834). He was knighted after the Battle of Waterloo. Maitland hated the Town of York and built his summer residence at Niagara.

MANNING AVENUE
Alexander Manning came to Upper Canada in 1834 and went on to become one of the most successful early builders, contractors and real estate developers. His projects included the Parliamentary Library in Ottawa, Toronto's Egerton Ryerson Normal School and the Welland Canal.

McCAUL STREET
The first principal of Upper Canada College was John McCaul, an Irishman who came here in 1838

MERCER STREET
Andrew Mercer was a pay clerk for the British forces during the War of 1812. After he died, his estate around King and Dufferin streets was taken over by the government and turned into the Mercer Reformatory for 'fallen women.'

PEARS AVENUE
This was the site of a brick works opened in the late 1800s by James and Leonard Pears.

PETER STREET
The name comes from 'Petersfield', which was the name of Peter Russell's estate that covered an area between Queen and Bloor, east of Spadina. Russell was Administrator of York until 1799

QUEEN STREET
Originally it was called Lot Street and formed the northern edge of the Town of York. Later it was re-named in honour of Queen Victoria.

REES STREET
Dr. William Rees was mainly responsible for the Provincial Lunatic Asylum, built in 1841. When he came to Canada from England in 1819 he served as assistant health officer at the Port of Québec.

RICHMOND STREET
Charles Lennox was the fourth Duke of Richmond, who came to Canada in 1818 from England to become Governor-in-Chief of British North America.

ROBERT STREET
Robert Baldwin laid out streets in this part of town. He was the son of Robert Baldwin Sr. who was a prominent politician in Upper Canada.

SCADDING AVENUE
Named after Rev. Henry Scadding, who was famous for writing an early history of the city.

SCOTT STREET
Thomas Scott was Attorney General of Upper Canada in 1880 and became Chief Justice in 1806

SHEPPARD STREET
This was the site of an early axe factory owned by Harvey Sheppard, an American from New England.

SUMMERHILL AVENUE
A 200-acre estate, named 'Summer Hill', was situated between Yonge Street and Bayview Avenue. Owner Charles Thompson fell on hard times and had to convert part of his mansion into a public dance hall to cope with rising debts.

TEMPERANCE STREET
Jesse Ketchum ran a tannery in this area. His father was an alcoholic and died, leaving his wife with 11 children. Jesse then became a strong supporter of the anti-liquor movement. Hence the name 'Temperance'.

UNIVERSITY AVENUE
The original name was 'College Avenue' and it was designed as a grand thoroughfare from Queen Street to King's College, later to become the University of Toronto.

WELLESLEY STREET
The first Duke of Wellington was Arthur Wellesley, who defeated Napoléon at the Battle of Waterloo.

WIDMER STREET
Dr. Christopher Widmer was best known for his work at the York General Hospital, founded in 1818, at the corner of King and Front streets. He also had many business interests and was a director of the Bank of Canada.

YONGE STREET
This was Toronto's first main street. It was named after Sir George Yonge, who was Secretary of War in Britain around 1790. He was also well known for his interest in Roman roads. See page 25

*City*Street index

190

191

*City*General index

198

200

Q

R

S